Titus Simons

Titus Simons
Father and Son Loyalists Who Fought in the American Revolution and the War of 1812

Ross D. Petty

Rock's Mills Press
Rock's Mills, Ontario • Oakville, Ontario
2024

Published by
Rock's Mills Press
www.rocksmillspress.com

Copyright © 2024 by Ross D. Petty.
All rights reserved. No part of this publication may be reproduced, distributed, or transmitted in any form or by any means, including photocopying, recording, or other electronic or mechanical methods, without the prior written permission of the publisher, except in the case of brief quotations embodied in critical reviews and certain other noncommercial uses permitted by copyright law. For permission requests, contact the publisher at:
customer.service@rocksmillspress.com

For adoption, trade, and bulk orders, contact the publisher at:
customer.service@rocksmillspress.com

All the images used in this book have been created expressly for this book or are in the public domain unless otherwise noted. Sources include: Figure 1.3. *Historical Atlas* by William R. Shepherd (New York: Henry Holt and Company, 1923). Figure 3.2. *Atlas of Windsor County, Vermont*, F.W. Beers, 1869. 4.1. A South-West View of St. John's by James Peachey, circa 1784. Figure 5.1. Reference: https://www.uelac.org/SirJohnJohnson/images/Refugee-Camps-HQ.jpg (from Sir John Johnson Centennial Branch UELAC and an article called "Loyalists in the Eastern Townships"), with revisions, redrawing, and corrections. Figure 5.2. Encampment of the Loyalists in Johnstown, a new settlement on the banks of the River St. Lawrence in Canada West, taken June 6th, 1784 (copied 1925); J. R. Simpson, after James Peachey. Museum Program Drawings, Department of Education. Reference Code: RG 2-344-0-0-89. Archives of Ontario, I0003081. Figure 5.3. Reference: http://uelac.org/st-lawrence/loyalists-of-sdg/, with revisions, redrawing, and corrections. Figure 5.4. https://commons.wikimedia.org/wiki/File:View_of_Cataraqui_1785.jpg. Also available at Library and Archives Canada, Acc. No. 1989-221-5. Figure 8.3. The Burning of Buffalo during the War of 1812, an engraving from Pictorial History of America, by Samuel G. Goodrich, published in 1847. The New York Public Library Digital Collections. Figure 9.1. Officers' barracks at Fort York. Adri/Wikimedia Commons (CCA-SA 2.0). Figure 9.4. Library of Congress.

Library and Archives Canada Cataloguing in Publication data has been applied for.

This book is a work of history, and in the interest of historical accuracy and understanding it reproduces quotations and images from the time period it describes. Some of the terms and expressions are no longer used, and some are now considered offensive and derogatory.

Dedication

This book is dedicated to all the archivists, librarians, and family
historians who assisted me with this research.
In particular, it is dedicated to Martha Hemphill,
a Simons descendant who generously shared her research and was
always available to bounce around ideas and strategies with me.
Much of the information contained in this book
was originally provided to me by Martha.

Contents

PREFACE | 1

Part One: Ancestors

1. THE NEW ENGLAND MIGRATION OF TITUS SIMONS' ANCESTORS | 5
To Salem and Vicinity | 8
Salem Village: James Hadlock and Richard Hutchinson | 10
Wenham: John Fairfield and John Abbe | 14
Conflict in New England | 16

2. CONVERGENCE ON NEW ENGLAND | 18
Thomas and Shubael Geer | 19
The Abbes and Simonses | 20
Henry Kingman and Robert Davis from Other Massachusetts Locations | 23
Conclusion | 24

Part Two: The Life and Times of Titus Simons Sr.

3. TITUS SIMONS GROWS UP IN ENFIELD AND MOVES TO VERMONT | 27
Upbringing | 27
Military Actions | 28
Political Unrest | 30
Settling Down | 31
Migrating to Vermont | 32

4. THE COMING OF THE AMERICAN REVOLUTION AND THE BATTLES AT SARATOGA | 38
Trouble in Westminster and Beyond | 38
Titus Fights for a Loyalist Regiment | 41
British Plan of Attack | 44
The Battles at Saratoga | 45
Retreat to St. Johns, Quebec | 47

5. TITUS SIMONS AND FAMILY BECOME REFUGEES IN CANADA | 49
Migration to Canada—At Last | 50
Refugee Camps | 51
Loyalist Militia Work | 54

6. From Kingston to Flamboro | 59
Deputy Sheriff of Montreal—At Last | 59
Private Lawsuits | 61
Titus Simons, Innkeeper | 65
Land Grant Petitions | 66
Jury Duty | 70

Part Three: The Life and Times of Titus Geer Simons

7. Titus Geer Simons, Government Printer and Public Citizen | 73
Becoming Known | 78
The Death of Titus Simons' First Wife and his Second Marriage | 82
Militia Activation | 84

8. Initial Militia Service and the Incorporated Militia | 88
Repelling Western Invasions | 89
Developing the Incorporated Militia | 91
Stoney Creek | 93
Fort Niagara and Black Rock (Buffalo) | 95

9. Messing with his Militia Record through the Battle of Lundy's Lane | 98
The Scuffle in the Officers' Mess | 98
Return to the Second York | 102
Wounded at Lundy's Lane | 104

10. Post-War Activities | 109
Pensions Claims | 109
Post-War Militia Service | 110
Land, Business, and Community Service | 113
Civic Service | 119

11. The Tar-and-Feather Outrage | 125
Background | 126
The Attack | 128
Rolph's Quest for Justice | 130
The Trial Proceeds | 131
The Appeal of the Civil Trial | 134
Criminal Prosecution | 136
The Aftermath | 139
Repercussions of the Ancaster Outrage | 142
Conclusion | 146

12. The Death of Titus Geer Simons | 148
Titus Simons' Will | 149
Titus Geer Simons' Estate | 152

13. Conclusion: From Loyalist to Tory in One Generation | 154

APPENDIX ONE: CHILDREN OF JOHN SIMONS AND SARAH GEER | 161

APPENDIX TWO: CHILDREN OF TITUS SIMONS SR. AND JERUSHA KINGSLEY | 162

APPENDIX THREE: CHILDREN OF TITUS GEER SIMONS | 164

APPENDIX FOUR: WILL OF TITUS GEER SIMONS, DRAFTED 1826, PROBATED IN 1829 | 166

INDEX | 169

List of Figures

1.1. Six-Generation Family Tree for Titus Simons' Ancestors | 7
1.2. Year of Migration for Some Titus Simons Ancestors | 8
1.3. Salem and Vicinity | 9
1.4. Salem, 1692 | 11
1.5. Salem Village (detail), 1692 | 11
1.6. Richard Hutchinson | 8
2.1. William and Sarah's Gravestone | 21
2.2. First Known Map of Enfield, from 1680 | 22
3.1. Sarah Geer's Gravestone | 27
3.2. Map of Windsor County | 36
3.3. Marriage Registration for Titus Simons and Jerusha Kingsley | 37
4.1. A South-West View of St. Johns, James Peachey, c. 1784 | 47
5.1. Loyalist Refugee Camps | 52
5.2. Loyalist Encampment in Johnstown by J. R. Simpson, after James Peachey | 54
5.3. Loyalist Townships, 1784 | 57
5.4. A South-East View of Cataraqui-Kingston by James Peachey (1785) | 58
6.1. Edward Walsh, "A View of Fort George, Navy Hall and New Niagara" (1804) | 67
6.2. Edward Walsh, "York ... as I Appeared in the Autumn of 1803" | 69
7.1 and 7.2. *Upper Canada Gazette* Masthead and Press | 74
7.3. Map of County of Wentworth | 79
8.1 and 8.2. The Capture of Fort Niagara | 96
8.3. The Burning of Buffalo during the War of 1812 | 97
9.1. The Officers' Barracks and Mess at Fort York | 99
9.2. Officers' Mess and Barracks at Fort York (diagram) | 100
9.3. Canister shot | 105
9.4. Battle of Niagara | 107
9.5. Titus Geer Simons' Uniform | 108
10.1 and 10.2. Old Free Church and Simons' Scroll | 118
11.1. Rolph, Hamilton, Robertson and Macauley | 132
12.1. Simons in Uniform | 149
12.2. New Grave Marker for Simons | 149
12.3. *Montreal Gazette* Auction Announcement | 153
13.1. Stormont | 158

Titus Simons

Preface

In the United States, the story of the American Revolution is well known, including famous leaders, military battles and commanders, but the story of the Revolution's impact on ordinary people is still being developed. John Adams estimated that about one-third of American colonists supported Great Britain (and one-third supported independence with the final third being neutral). One source estimates that these loyalists fought in 576 of the Revolution's 772 battles and skirmishes.[1] After the war, about 5,000 to 7,500 of these loyalists migrated to Upper Canada (now Ontario) with many more relocating to the Maritime Provinces, Lower Canada (now Quebec) and elsewhere.

Decades later, the British fought against France under Napoleon in Europe and the United States and Britain once again battled in North America in what Americans sometimes call the Second War for Independence. The Americans hoped they could acquire some or all of Canada but the British and Canadians thwarted this plan. Because of their success, the War of 1812 is probably celebrated more in Canada than in the U.S.

This book tells the story of a father, Titus Simons (1743–1824), originally from Connecticut, who moved to what is now Vermont and then fought for Britain in the American Revolution. In 1779, he migrated with his family as refugees to Upper Canada. Loyalists generally were not welcome to return to their previous property, which had been sold to others to raise money for the war. One important member of Titus' family was his oldest son Titus Geer Simons, sometimes referred to as Titus Simons Jr. (1765–1829). As a boy refugee he grew up migrating to various locations in Upper Canada. Eventually he and many of his siblings would receive government land grants in Upper Canada based on his

---

1. Thomas B. Allen, *Tories: Fighting for the King in America's First Civil War* (New York: Harper-Collins, 2010), xix, xx.

father's standing as a loyalist. Titus Jr. was able to fight for the crown in the War of 1812 as a major in the militia while his father ran the family businesses. Titus Geer Simons was disabled in the Battle of Lundy's Lane (1814) near the end of the war and then continued his father's efforts to support the family. He also served the community including a stint as sheriff of the Gore District and later as a magistrate. Simons Jr. also sought to make a name for himself and entrench himself within the ruling class by opposing government reform and attacking reformers, including the tar-and-feathering of the brother of a well-known reformer.

By traveling across generations and wars, this book adds to the existing literature about loyalists. Book-length biographies of Revolutionary War American loyalists are rare;[2] chapter biographies are more common.[3] Although rare, other father-and-son biographies from this era exist. Perhaps the best known are the stories of John and John Quincy Adams, the second and sixth American presidents who supported and led the United States in both the Revolution and the War of 1812.[4] Other fathers and sons were not so fortunate to be on the same side—for example, revolutionary Benjamin Franklin and his son William who was the loyalist governor of the New Jersey colony.[5]

This book may be the first to detail the struggles of both a father and son loyalist during two wars and peace time. It tells their stories from their perspective as loyalists. While their stories are unique, many other loyalists faced similar trials and issues and had similar experiences. This book also seeks to advance the loyalist and early war literature by examining the likely motivations of father and son in their particular social contexts and how their beliefs were passed on from senior to junior.

Although the author is grateful to many for assistance, he particularly

---

2. For rare exceptions see for example Mary Beacock Fryer, *Buckskin Pimpernel: The Exploits of Justus Sherwood, Loyalist Spy* (Toronto: Dundurn Press, 1981); Daniel Lovelace, *Tory Spy: A New York Frontier Family's War Against the American Revolution* (Westminster: Heritage Books, 2009); and Jennifer S. H. Brown, *Col. William Marsh: Vermont Patriot & Loyalist* (Denver: Tiger Rock Press, 2013).
3. See for example Mark Jodoin, *Shadow Soldiers of the American Revolution: Loyalist Tales from New York to Canada* (Charleston: The History Press, 2009), and Phyllis R. Blakeley and John N. Grant (eds.), *Eleven Exiles: Accounts of Loyalists of the American Revolution* (Toronto: Dundurn Press, 1982).
4. Nancy Isenberg and Andrew Burstein, *The Problem of Democracy: The Presidents Adams Confront the Cult of Personality* (New York: Viking, 2019).
5. Daniel Mark Epstein, *The Loyal Son: The War in Ben Franklin's House* (New York: Ballantine Press, 2017).

wishes to thank Martha Hemphill for sharing her vast research on this family and the late H.H. Robertson who published biographical articles on this family over a century ago. Some of the material in this book was published in Ross D. Petty, "Titus Simons of Hartland, Vermont, and Flamborough, Ontario," *Vermont Genealogy*, Vol. 25, No. 2, pp. 99–110 (Fall 2020) and Ross D. Petty, "The 1826 Ancaster Tar and Feathers Outrage: Three Defendants' Perspectives," *Ontario History*, Vol. 114, No. 2, pp. 196–220 (Autumn 2022).

Part One
Ancestors

CHAPTER ONE

The New England Migration of Titus Simons' Ancestors

In order to understand the father Titus Simons and son Titus Geer Simons—the loyalists who are the subject of this book—this chapter and the next explore the lives and experiences of their ancestors in migrating from England to settle in New England. Richard Bushman posits that this migration started with the Pilgrims, who sought to separate from the Church of England and establish local control of congregations and a focus on the Bible rather than being directed by the English monarch, the head of the Church of England. The Pilgrims were followed by the Puritans who shared similar beliefs about the Church of England and felt it was too similar to the Catholic Church but who also believed the Church of England could be reformed from within. As a group, the Puritans were wealthier than the Pilgrims and sought to invest in land and other resources in the New World. The Puritans officially received a royal charter for the Massachusetts Bay Colony in 1629 and started migrating there in 1630. Ten years later, the Massachusetts Bay Colony was a Puritan stronghold of 20,000, while humble Plymouth Colony was home to just 2,600 Pilgrims. Massachusetts Bay descendants, including the Simons' ancestors, would grow to 100,000 in number by 1700.

These ancestors migrated during a period called the Great Migration that started in 1629 when Charles I tried to rule England without a Parliament. The Anglican Archbishop at this time decided to purge the church of its Puritan members. To make matters worse, England suffered epidemic disease and an economic recession. From the English perspective, this period was the great exodus as people migrated to Ireland, the Netherlands, the West Indies, and Massachusetts. The migration ended abruptly by 1641 with the outbreak the next year of the first

English Civil War between the Royalist forces supporting the absolute rule of King Charles and Parliamentarians supporting a constitutional monarchy where the Parliament held authority over the Crown. Many Massachusetts Puritans returned to England to fight against the king who, with his bishop, had prosecuted the Puritans.[1]

Titus Simons' migrating ancestors were Puritans[2] who sought to establish their version of the Church of England in the new world. Each settlement had a Congregational Church and church and town leaders (who were often the same) sought to control the behaviors of the town citizens.[3] By 1765, when the son Titus Geer Simons was born, these Puritans had become Yankees who tended to favor individual freedom and commercial entrepreneurship over community conformity.[4] However, this Yankee independence was counterbalanced in many cases by a strong interest in religion and membership in a church community.

Opposite (Figure 1.1) is a six-generation family tree from familysearch.org for the ancestors of Titus Simons.[5] As the tree indicates, all four of Titus Simons' grandparents and four of eight of his great grandparents were born and raised in New England. While his parents could tell stories of his ancestors migrating from England, neither they nor their parents had lived in England. One of Titus' great-great-grandparents, Sarah Skepper, was even a pure New Englander, being born in 1639, the year her parents migrated.[6] The table below (Figure 1.2) identifies several other ancestors who settled initially in Massachusetts during the Great Migration more than a century before Titus Simons Sr. was born.[7]

1. David Hackett Fischer, *Albion's Seed: Four British Folkways in America* (New York: Oxford University Press, 1989), 16–17.
2. Margaret Houghton, *The Hamiltonians: 100 Fascinating Lives* (Toronto: James Lorimer & Co., 2003), 135.
3. Kenneth S. Lynn, *A Divided People* (Westport: Greenwood Press 1977), 97.
4. Richard L. Bushman, *From Puritan to Yankee: Character and Social Order in Connecticut 1690–1765* (Cambridge: Harvard University Press, 1967).
5. Familysearch.org is free for registered users and seeks to have users agree on a single universal family tree rather than have each user construct her own family tree. Since Titus' first wife, Sarah Simons, was also his cousin half of her ancestry is duplicative with his. Since she died about 1770 when Titus Geer Simons was quite young, he would not have heard nor remembered stories about her mother's (Dorcas Foster's) separate ancestry.
6. Sarah and her father Rev. William Skepper are descendants of Edward I, King of England, and other royalty, but there is no indication that Titus Simons knew this. Gary Boyd Roberts,, *The Royal Descents of 600 Immigrants* (Baltimore: Genealogical Publishing Co., 2004), 149, 152. See also Mary Lovering Holman, "The Skepper Family," *American Genealogist* 20 (1943–44): 76–85.
7. See Robert Charles Anderson, *The Great Migration Directory: Immigrants to New England 1620–1640* (Boston: New England Historic Genealogical Society, 2015), ix.

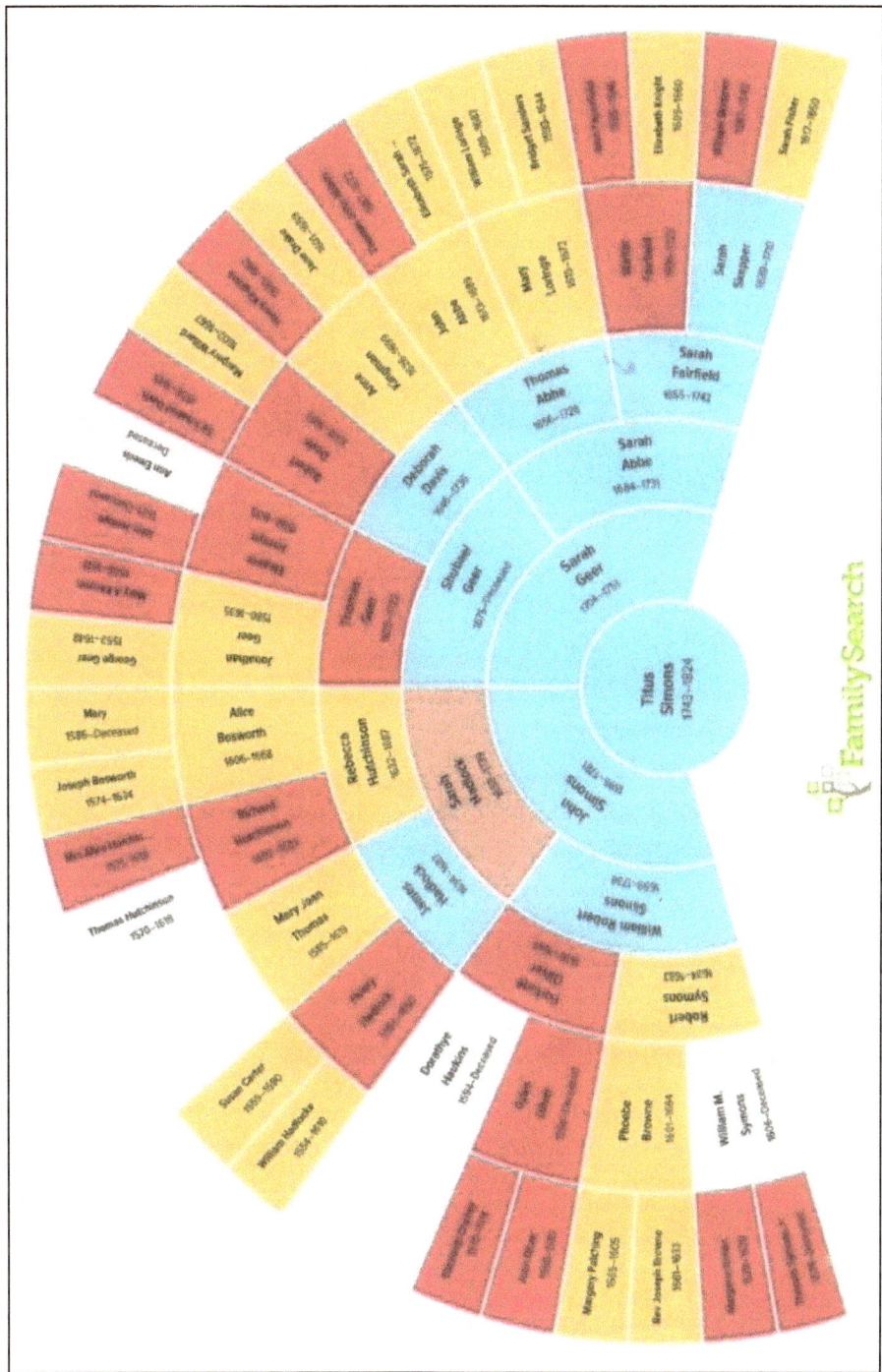

Figure 1.1. Six-Generation Family Tree for Titus Simons' Ancestors
(A larger version of this image can be found on the catalogue listing for this book at www.rocksmillspress.com).

Figure 1.2. Year of Migration for Some Titus Simons Ancestors

Year	Name	Comments (see footnote 12 for a citation to Anderson)
<1634	James Hadlock	Believed born in Charlestown circa 1634; married and moved by 1654 to Salem
1634[8]	Richard Hutchinson	Lived in Salem; Anderson, p. 176, says migrated 1636
1635	Thomas Geer	Probably moved from Boston to Salem; to Enfield in 1682.[9]
1635	Henry Kingman	On *Marygould*; Lived in Weymouth; Anderson, p. 195
1636	John Abbe	Lived in Salem/Wenham; Anderson, p. 1
1638	Robert Davis	On *Confidence*; Lived in Sudbury; Anderson, p. 90
1639	Rev. William Skepper	Lived in Boston or Lynn; Anderson, p. 307
1639	John Fairfield	Lived in Salem; Anderson, p. 111

The table above suggests that many of Titus Simons' ancestors came from England to the Salem area. A couple of generations later they migrated to Enfield on the Connecticut river valley south of Springfield and north of Windsor (see the map opposite).[10] From 1680 to 1683, Enfield saw nearly thirty families migrate from the Salem area, so Enfield has been referred to as a Salem colony.[11] Originally Enfield was thought to be in Massachusetts (under the parent town of Springfield) until careful surveys revealed it was in Hartford County in Connecticut. Enfield seceded from Massachusetts to join Connecticut in 1749—six years after Titus Simons was born. Later, as discussed in Chapter Three, Titus would move about 120 miles north on the Connecticut River to what would become Hartland, Vermont. Several relatives would move to Andover, Vermont.

To Salem and Vicinity

Salem Town was founded in 1626 by Roger Conant and a group of immigrants from Cape Ann known as the "Olde Planters."[12] At first the set-

---

8. Walter Goodwin Davis, *The Ancestry of Sarah Johnson* (Portland: The Anthoensen Press, 1960), 63–65.
9. Walter Geer, *The Geer Genealogy* (1923), 5–8, 297–299.
10. https://vlc-uk.tumblr.com/post/178055111563/the-new-england-colonies.
11. Francis Olcott Allen, ed., *The History of Enfield Connecticut, Volume I* (Lancaster, PA: The Wickersham Printing Co., 1900), 13.
12. There is a Walter Knight who was an "Olde Planter" but he was not the Walter Knight who married Elizabeth Gunne in England in 1618 and came to Wenham, having a daughter Elizabeth

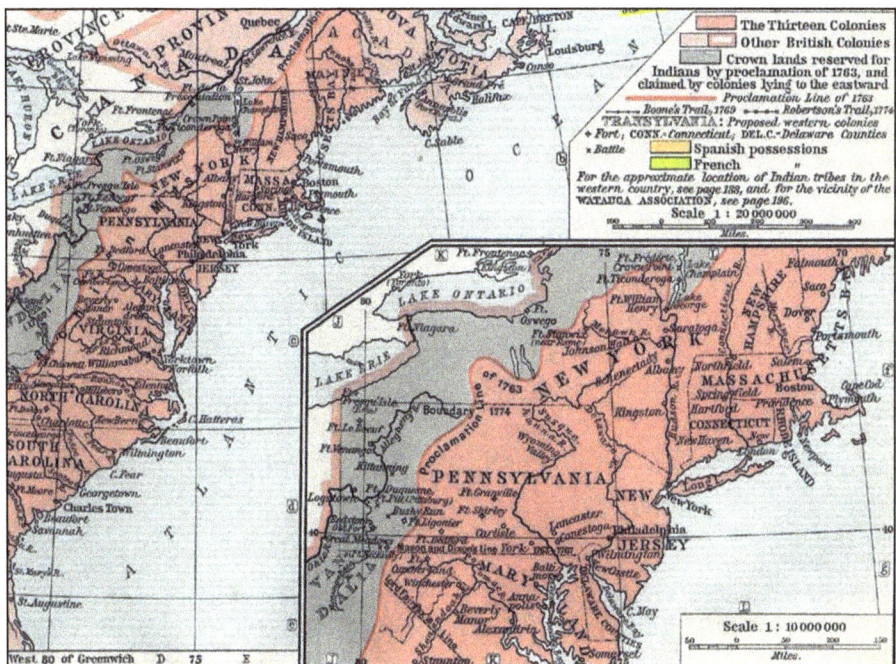

Figure 1.3. Salem and Vicinity

tlement was named Naumkeag but the settlers preferred to call it Salem, derived from the Hebrew word for "peace." In 1628, they were joined by another group, led by John Endecott, from the soon-to-be-chartered Massachusetts Bay Colony. The following year the Town of Salem received a royal charter authorizing self-rule. By June 1630, Puritans began their mass migration of ships landing at Salem. Salem's first public market was opened in 1634 and in 1649 Salem Custom House built to collect taxes on imported cargoes. It became a prosperous port engaged in commerce, fishing, ship building and other activities. Over a century later, Salem would become a hotbed of threatened and actual tar-and-feathering of customs officials after the passage of the 1767 Townshend Act that levied taxes on glass, paint, paper and tea and increased duties on other imported goods such as molasses and wine. At least one historian has (incorrectly) accused Salem of inventing both tar-and-feathering and witchcraft trials.[13]

---

who married John Fairfield in 1632. For the "Olde Planter" Walter Knight, see Robert Charles Anderson, *The Great Migration Directory: Immigrants to New England 1620–1640* (Boston: New England Historic Genealogical Society, 2015), 198. For the Simons ancestor Walter Knight, see Kathryn Fairfield Knight, *The Fairfields: Ancestors and Descendants* (2016), 21.

13. Benjamin H. Irvin, "Tar, Feathers, and the Enemies of American Liberties," *The New England Quarterly* 76, no. 2 (June 2003): 197–238 at 201–202, 220.

However, the land of Salem Town was not fertile, so settlers with farming ambitions would seek land outside the town. Titus Simons' ancestors tended to settle in a couple of Salem-area locations. Wenham was first settled in 1635 as part of Salem and then became the first town to be separately incorporated from Salem in 1643. Wenham town history is vague for many years and inhabitants were careless about attending town meetings to the point where fines were assessed for such laxness. A second popular settlement location was Salem Village (home of the famous witchcraft trials and now called Danvers). It started in 1636 as a fast-growing agricultural area located about five to seven miles from the Salem Town meeting house. The town permitted the village to hire its own minister in 1672 but the village would not gain complete independence until 1752. The maps on the next page illustrate the relative locations of Salem Town, Salem Village and Wenham.[14]

Salem Village: James Hadlock and Richard Hutchinson

The Simons ancestor who appears to have first migrated to New England is one we know little about. Some sources seem to agree that James Hadlock was born in Massachusetts but records to support this or to identify his parents are lacking. In contrast, familysearch.org suggests James' presumed parents Henry Hadlock and Mary Thomas were born, married and died in England. Mary died after giving birth to their seventh child in 1619, but then Henry presumably moved to New England, remarried, and had a son James, born in 1634 in Charlestown. Henry then returned to England before he died there in 1650. This seems unlikely but is possible. Others suggest James was the brother of Nathaniel of Charlestown, son of an earlier Nathaniel Hadlock,[15] but this is not accounted for in the familysearch.org tree.

The first documentation of James Hadlock is his marriage to Demaris Fosdick in 1652 in Charlestown where they both may have lived. They moved to the Salem area by 1654 where their first child was born. Their second child was born in July 1657 in Salem and Demaris died after childbirth. James then married Rebecca Hutchinson (Titus Simons'

---

14. See respectively https://www.sutori.com/en/item/untitled-d8a5-8af4 and Sidney Perley, *The History of Salem Massachusetts*, vol. 2 (Salem: Sidney Perley, 1926), 440–441.
15. Donald Lines Jacobus, *The Granberry Family and Allied Families* (Hartford: Edgar F. Waterman, 1945), 238.

ancestor) in May 1658, still in Salem.[16] In 1659, they lived in Salem "on the westerly side of Pine Street, about midway between Holton and Hobart Streets in Danvers" (Salem Village)[17] as depicted on the map of Salem Village (Figure 1.5). Their daughter Sarah, born in Salem in September 1659, would marry William Simons in Salisbury, Connecticut, about 1677. William and Sarah Simons had moved to Enfield by 1686 when their first child was born there.

Rebecca Hutchinson, second wife of James Hadlock and mother of Sarah Hadlock, was the daughter of Richard Hutchinson who migrated to Salem about 1634. The Richard Hutchinson home also is depicted on the map in

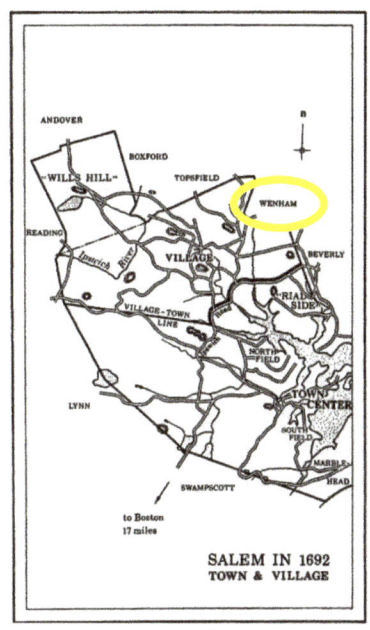

Figure 1.4. Salem, 1692

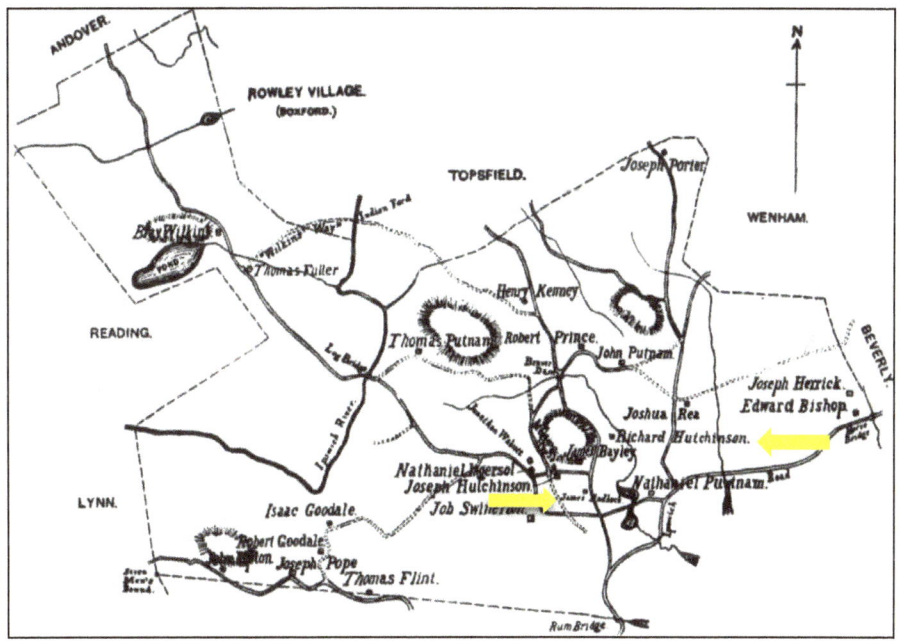

Figure 1.5. Salem Village (detail), 1692

16. Ibid., 235–238.
17. Perley, vol. 2, 375.

Figure 1.6.
Richard Hutchinson

Figure 1.5. Richard Hutchinson was born about 1602 in England, married Alice Bosworth at Cotgrave, Nottingham, on December 7, 1627, and was the father of three daughters baptized in neighboring parishes between 1628 and 1630, two of whom bore the names of Richard Hutchinson's two oldest daughters that were with him in Salem. Titus Simons' ancestor Rebecca Hutchinson apparently was not baptized but born in England in 1632. The family emigrated in 1634 and Richard Hutchinson was sworn in as a Salem freeman on March 4, 1634/35.[18] By December 1636, they were members of the First Church of Salem when they baptized their first New England born daughter.

Richard Hutchinson was not known for public service but he was one of the few people to own a plow (Figure 1.6). He received an additional 20 acres from Salem on the condition that he set up plowing within two years.[19] He also acquired four hundred acres of land and bought another 560 acres as part of a four-person partnership, making him one of the largest landowners in the area. Most of his land was located in what is now called Danvers and he distributed much of it to family members before he died. Richard Hutchinson of Salem made his will on January 19, 1679/80 and it was proved September 28, 1682. He left ten acres of land to each of his two granddaughters, Bethia Hutchinson and Sarah Hadlock. In November 1687, Sarah and her new husband, William Simons, sold the land in Salem she inherited from her grandfather and moved to Enfield where she would give birth to John Simons, Titus' father.[20]

Richard Hutchinson and James Hadlock could not avoid the religious controversies of their time at Salem Village. In 1644, the former was appointed as one of a list of patrol men who would walk around town on

---

18. Davis, *Sarah Johnson*, 63–65.
19. The image and the plow story are from "Richard Hutchinson of Salem Massachusetts" at http://freepages.genealogy.rootsweb.ancestry.com/~rhutch/richard_hutchinson.html. In addition, see http://catnip13.tripod.com/Hutchinson.html.
20. John Robinson Simons, "The Fortunes of a United Empire Loyalist Family," *Ontario Historical Society Papers and Records* 23 (1926): 470–483. Alternatively, the inherited land may have come from or through her mother Rebecca Hutchinson who died in 1687.

Sunday to see who was not in church. Those who lied about being in church or did not have a good excuse were to be reported to the magistrate for prosecution.[21] As constable, Hutchinson also was obligated to inspect individual households to make sure "good order" had not broken down within them.[22] Both Hutchinson and Hadlock signed a petition in 1667 to be excused from constable watch and they successfully received exemptions for anyone who lived move than four miles away from the town meeting house.

Operating such an intimate community inevitably led to size and distance limitations. Settlers wanted new towns and meeting houses closer to their homes. When the town of Salem was considering building a new meeting house in 1670, Hutchinson, Hadlock and several others signed a petition asking that they be exempt from contributing to the new town meeting house unless the town agreed to contribute to the building of a Salem Village meeting house. In 1672, the town allowed the village to avoid paying town church and minister fees so long as they hired and maintained their own village minister. The village agreed to do so but failed to build a dwelling house for the first minister, who then built his own house on land donated by Richard Hutchinson.[23]

There were ongoing disagreements about the early ministers of Salem Village. Richard Hutchinson and James Hadlock both signed a petition in 1679 supporting the first minister, Rev. James Bayley, and both signed a petition later that year to the General Court requesting that it instruct the Church of Salem (Town) to allow a vote by Salem Villagers on whether they wish to continue supporting this minister.[24] The Salem Village Book of Records indicates that in 1681, Richard Hutchinson would pay 2 pounds, 9 shillings and 6 pence (2/9/6) to support the meeting house and ministry costs and James Hadlock Sr. would pay 1/9/3. The latter would still owe 0/2/6 in February 1682.[25] A decade later in 1689 the Village finally hired its first ordained minister (who could administer communion) but this was after many Salem settlers moved to Enfield.

---

21. Perley, vol. 2, 165.
22. Fischer, *Albion's Seed*, 72.
23. Perley, vol. 2. 438–441.
24. Paul Boyer and Stephen Nissenbaum, eds., *Salem-Village Witchcraft: A Documentary Record of Local Conflict in Colonial New England* (Boston: Northeastern University Press, 1972), 247–251. In 1679, James Hadlock was paid ten shillings to sweep the meeting house (318).
25. Ibid., 320–322, 329.

Wenham: John Fairfield and John Abbe

Like the Hadlocks and the Hutchinsons, the Fairfield and Abbe families settled in another area near Salem called Wenham. John Fairfield and John Abbe were two of the earliest settlers there.[26] John Fairfield (1595–1646) was the father of Walter Fairfield and grandfather to Sarah Fairfield—all ancestors of Titus Simons. John, his wife Elizabeth Knight and their three-year-old son Walter, who was probably christened on December 21, 1631 at Copford Parish in Essex, England, migrated to New England in 1638 or 1639. Some say they landed in Charleston and bought property there like James Hadlock.[27] By 1639, John Fairfield received membership in the Salem Church and 80 acres of land for a farm in Salem, so he presumably sold any property he had in Charleston. In 1640, John was admitted to Salem as a freeman. He had a few land transactions and in 1643 he was fined 30 shillings for "attempting the chastity of wife of Goodman Goldsmith." He is considered one of the original proprietors of Wenham and died there in 1646. His wife re-married to Peter Palfrey, who gained control of the Fairfield lands in Wenham and became guardian to Walter's two younger brothers. Walter lived separately from the Palfrey family but they all moved to Reading in 1652. Palfrey rented out the Fairfield property in Wenham with a lease that ultimately expired in 1666.

In December 1654, Walter Fairfield married Sarah Skepper, daughter of Rev. William Skepper and Sarah Fisher in Reading. Rev. William Skepper was baptised in Boston, Lincolnshire, England on November 27, 1597 and died in New England between 1640 and 1650. William's first wife is not known but his second marriage was to Sarah Fisher on January 17, 1638/39 in Boston, England. He attended Sidney College, Cambridge, receiving a B.A. in 1617/18. By 1630, Rev. William Skepper was a vicar in Thorpe by Wainflete. He migrated to New England in 1639, but died on May 14, 1640 in Lynn shortly after the birth of his daughter Sarah in 1639. Sarah died at age 71 and was buried in Wenham.[28]

In 1664, Walter Fairfield, his surviving brother John (for whom he was briefly guardian) and his wife Sarah Skepper and their two children left Reading and returned to Wenham. Walter was sworn in as town consta-

---

26. Myron O. Allen, *The History of Wenham: Civil and Ecclesiastical from its Settlement in 1639 to 1860* (Boston: Brazin and Chandler, 1860), 28.
27. Knight, *The Fairfields*, 3.
28. Holman, "The Skepper Family": 77–85.

ble in November of that year.[29] Almost immediately, he began serving on juries and committees. He also was treasurer and constable of Wenham in 1676. He kept an "ordinary" (a tavern or inn that served a complete meal at a fixed price), licensed in 1680 (recorded in court in 1681) and 1686 (licensed to sell liquor).[30] Lastly, he was a selectman several times between 1668 and 1709, and between 1706 and 1709 he also was the moderator of the Wenham town meeting. Fairfield was an attorney and involved in many litigations, some involving his own violent outbursts of language and action, most famously as a tax collector.[31] In 1688 King James was replaced by William and Mary on the British throne after a war with France that caused the French to arm natives in North America. Ensign Walter Fairfield was appointed to the Wenham Committee of Safety to urge the resumption of the Massachusetts Bay charter and plan for the fortification of Wenham.[32]

The fact that Walter was a prosperous innkeeper and active in town affairs did not prevent his daughter Sarah from being prosecuted for fornication in 1680–81—particularly after she gave birth to an illegitimate son, named Philip Parsons after his father. She failed to appear in court and forfeited her bond. Walter probably paid a fine as well since his daughter and grandson likely lived with him. Despite this scandal, Sarah Fairfield married Thomas Abbe on December 17, 1683 in Marblehead and they moved to Enfield for a fresh start before the end of the year.[33]

Between 1692 and 1700 Walter Fairfield was the Wenham Representative to General Court (the state legislature) for which he was paid two shillings per day. He would have voted in December 1692 on a bill "Against Conjurations, Witchcraft and Dealing with Evil and Wicked Spirits." Once enacted, this law became a legal basis for the infamous Salem Village Witch trials. William Fairfield was the constable who recruited jury members and John Abbe was recruited as a jury member. These men were brothers to Titus Simons' ancestors Sarah Fairfield and Sarah Abbe, respectively. All of Titus Simons' other ancestors except for Walter Fairfield had left Salem by the time of the witchcraft trials. As a member of the Wenham town elite, Walter Fairfield never moved to

---

29. Connie Fairfield Ganz, *The Fairfields of Wenham* (2013), 43.
30. Ibid., 59.
31. http://www.fairfieldfamily.com/records/court%20documents/court_index.html.
32. Ganz, *The Fairfields*, 62.
33. Ganz, *The Fairfields*, 58.

Enfield like his daughter. He died on July 20, 1723 at Wenham at the age of about 92.[34]

Titus' second Wenham ancestor, John Abbe (1613–1689), migrated to New England in 1636 and was received as an inhabitant of Salem in about 1637. As was the custom at the time, he received a one-acre lot for a house in the village (near the gunsmith) and three acres outside of the village for planting. He had ten more acres granted in 1642 that became part of the area incorporated as Wenham the following year. Over the years, John engaged in many land transactions in Wenham. He appears as constable in 1669 and 1671. John's son Thomas Abbe (1656–1728) took care of his elderly parents in Wenham until he was dismissed for "bad behavior" in 1683 and replaced by his brother John Jr.[35] As noted above, this is when Thomas Abbe married the scandalized Sarah Fairfield and they moved to Enfield.

Conflict in New England

Military concerns were of great importance to the colonists. King Philip's War started in the summer of 1675, when native troops attacked several English settlements. On October 5, 1675, 60 houses in Springfield, Massachusetts were burned to the ground. Colonists raised troops for war. Thomas Abbe was wounded in the "Great Swamp Fight" under Captain Appleton at Narrangansett, Rhode Island on December 19, 1675. He had volunteered for what has been called the bloodiest battle per capita in North American history.[36] It is estimated that about 5 percent of the English population and 40 percent of the natives died in this bat-

---

34. Knight, *The Fairfields*, 7–8.
35. Cleveland Abbe and Josephine Genung Nichols, *Abbe–Abbey Genealogy: In Memory of John Abbe and his Descendants* (New Haven: The Tuttle, Morehouse and Taylor Co., 1916), 2.
36. The Great Swamp at South Kingston, Rhode Island, was the site of the last stand of the Narragansetts in King Philip's War against the colonists. In the bloody engagement which took place there on Sunday, December 19, 1675, troops from the colonies of New England attacked what would ordinarily be an impenetrable fort on an island in the swamp, but the swamp was frozen enabling the English to attack. At first repulsed, the English continued the assault, though with heavy losses. They contested almost every foot of ground until the Narragansetts, also suffering many casualties, were driven gradually from their fort into the swamp and woods. The English had set fire to the wigwams, some 600 in number, and flames swept through the crowded fort. The English lost five captains and 20 men and had some 150 wounded. A return march to New England took a toll of 30 or 40 more lives. The natives reported a loss of 40 fighting men and one sachem killed and some 300 old men, women and children burned alive in the wigwams (Daniel R. Mandell, *King Philip's War: Colonial Expansion, Native Resistance, and the End of Indian Sovereignty* (Baltimore: The John Hopkins University Press, 2010), 87–89).

tle of King Philip's War. James Hadlock also fought in King Philip's War and died shortly thereafter on November 14, 1678.[37] His daughter Sarah lived with her grandfather until she married William Simons in 1684.[38] Private Walter Fairfield also fought and was promoted to militia sergeant after the war in 1683 and to ensign in 1695.

In 1686, nine years after the end of King Philip's War, England re-asserted control over the Massachusetts Bay Colony by cancelling its charter and integrating it into the Dominion of New England that included Plymouth, Connecticut, New York and New Jersey.[39] Since cancelling colonial charters also cancelled the land titles of colonists, many towns sought to reaffirm their land titles by seeking to verify sales with remaining natives. Other restrictions were imposed on local governments such as restricting town meetings to one per year.

Two years later, the Glorious Revolution in England began and within another year, Catholic King James II was replaced by his daughter Mary and her husband William of Orange. This led to the Dominion being overturned and its colonial administrators being arrested and replaced with the previous colonial administrators. Massachusetts received a new colonial charter now including Plymouth to prevent complete domination by the Puritans. The Puritans accepted this change because they were no longer forced to accept the Church of England as under the Dominion.[40] These were just the first of the conflicts between New England colonists and native Americans and the British government that would shape Titus Simons' heritage.

---

37. On March 24, 1675/76, James Hadlock is listed in the company of Captain Samuel Wadsworth and would have fought in the Sudbury campaign the following month. On September 23, 1676, James Hadlock was listed as a soldier in the company of Captain John Holbrooke of Weymouth, Massachusetts. George Madison Bodge, *Soldiers in King Philip's War* (Boston: George M. Bodge, 1696), 221, 281. I don't know if this is the same man or two different men.
38. Simons, "Fortunes," 471.
39. Wim Klooster, *Revolutions in the Atlantic World: A Comparative History* (New York: New York University Press, 2018), 15.
40. Mandel, *King Philip's War*, 138.

CHAPTER TWO

Convergence on Enfield

Land grants had been issued for what would become Enfield starting in 1674 and the following year a sawmill in Enfield was burned in the wake of King Philip's War. However, settlement of Enfield did not take off until 1679, when two brothers migrated from Salem and camped in Enfield for the winter until their families came to help them build houses the following spring. The succeeding three years saw nearly thirty families migrate from the Salem area, so Enfield has been referred to as a Salem colony, as noted above.[1]

The first Enfield town meeting was held on August 14, 1679 and a committee of five were appointed by men from Springfield—the parent town at the time. Enfield was incorporated in Massachusetts on May 16, 1683 as the Freshwater Plantation. Five years later, on March 16, 1688, the townspeople purchased Enfield from a Podunk Native American named Notatuck for 25 pounds sterling. It is unclear what claim Notatuck actually had to the land but this purchase would re-affirm the town's right to it. Around 1700, the town changed its name to Enfield, after Enfield Town in Middlesex, and in keeping with other towns in the area with "field" in their names, such as Springfield, Westfield, and Suffield. In 1749, following the settlement of a lawsuit in which it was determined that a surveyor's error placed a section of present-day Hartford County (including Enfield) within the boundaries of Massachusetts, the town seceded from Massachusetts and became part of Connecticut. This change in colonial status probably meant nothing to six-year-old Titus Simons.

---

1. Francis Olcott Allen, ed., *The History of Enfield Connecticut, Volume I* (Lancaster, PA: The Wickersham Printing Co., 1900), 13.

Thomas and Shubael Geer

Once the Pease brothers from Salem established Enfield, Titus Simons' ancestors began to migrate. Thomas Geer was an early settler of Enfield arriving in town in 1681 or 1682.[2] He was a tanner and extensive land owner and in 1691 was chosen as a town moderator. Thomas Geer was born in 1623 in Heavitree, near Exeter in Devon, England. He and his older brother George (born about 1621 in the same place) were the sons of Jonathan Geer who died prior to 1635 soon after the death of his wife. Their two sons became wards of their uncle who wanted to control their apparently extensive estate, so he reportedly tricked them to get on a ship to America that arrived in Boston in 1635. Neither boy knew anyone in America and neither could read or write. Nevertheless, both became successful settlers, George in New London and Thomas in Enfield.

Thomas Geer and Deborah Davis had a son, Shubael, born on March 19, 1675/76, in Wenham, Essex County, Massachusetts. So, technically, Thomas could be considered as a settler who started in Wenham and then migrated to Enfield. Unfortunately, there is no other history of his activities in Wenham or other areas before his settlement in Enfield. After forty years in Enfield, Thomas died there in 1722 at the age of 99 and Deborah died there in January 1735/6 at the age of 90.[3] Puritans respected the elderly as being selected by God for long life in order to guide and provide wisdom to younger people. Thomas and Deborah would have been seated near the front of the meeting house.[4]

Thomas and Deborah's son Shubael Geer also was active in Enfield town affairs, serving on committees and as fence viewer, field driver, highway surveyor and searcher and gauger (that is, one who measures the alcohol content in beer and collects the appropriate taxes). At one point he also was appointed constable. Shubael Geer married Sarah Abbe in 1702/03. They had ten children including Sarah Geer, the mother of Titus Simons.[5] Shubael's death date is not known, but he appears to

---

2. Ibid., 13; Walter Geer, *The Geer Genealogy* (1923), 8, 123.
3. Ibid., 7–8, 123–127.
4. David Hackett Fischer, *Albion's Seed: Four British Folkways in America* (New York: Oxford University Press, 1989), 103–104.
5. Geer, *Genealogy*, 126–127; Cleveland Abbe and Josephine Genung Nichols, *Abbe–Abbey Genealogy* (New Haven: The Tuttle, Morehouse and Taylor Co.. 1916), 25. Note that it is often said that Shubael Geer was at the Great Swamp fight in 1695 with his future father-in-law. However, Shubael was born about the time of the fight so this is not possible.

have been chosen as a committee member at the February 2, 1769, town meeting and presumably died after that.[6]

The Abbes and Simonses

In 1683, one year after Thomas Geer arrived in Enfield, he was followed by Thomas Abbe who had been dismissed from taking care of his parents in Wenham. Thomas Abbe is included in many of the Enfield town records, serving as a selectman numerous times (1686, 1689, 1706, 1707, 1709, 1710) and as an assessor in 1705, and also appears on many property records. When his brother John Abbe Jr. died about 1700, Thomas Abbe challenged his disposition of their father's estate using his father-in-law Walter Fairfield as his attorney.[7] Thomas Abbe made his will December 12, 1726 (probated August 30, 1728). He styled himself Thomas Abbey Sr., a husbandman. He left his cattle to his two daughters, Sarah Geer and Tabitha Warner.[8] As noted above, Thomas Abbe married Sarah Fairfield, a daughter of Walter Fairfield and his wife Sarah Skepper of Reading, before moving to Enfield. Their granddaughter Sarah Geer became the mother of Titus Simons after she married John Simons of Enfield, son of William Simons and Sarah Hadlock.

John Simons' father William Robert Simons is commonly reported as being born in Salem, Massachusetts in 1659 but there is no documentation. There also appears to be a possible christening record in 1657 in England. According to the latter record, his parents were Robert Simons and Fortune Olaver (Oliver). Robert Simons was born in 1634 in Hurst, Berkshire England and Fortune was born in 1630 in Walkern, Hertfordshire, England. According to familysearch.org, Robert and Fortune were married in 1651 in Ardeley Hertfordshire and both died and were buried in 1665 in Whitechapel, Middlesex County, England.

Although we are not sure of his parentage or migration, William Simons—a farmer in Salem—married Sarah Hadlock in 1684 in Salisbury, and then moved to Enfield in 1687 as mentioned above. According to the minutes of the committee for Enfield, dated December 20, 1686,

---

6. Allen, ed., *History of Enfield, Volume I*, 438. Shubael Geer Jr. was appointed a surveyor in the December 1756 town meeting so at least at that time there was a clear distinction between Shubael Sr. and Jr. Being appointed to the town committee was a prestigious position and likely to go to senior town citizens.
7. Abbe and Nichols, *Abbe–Abbey Genealogy*, 12–14; William Weaver, *History of Ancient Windham, CT: Genealogy* (Willimantic: Waver & Curtiss 1864), 9–14, 25–26.
8. Abbe and Nichols, *Abbe–Abbey Genealogy*, 12.

William Simons was admitted as an inhabitant of Enfield, with a grant of a home lot of 12 acres and a field of land of 35 acres and some meadows, provided he settle there for seven years. His home lot was situated along the Connecticut River, south of "Terry Lane," between those of Thomas Geer and John Burroughs. A deed dated November 10, 1687 in Salem shows William and Sarah Simons sold ten acres of land in Salem to Jonathan Walcott. The map on the next page shows lots belonging to William Simons and his family members Thomas Abbe and Thomas Geer.[9]

The records of Enfield make several references to William Simons and Sarah his wife. At a town meeting on December 28, 1691, he was one of those warned that they would be fined 2 shillings, 6 pence if they failed to perform their day's work of cutting brush on the town commons. There are several instances of William acquiring land and by 1710 he is listed as owning 137 acres of land. On February 25, 1709/10 he signed an agreement for a dam and grist mill on a stream running through his property. William Simons and Sarah Hadlock Simons are both buried in the Enfield Street Cemetery, Enfield, Conn. Their masonically decorated gravestone is still standing but no record of a will has been found. Their third son John Simons lived his entire life in Enfield, marrying Sarah Geer in 1723 and dying in 1781 after having eleven children including Titus Simons born on June 7, 1743.

Figure 2.1. William and Sarah's Gravestone

The first forty years of the Enfield settlement had been prosperous in the pursuit of husbandry, the conversion of wilderness into fields, and the construction of buildings and roads. Enfield's settlers initially avoided any warfare with the Indians. However, one town historian concluded the original settlers were "not remarkable for their skill or industry in agricultural employments." Prior to 1770, wolf, bear, catamount (an umbrella term for wild cats, including cougars) and deer abounded near town and shad and pigeons continued to be plentiful

---

9. This map appears on the Enfield Historical Society website at https://enfieldhistoricalsociety.org/old-town-hall/the-settling-of-enfield/.

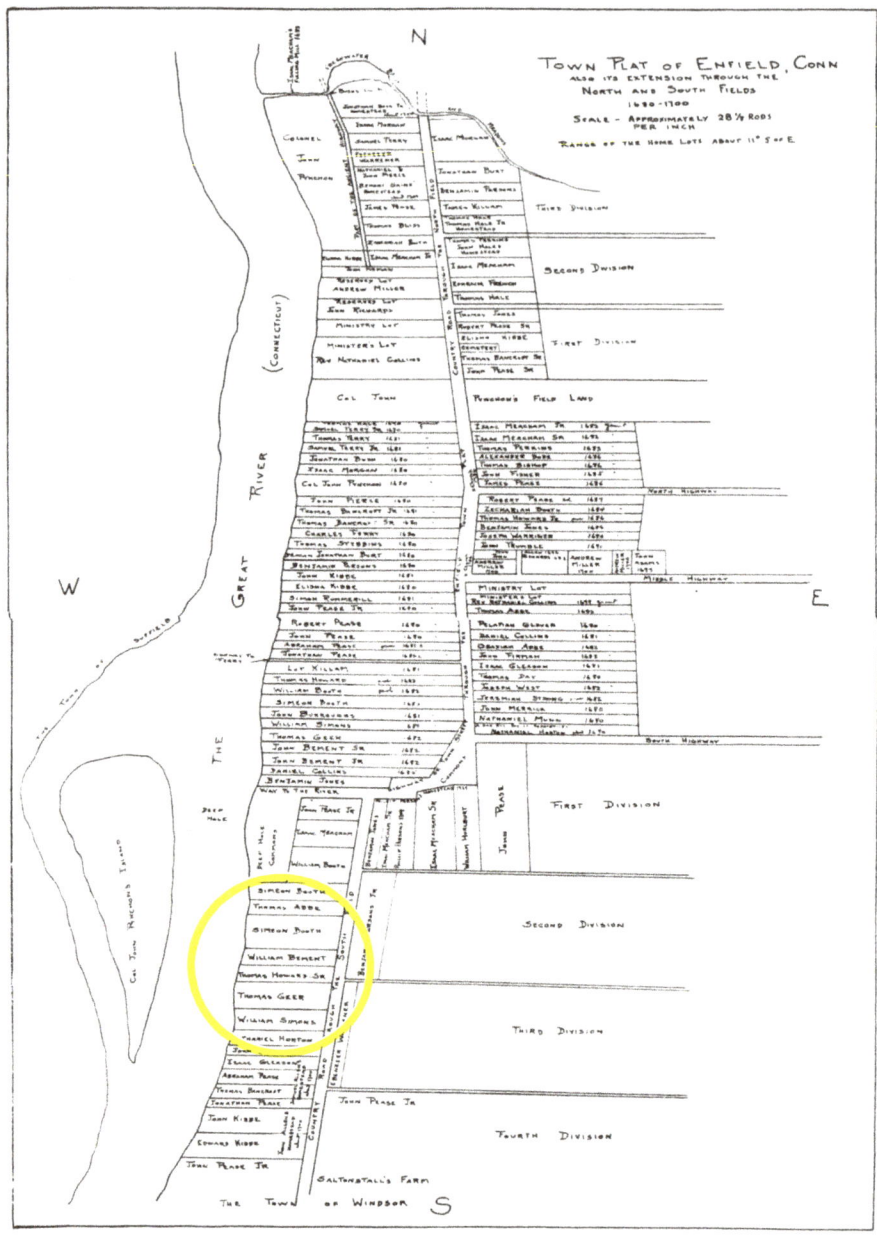

Figure 2.2. First Known Map of Enfield, from 1680

after that time. The early settlers annually burned the hardwood forests to allow the cattle to forage, but that left the soil sterile. They never exploited the forests to actually sell timber.[10] Despite these shortcomings

10. Allen, ed., *History of Enfield, Volume I*, 49.

revealed in hindsight, these settlers chose an area rich in resources and were able to exploit those resources.

Henry Kingman and Robert Davis from Other Massachusetts Locations

Two Titus Simons ancestral families followed a path different from the Salem-to-Enfield migration. First was Henry Kingman and family. He was part of the expedition run by the Rev. Joseph Hull that arrived in Boston on May 6, 1635. Henry was admitted as a freeman to the Town of Weymouth on March 3, 1636. He was a member of the Congregational church. He was licensed to keep a ferry and an inn or house of entertainment. He received many tracts of land and served on various committees and other public duties. In 1638, 1652 and 1657, Kingman was selected Deputy for Weymouth for the General Court of Elections. In 1648, he was a member of a committee to build a road from Weymouth to Dorchester. Henry and his wife Joanne (or Jane) had about eight children and their daughter Anne, born in 1626, received ten pounds in his will.

Anne Kingman married Tobias or Robert Davis on December 13, 1649 in Barnstable where Robert had been living since 1645. Robert Davis also did not follow the Salem-to-Enfield migration pattern. Davis was born in 1608 in England. He came from South Hampton in 1638 as servant to Peter Noyes. He had a farm in Yarmouth in 1639 and married Anne there in 1643. He was listed as a man who was able to bear Arms in Yarmouth in August 1643. Robert and Anne moved to Barnstable, Mass., in 1645 but Anne did not join the church until 1685. Robert was said to be neither rich nor involved in politics, but simply was an honest, hard-working, good man.[11] Robert's will was written on April 14, 1688 and probated June 29, 1693. Anne was born in 1608 and died in 1701. Her will was written May 6, 1699 and probated on April 1, 1701. They had ten children, the eldest being Deborah Davis, born January 1645 at Barnstable who married Thomas Geer about 1667, probably in Barnstable. Deborah Davis and Thomas Geer moved from Wenham to Enfield in 1682 as noted above.

---

11. Amos Otis, *Genealogical Notes of Barnstable Families* (Barnstable: F. B. & F. P. Goss Publishers, 1888), 276–278.

Conclusion

Migration had become a regular part of life for Titus Simons' ancestors over the course of several generations. The dangerous and lengthy seafaring migration to the New World was followed by more mundane overland migration seeking land that was less expensive and more fertile. Frontier colonists sought to co-exist with native peoples but also were mindful that hostilities could erupt at almost any time. They were willing to fight if necessary.

Nearly all of Titus Simons' ancestors seem to have run some sort of farming operation as was common at this time. Many operated other businesses and many were active in town affairs, some at the leadership levels. Others, while not local leaders, appeared to be solid citizens who served the local government or church when requested. Religion and the local church were an important part of everyday life, although the importance diminished as settlements became more spread out and less populous, making it difficult for every small village to support a church.

The changes that occurred during the first century–plus of New England settlement were subtle. The opportunity to own land was available to most people.[12] Strict adherence to the local community church diminished while interest in commerce and enterprise and the freedom to pursue commercial interests increased. However, organized religion did not fade into obscurity. It diversified with new Protestant sects. In 1741, Jonathan Edwards preached his famous sermon, "Sinners in the Hands of an Angry God," in Enfield, Conn. The sermon emphasized the reality of hell and the terrible eternal suffering there for those who did not embrace Jesus Christ. The congregation was so upset that Edwards could not finish the sermon and other pastors had to circulate amongst the congregation to provide comfort. This led to at least some colonists re-committing to church attendance and beliefs and is considered part of the so called "Great Awakening"—the emergence of Anglo-American evangelicalism/revivalism as a trans-denominational movement aiming to persuade colonists to rejoin the church by embracing Jesus Christ and his teachings. Titus' brother John Simons Jr. reportedly was a member of a "New Light" congregation, at least after he moved to Vermont.[13]

---

12. Richard L. Bushman, *From Puritan to Yankee: Character and Social Order in Connecticut 1690–1765* (Cambridge: Harvard University Press, 1967).
13. *Early Vermont Settlers Index Cards, 1750–1784* (online database: *AmericanAncestors.org*, New England Historic Genealogical Society, 2019), 392.

Despite these changes, colonial society remained an aristocracy. Landed gentry were in the highest class and over time members of professions (such as merchants, lawyers, clerics and others) became the second-highest level of gentlemen. Such distinctions of rank and status were thought to be beneficial to society and part of the natural order, both by colonists who ended up favoring revolution as well as those who stayed loyal to the crown and their British heritage.[14]

14. Tom Cutterham, *Gentlemen Revolutionaries: Power and Justice in the New American Republic* (Princeton, Princeton University Press, 2017), 1, 31.

Part Two
The Life and Times of Titus Simons Sr.

CHAPTER THREE

Titus Simons Grows Up in Enfield and Moves to Vermont

Upbringing

As Appendix One indicates, Titus Simons was the youngest of six surviving children of John Simons and Sarah Geer (five additional children died young). Titus grew up in Enfield where his father John married his mother Sarah Geer in 1723. Sarah Geer died in 1751 when her son Titus was just eight years old and just six months after three-month-old baby Edward died. Her gravestone is pictured in Figure 3.1. Titus was 11 when his six-year-old younger sister Bathsheba died and the next year Titus' older brother Ebenezer passed away. Perhaps Titus' sister Charity Simons (1738–1895) helped raise him before her marriage to John Abbe III in 1761. Titus would have been 18 years old at the time of that marriage. John Simons survived his wife Sarah Geer Simons by thirty years with no indication that he re-married.

Figure 3.1. Sarah Geer's Gravestone

This rather large nuclear family also enjoyed a large extended family in Enfield. John Simons had four brothers and Sarah Geer had nine siblings. As Appendix One indicates, many of John Simons' children had children, so Titus Simons had numerous aunts and uncles and even more cousins living in Enfield. We don't know what ancestral stories he may have heard about family, their farming and other business interests, and their religious or military struggles. Titus Simons named a son from his second marriage Walter William—perhaps after his grandfather William Simons and his great grandfather Walter Fairfield.

Titus' father John Simons, like many of his ancestors, served his community. In 1724, the year after his marriage, John Simons was chosen at the town meeting as a fence "veuer" (inspector). Twenty years later he was selected as a hog "reves"—a person who assessed the damage caused by free-roaming hogs.[1] Like many of his relatives, John Simons was paid for working on the Scantick highway in 1736 and other highway work the following year when he was appointed to be one of the surveyors of the highways. He was appointed to that task again in 1748/49.[2] In 1752 John Simons was appointed to a committee to determine what bridges were needed and should be constructed by the town. Two years later he was on a committee that was deciding where to build schoolhouses in the town. He became one of the tything (tithing) men (supervisors of church attendance and behavior on the Sabbath) in 1755.[3] He was back on the school committee in 1770.[4]

Military Actions

Growing up, not only did Titus observe the community service of his father and other relatives, he also observed two military engagements. In the summer of 1744, when Titus was a baby, a French and Native American force sailed from Louisbourg, a port city on Cape Breton, to the nearby British fishing port of Canso, attacking a small fort on Grassy Island and burning it to the ground, taking prisoner 50 British families. This port was used by the New England fishing fleet; however, the Canso Islands (including Grassy Island) were contested by both Britain and France.

The French, military and civilians alike, were not in the best of condition at Louisbourg. Supplies were short in 1744, and the fishermen were reluctant to sail without adequate provisions. The military rank and file claimed that they had been promised a share of the spoils from the Canso raid, which had instead gone to officers, who sold those same provisions and profited in the endeavor. In December 1744, the troops mu-

---

1. Francis Olcott Allen, ed., *The History of Enfield Connecticut, Volume I* (Lancaster, PA: The Wickersham Printing Co., 1900), 246, 400.
2. Ibid., 376, 382, 387, 410.
3. Ibid., 417, 420, 421; David Hackett Fischer, *Albion's Seed: Four British Folkways in America* (New York: Oxford University Press, 1989), 72.
4. Allen, *History of Enfield, Volume I*, 441

tinied over the poor conditions and pay that was months overdue. Even after acting Governor Louis Du Pont Duchambon managed to quiet the discontent by releasing back pay and supplies, the following winter was extremely tense, as the military leadership maintained a tenuous hold on the situation.

Ultimately the British prisoners were released and most traveled to Boston, reporting on the tense conditions at Louisbourg. In 1745, the governor of the Province of Massachusetts Bay, William Shirley, secured by a narrow margin the support of the Massachusetts legislature for an attack on the fortress. He and the governor of the province of New Hampshire, Benning Wentworth, sought the support of other colonies. Connecticut provided 500 troops, New Hampshire 450, Rhode Island a ship, New York ten cannons, and Pennsylvania and New Jersey funds. The force was under the command of William Pepperrell of Kittery (in the portion of the Massachusetts colony that is now the state of Maine), included several men from Enfield, and a fleet of colonial ships was assembled and initially placed under the command of Captain Edward Tyng. The expedition set sail from Boston in stages beginning in early March 1745, with 4,200 soldiers and sailors aboard a total of 90 ships.

While the siege resulted in an almost bloodless victory, the climate, famine, and disease killed 19 Enfield men, including members of the Abbe and Geer families who were relatives but not ancestors of Titus Simons. Louisbourg was returned to the French with the 1748 peace treaty. Titus Simons undoubtedly learned of these events when he was old enough to understand this was a victory over the French.

A decade or so later, the French and Indian War (1754–1763) took the lives of other Enfield settlers.[5] At the age of 12, Titus would be aware that his eldest brother (by 19 years) John Simons Jr. and the brother closest in age to Titus (Asahel, nine years older) both participated in and survived this war. Two other brothers, Ebenezer and Paul, apparently did not participate. Asahel reportedly participated in the expedition to reinforce Fort Edward in October 1757 but militia records only show him as serving from March 9 to August 4, 1757 in Major Payson's Company of Col. Lyman's Regiment. His departure date was the beginning of the siege of Fort William Henry, which was captured by the French. Natives then attacked British and Colonial troops being escorted by the French under

5. Ibid., 17–20.

the terms of surrender to nearby Fort Edward, which was still held by the British. John Simons Jr. served in Captain Durnham's militia company for 15 days in August 1757 so he was probably involved with the transfer of troops from captured Fort William Henry to Fort Edward.[6]

Militia service continued for three more years. On October 19, 1758, John "Simmins" is listed at Fort Edward as part of the 3rd Company under Major Israel Putnam within the 3rd Connecticut Regiment under Colonel Eleazer Fitch. They may have been recovering from the July 8, 1758 Battle of Fort Carillon (Ticonderoga). The British suffered numerous casualties at this French victory. In 1759, John Simons Jr. served from April 5 to November 20 in Captain Samuel Elmore's company of the 3rd Regiment of Connecticut under Colonel David Wooster. This service occurred during the Ticonderoga expedition and another battle in July lasting three days near Fort Carillon. This time the British were successful.

In 1760, both brothers again served. Payroll records indicate John served in Captain Christopher Palmer's Company of the 4th Connecticut under Col. Eleazar Fitch from March 25 to August 4, apparently fighting in the unsuccessful Battle of Sainte-Foy (near Quebec) on April 28 but departing just before the Battle of the Thousand Islands, one of the last engagements in North America. Asahel Simons also served from April 5 to May 2, 1760 during the French victory at the Battle of Quebec. He served with the First Connecticut Regiment, 9th Company, under Capt. David Parsons of Enfield.[7]

Political Unrest

As previously noted, a surveying error originally established Enfield's location as being in Massachusetts. This error was finally corrected when in 1749 Enfield left the colony of Massachusetts to join the colony of Connecticut. Connecticut colonists were proud of their long history of relatively autonomous rule dating back to the colonial charter from King Charles II in 1662. Given this history of relative independence, most Connecticut colonists were displeased when Parliament imposed the 1765 Stamp Act on the colonies without any input from them. They argued colonists should be consulted on or approve of taxes. Some even

---

6. *Rolls of Connecticut Men in the French and Indian War, 1755, 1762*, Vol. I (Hartford: Connecticut Historical Society, 1905), 173–174, 220.
7. *Rolls of Connecticut Men in the French and Indian War, 1755, 1762*, Vol. II (Hartford: Connecticut Historical Society, 1905), 57–58, 153–156, 187–188, 220–221.

argued that Parliament had no authority over the colonies because they were established by the crown alone.[8] The act imposed a tax (represented by a stamp) on various forms of papers and documents including colonial newspapers, professional certifications and college degrees. The act sought to raise money to pay for debts from the Seven Years' War, fought in North America as the French and Indian War, and to pay for future British troops stationed in North America.

The act was repealed promptly due to protests and threats upon the tax collectors but other taxes were adopted by Parliament without input from the colonies, leading to the American Revolution. For instance, the 1767 Townshend Act increased duties on molasses and wine and added new duties on glass, paint, paper and tea. Protests against these duties included the tar-and-feathering of some customs officials in Salem[9]— the ancestral home of many Enfielders and members of Titus Simons' extended family.

Enfield residents were nearly unanimous in their condemnation of taxes and other oppressive acts by Great Britain against the American colonies.[10] In 1766, the Whigs in Connecticut, backed by the Sons of Liberty, gained control over the Connecticut General Assembly and in 1769, Whig Jonathan Trumbull became governor. He was the only colonial governor to champion the patriots' cause and remained in office throughout the revolution.

Settling Down

Meanwhile ordinary life continued. Titus was too busy with family life to become involved in politics. On January 20, 1763, Titus, now age 20, married his first cousin Sarah Simons, age 23, the seventh child out of nine of James Simons of East Windsor, a brother of Titus' father John Simons. James Simons had married Dorcas Foster in Enfield in January 1731 and died in East Windsor in 1761 leaving Sarah some inheritance.[11]

---

8. Eric Nelson, *The Royalist Revolution: Monarchy and the American Founding* (Cambridge, MA: Harvard University Press, 2014).
9. Benjamin H. Irvin, "Tar, Feathers, and the Enemies of American Liberties," *The New England Quarterly* 76, no. 2 (2003): 197–238 at 201–202.
10. Allen, ed., *History of Enfield, Volume I*, 21.
11. James Simons divided his estate among eight surviving children with the five sons receiving twice as much as the three daughters. LDS Film 0,004,555 Probate Records, 1649–1932 Connecticut. Probate Court (Hartford Dist.) v. 17–19 1753–1770 Will of James Simons (18:235–36) p. 235.

Dorcas was born in September 1705 in Chelmsford, Mass., to Eli Foster (1653–1718) and Judith Keyes.

Titus and Sarah had two children in rapid succession: Titus Geer Simons, born January 30, 1765, and Sarah Simons, born July 1, 1767 (some sources say 1765 or 1768). Sadly, tragedy struck this new little family. Records indicate that Titus Simons, son of Titus and Sarah Simons, died on June 14, 1771.[12] However, since we know their son Titus Geer Simons lived until 1829, this death notice may be for baby Sarah Simons or a new unnamed child who died at birth. It also might be for Sarah Simons, wife of Titus Simons.[13] There is a grave marker in the Enfield Street Cemetery for "Mrs. Sarah Simons" but the stone is well worn and provides no additional information.[14] Neither this 1771 death record nor marker are for Mrs. Sarah Geer Simons, Titus's mother, who has the different grave marker pictured at the beginning of this chapter.

After his marriage Titus, like his father and many of his ancestors, appears to have done some work for the town of Enfield. The Treasurer's book shows him receiving periodic payments: 1 pound/8 shillings/11 pence on January 18, 1768 (in part for building Scantick bridge); 1/08/0 on January 25, 1768; 6/1/1 on August 1, 1768 (building the Scantick bridge); 0/3/6 on June 22, 1769; and 0/3/6 on December 15, 1769.[15]

Migrating to Vermont

The death of his wife (and probably baby daughter) apparently caused Titus Simons to reconsider his situation in Enfield and decide to make a fresh start by moving to what would become Vermont (generally called the "New Hampshire Grants" at the time). Since he had married a first cousin, Titus may have had too many Enfield relatives who reminded him of his late wife. As shown in Chapters One and Two, migration was part of his heritage and not unusual as settlers sought new land and sometimes religious freedom.

There may be several other reasons for Titus' decision to migrate.

---

12. Allen, ed., *History of Enfield, Volume II*, 1874; also repeated in Cleveland Abbe and Josephine Genung Nichols, *Abbe–Abbey Genealogy* (New Haven, 1916), 47.
13. Abbe and Nichols, *Abbe–Abbey Genealogy*, 47; Allen, ed., *History of Enfield, Volume II*, 1667, 1681, 1874.
14. Hale Cemetery Inscriptions and Newspaper Notices, Connecticut Headstone Inscriptions, vol. 15.
15. Allen, ed., *History of Enfield, Volume II*, 961–963, 991, 1144–1145. The monetary designation here is pounds/shillings/pence.

First, he was the fourth son in line for any inheritance from his father at a time when most land was inherited by the oldest son. The tradition in Enfield was that all sons would inherit some land and some moveable property while daughters inherited the bulk of moveable property.[16] Second, resources such as wild game and fertile farm land were no longer plentiful in Enfield in contrast to less settled areas like Vermont. Third, even at this young age, Titus may have been loyal to the British crown or at least neutral about the evolving question of independence. We know he was inclined more toward being a merchant than a farmer so he probably favored conducting trade as part of the largest empire in the world.[17] Perhaps as the youngest male child, he rebelled against his older siblings' eventual support of the Revolution. As discussed below, at least two of Titus' brothers would fight with the patriots during the American Revolution. Titus Simons may not have been a full-fledged loyalist when he moved to Vermont but he might have sought a more politically tolerant town.[18]

So why pick Vermont? There was little non-native settlement in Vermont before the end of the French and Indian War (1754–1763). The war almost completely stopped the flow of settlers. However, the war also brought reports of the new land so green and unsettled.[19] Titus probably heard such stories from his brothers and other towns people who fought in that war. He likely also knew there was a dispute between those who claimed to purchase land from New Hampshire and those who claimed title from New York.

In 1749, New Hampshire Governor Benning Wentworth began to sell land grants. These grants were in "freehold," giving full title to the purchaser from the crown, in contrast to New York grants that provided rights under a patent issued by the crown to a private party—the

---

16. Allen, ed., *History of Enfield, Volume I*, 49; Fischer, *Albion's Seed*, 172–173. A 1648 Massachusetts statute required that a double portion of land go to the eldest sons in cases where there was no will so this would be a familiar practice even after Enfield joined Connecticut.
17. Wim Klooster, *Revolutions in the Atlantic World: A Comparative History* (New York: New York University Press, 2018), 41.
18. Kenneth S. Lynn, *A Divided People* (Westport: Greenwood Press, 1977), 40, suggests that loyalists were either dominated by their fathers or suffered from a lack of paternal guidance and therefore sought the king as a substitute authority picture. As the fourth son either category might have applied to Titus Simons but the fact that he decided to move suggests he was not dominated by his father.
19. Scott Andrew Bartley, *Migration: A Story of Vermont Before 1850*, at https://www.americanancestors.org/features/vermontmigration.

patent holder. The New Hampshire prices also were substantially lower. Township grants from New Hampshire cost £20 for 15,000 acres compared to £330 for comparable acreage purchased from New York. The quitrent paid to the king for 100 acres was one shilling for a New Hampshire grant and two shillings sixpence for a New York grant of the same acreage.[20]

Fourteen years later, in 1763, New York's Lt. Governor Cadwallader Colden argued that land grants sold by New Hampshire in the Green Mountains west of the Connecticut River were invalid since this territory was part of New York.[21] In July 1764, the King supported New York's claim, leaving the New Hampshire settlers little recourse. By 1770, all of the court cases ruled for New York petitioners, which convinced many with New Hampshire grants in the Green Mountains that the courts were biased against them.[22]

Despite these conflicts, the land and location were highly sought after and settlers came from Connecticut, Massachusetts and the British Isles.[23] For example, the famous Vermont patriot Ethan Allen also moved from Connecticut to Vermont about the same time as Titus. While the vast majority of Vermont settlers purchased New Hampshire grants, Hartland was initially settled under a New York grant and Titus took his land under the New York land patent. Titus simply followed the Connecticut River 120 miles north of Enfield to settle his new property at the "far southeast corner" of Hartland (called Hertford at the time), Vermont.[24]

There is some question of the exact date of Titus' move to Vermont. Family legend says he moved to Vermont in 1771—the "next year" after his wife reportedly died in 1770.[25] As discussed above, his wife may

---

20. Jessie Haas, *Revolutionary Westminster: From Massacre to Statehood* (Charleston: History Press, 2011), 23.
21. Michael A. Bellesiles, *Revolutionary Outlaws: Ethan Allen and the Struggle for Independence on the Early American Frontier* (Charlottesville: University Press of Virginia, 1993), 33.
22. Robert E. Shalhope, *Bennington and the Green Mountain Boys: The Emergence of Liberal Democracy in Vermont, 1760–1850* (Baltimore: Johns Hopkins University Press, 1996), 75.
23. Paul R. Huey, "Charlotte County," in Joseph S. Tiedermann and Eugene R. Fingerhut, eds., *The Other New York: The American Revolution Beyond New York City* (Albany: State University of New York Press, 2005), 199–222.
24. Hamilton Vaughn Bail, "Zadock Wright: That 'Devilist' Tory of Hartland," *Vermont History* 36 (Autumn 1968): 186–203 at 194.
25. John Robinson Simons, "The Fortunes of a United Empire Loyalist Family," *Ontario Historical Society Papers and Records* 23 (1926): 470–483 at 470.

have died in June 1771, making it more likely that Titus moved in 1772. Furthermore, Titus Simons was not listed as one of 25 heads of household (there were 32 men over age 16 and 144 people total) in the April 1771 New York Census of Hartford.[26] He also was sought in Enfield in October 1771 to collect a debt from May 1769.[27] Finally, Titus was listed in Enfield town records as late as January 1772 as the town collector appeared to be waiting on the "sundry person rates" for seven people, including Titus Simons.[28]

It seems likely that Titus Simons moved to Hartland during or sometime before the spring of 1772 in order to plant crops there. In any event, Titus Simons can be documented as living in Hartland on October 10, 1772 when he witnessed an indenture for Zadock Wright of Hartland.[29] D. A. Smith's research notes indicate that Titus "Simonds" settled in Hartland in 1773, having purchased 150 acres under a New York grant making him a yeoman (small landowner). The notes are unclear but he may have purchased part of the estate settled by Charles Ward Apthorpe. His occupation is listed as a merchant.[30] An indenture dated April 19, 1774, also describes Titus as a merchant.[31] Over the next two years, he witnessed several other indentures for Wright.[32]

Titus was not the first nor would he be the last Enfielder to move to Vermont. His uncle Shubael Geer and others traveled to Andover, Vermont, in 1768, attempted a settlement, but quickly abandoned it. In December 1774 the proprietors of Andover held a meeting at John Simons Jr.'s house (Titus's eldest brother) in Enfield to draft property lots. They also voted to lay a road from Chester to Andover. John Simons Jr. was

---

26. Jay Mack Holbrook, *Vermont 1771 Census* (Oxford, MA: Holbrook Research Institute, 1982), ii, xix–xx.
27. Letter from Henry Wilmot of New York to Titus Simons of Endfield (*sic*), October 5, 1771, New Jersey Historical Society, MG 824, Box 115, Folder 62.
28. Allen, ed., *History of Enfield, Volume II*, 971, 1150. Presumably Titus was still in Enfield at this time. Titus Simons' rates are mentioned in town records again in November 1772 first by an estate that apparently was owed the rate and later by a different party seeking abatement of the rate for five men including Titus Simons and Shubael Geere. Perhaps Titus was seeking an abatement because he had left town.
29. Scott Andrew Bartley, "Cumberland County, New York, Land Deeds, Vol. 1, 1761–1774," *Vermont Genealogy* 13 (2008):44.
30. *Early Vermont Settlers Index Cards, 1750–1784*. (Online database: *AmericanAncestors.org*, New England Historic Genealogical Society, 2019). From source materials for *Legacy of Dissent: Religion and Politics in Revolutionary Vermont, 1749–1784* (Worcester, MA: D.A. Smith, 1980).
31. Bartley, "Deeds": 48.
32. Ibid.: 46.

elected to be treasurer and a member of the road committee. In June 1776, John Simons Jr. and about thirteen families, including several from his militia unit and reportedly Titus' father John Simons Sr., would make a successful second attempt to settle there.[33] This group migration from Enfield is reminiscent of the original group migration from the Salem area to Enfield nearly a century earlier. John Simons Jr. built the first saw and grist mill in Andover.[34]

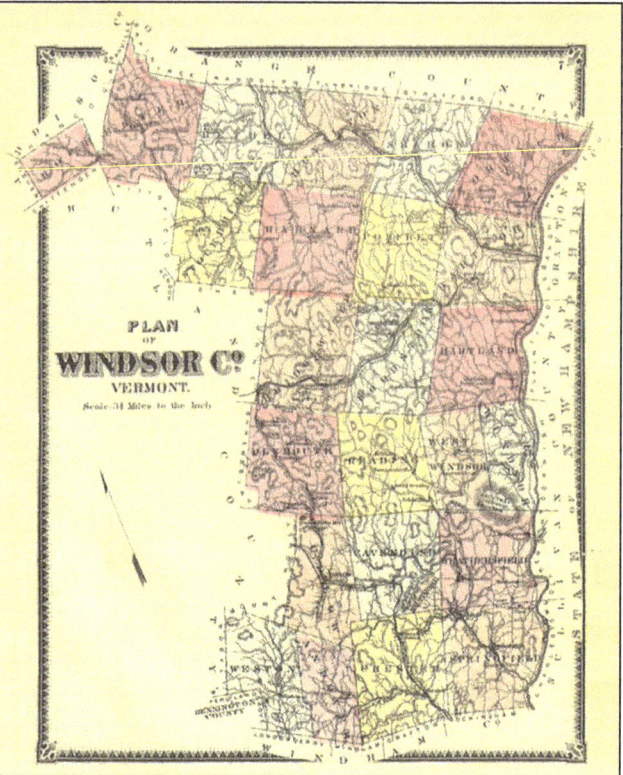

Figure 3.2. Map of Windsor County

John Simon[d]s was listed as Andover's representative to the General Assembly in 1781–82; this also probably refers to John Jr., since John Sr. died and was buried in Enfield in 1781.[35] John Jr. is listed as representative in 1784 while he served as Town Clerk from 1783–1785 and then as Town Treasurer from 1787–1792. John Simon[d]s also served as a Se-

---

33. Lewis C. Aldrich and Frank R. Holmes, *The History of Windsor County, Vermont*, transcribed by Jan Grant (1891).
34. Dennis Flower, *Hartland in the Revolutionary War with Associated History* (Hartland: Solitarian Press, 1914), 38; Henry P. Johnston, ed., *Record of Service of Connecticut Men in the War of the Revolution* (Hartford: Case, Lockwood and Brainard Co., 1889), 10, 381. There is some confusion regarding records identifying John Simons Jr. Titus' father John Simons, Sr. died in 1781. John Jr. (1724–1797), Titus's brother, is sometimes labeled Captain John Simons. This John Simons also had a son of the same name who was born in January 1751 in Enfield, married Ann Harper in December 1776 in Hartford County, and then moved to Andover, Vermont. This younger John died in 1814, reportedly in New York. He may have accounted for some of the references to John Simons Jr after his grandfather had died.
35. John Simons, Find A Grave, https://www.findagrave.com/memorial/32603282/john-simons.

lectman from 1780–1786 and in 1792.³⁶ Both Andover and Hartland are within Windsor County with Andover to the south and west of Hartland as illustrated by the map opposite (Figure 3.2).

Arriving in Vermont by spring 1772 would leave Titus nearly two years to meet and court his second wife. The marriage registration below (Figure 3.3) shows that on February 1, 1774, Titus Simons was married to his second wife Jerusha Kingsley by Zadock Wright, a Justice of the Peace of the Province of New York, who had been in Hartland since April 1772. Wright also was one of the original Hartland settlers under the New York patent. Jerusha was reportedly born on September 17, 1743 in Windham, Vermont, the daughter of John Kingsley (born about 1721)³⁷ and his wife Elizabeth.

As was the case with his first marriage in Enfield, Titus and his new wife probably attempted to settle down and enjoy family life. They were blessed with their first child together, who was born March 17, 1775 and named Jerusha for her mother.³⁸ Ten-year-old Titus Geer Simons now had a baby sister. They enjoyed about three years of a fairly normal life interspersed with some political intrigue. Unfortunately for their dreams of a quiet life, tensions between New Hampshire grant holders and the government of New York and tensions between colonists and the crown continued.

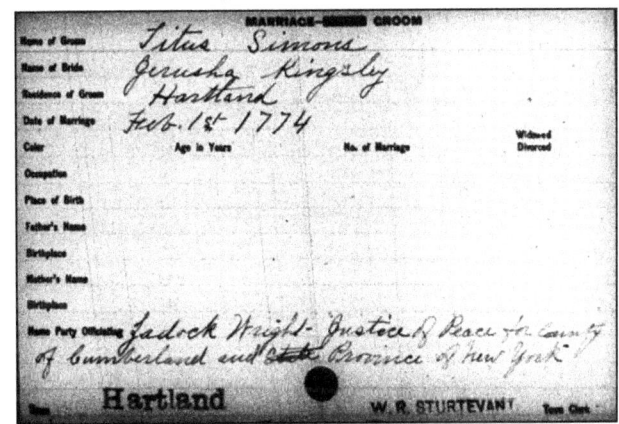

Figure 3.3. Marriage Registration for Titus Simons and Jerusha Kingsley

---

36. Lewis C. Aldrich and Frank R. Holmes, *The History of Windsor County Vermont*, 622–626.
37. *Early Vermont Settlers Index Cards, 1750-1784*. https://www.americanancestors.org/databases/early-vermont-settlers-index-cards-1750-1784/image?volumeId=56488&pageName=1428&rId=1425781151.
38. She would marry John Detlor in 1790 and have several children before her death in 1847.

CHAPTER FOUR

The Coming of the American Revolution and the Battles at Saratoga

After the Boston Tea Party in December 1773, Britain enacted the so-called Intolerable or Coercive Acts in June 1774 that closed the port of Boston and decreed that all judges and representatives in Massachusetts government would be appointed by the crown. Town meetings were limited to one per year. This led New England towns to organize and muster militia as well as stockpile ammunition. In August and September 1774, large crowds shut down the courts in several New England cities. In October 1774, the First Continental Congress adopted Articles of Association where the colonies (except for New York) agreed to cut off all trade with Great Britain, Ireland, and the East Indies.

Trouble in Westminster and Beyond

Westminster, in what is now Vermont, 35 miles south of Hartland, hosted a two-day convention to condemn the actions of Parliament—not as revolutionaries but as loyal British subjects. Two more conventions were held at Westminster in November 1774 (when Cumberland County, New York, voted to adhere to the provisions of the Articles of Association despite New York's reluctance) and February 1775.[1]

In March 1775 not only was Titus' daughter Jerusha born, but a riot also occurred at nearby Westminster. There a group of local settlers occupied the court house in order to prevent the court from conducting its business of hearing several mortgage forfeiture cases. The New York sheriff showed up with a posse and ordered his men to take the court house by force, which they did. Two of the occupiers were killed. The

---

1. Jessie Haas, *Revolutionary Westminster: From Massacre to Statehood* (Charleston, SC: The History Press, 2011), 43–47.

next day the militia known as the Green Mountain Boys arrived and arrested members of the court and the sheriff, sending them to Massachusetts. These latter events inflamed residents who called for another Cumberland County convention at Westminster for April 11, 1775 to discuss them. This convention was focused on court maladministration and rebelling against the colony of New York for not agreeing with the Articles of Association.[2]

Some claim the Westminster "massacre" was the true start of the American Revolution[3] but it was soon overshadowed by the famous battles at Lexington and Concord that were fought one month later on April 19, 1775.[4] Neither set of events had a direct impact on Titus and his family in Vermont but after Lexington and Concord, men from Connecticut and other colonies "marched for the relief of Boston." From Enfield those militiamen included Titus' brother, Captain John Simons Jr., as well as several cousins. Captain John served for six days before returning home. As George Washington organized the Continental Army, three regiments of militia from Connecticut occupied Boston from January through March 1776. Colonel Wolcott's regiment included Captain John Simons' company and Captain Jonathan Wells' company from Hartford, which included Titus' brother Private "Ashna" (Asahel) Simons.[5]

Most Vermonters supported protests against British actions. In May 1775, the Second Continental Congress met in Philadelphia. Benjamin Franklin later wrote, "I never had heard in any Conversation from any Person drunk or sober, the least Expression of a wish for a Separation, or Hint that such a Thing would be advantageous to America."[6]

Roughly seven months later in January 1776, Thomas Paine published his famous pamphlet *Common Sense* advocating independence from Britain (Paine would later coin the name "United States of America"). Now protesting colonists had to decide if they favored independence or reconciliation with Britain and American's continued membership in

---

2. Jennifer S. H. Brown and Wilson B. Brown, *Col. William Marsh: Vermont Patriot and Loyalist* (Denver: Tiger Rock Press, 2013), 100–101; Haas, *Westminster*, 87.
3. Haas, *Westminster*.
4. Theodore Corbett, *No Turning Point: The Saratoga Campaign in Perspective* (Norman, OK: University of Oklahoma Press, 2012), 79.
5. Henry P. Johnson, ed., *The Record of Connecticut Men in the Military and Naval Service During the War of the Revolution 1775–1783*, Vol. 1–3 (Hartford, 1889), 10, 381, 384.
6. Benjamin Franklin, quoted in Arendt, *On Revolution*, 44, from Clinton Rossiter, *The First American Revolution* (New York, 1956), 4.

the British Empire. The Second Continental Congress would draft and adopt the Declaration of Independence and become the de facto independent government for the colonies during the American Revolution. In January 1776, it also would pass the Tory Act, stating that those supporting the revolution should first try to persuade those who were loyal to the crown. However, those who explicitly supported the cause of the crown should be dealt with by local councils of safety and should be disarmed and perhaps imprisoned.

In attempt to control their own fate, the future Vermonters held another Vermont convention at Westminster in January 1777. This was the first convention to include 22 representatives from 16 towns including both those who favored New York grants and those who favored New Hampshire grants. The convention voted to declare the area known as the "New Hampshire Grants" as an independent entity initially called New Connecticut but renamed Vermont six months later. It also petitioned for statehood to the Continental Congress but that body rejected the petition based on opposition by New York which still claimed the territory. Vermont then declared itself to be an independent republic.[7]

As Vermont was trying to determine its own fate, the British made plans to suppress the revolution. In order to separate the most troublesome New England colonies from the others, British commander General John Burgoyne planned to invade New York from Canada and meet up with similar armies from the west and south thereby controlling the Hudson River and isolating New England. Burgoyne successfully recaptured Fort Ticonderoga on July 5, 1777 and then engaged the withdrawing rebels including local militia at Hubbardton, Vermont, two days later.[8] Vermonters were nervous about being attacked so a 13-person committee of safety was appointed to act statewide on July 8, 1777 in order to seize loyalist property and sell it in order to raise funds for a Vermont militia.[9] The committee called on neighboring states for aid on July 15 but three days later it authorized a three-regiment brigade be commanded by John Stark.[10]

---

7. Haas, 106; Brown and Brown, Marsh, 109–125.
8. Corbett, *No Turning Point*, 127–132.
9. Mary Greene Nye, "Loyalists and their Property," *Proceedings of the Vermont Historical Society* 10, no. 1 (1942): 36–44.
10. Michael P. Gabriel, *The Battle of Bennington: Soldiers and Civilians* (Charleston: History Press, 2010), 106.

To finance the newly formed Vermont militia, the various local committees of safety, authorized at the Windsor convention in June 1777, began condemning those who were loyal to Great Britain. On July 25, 1777, just two weeks after the Vermont-wide committee of safety was formed, Titus was among the first to be brought before the Committee of Safety at Hartland. Apparently, he had enough integrity to not try to hide his support of the crown and his loyalty to Britain was well known. His trial seems to have taken a half day. According to bills submitted to cover the cost of Simons' half-day trial in Hartland, the following people were paid to be present: billing 18 shillings (20 shillings = £1) for 1½ days' work: Stephen Tilden, William Dean, Darius Sessions, and Secretary Amos Robinson; billing 12 shillings for one day: Elijah Hore, Capt. Abel Marsh, Dr. Joseph Marsh (later Lieutenant Governor). Dr. Stephen Powers billed for just half a day. All of these people and others also billed half a day for the trial of Jonathan Pirce that occurred on the same day.[11] Only Robinson, Dr. Marsh and Commissioner Benjamin Emmons attended additional trials in the fall of 1777. There were no reimbursement records suggesting that Titus Simons called any witnesses in his own defense.

By the time of the trial, Simons had likely been arrested, jailed and his property placed under control of the committee. The bill includes funding for guards who would not have been necessary had Titus not been under arrest. At this time only personal property was confiscated. The confiscation of land was not authorized until March 1778.[12] The family story is that he was imprisoned for his loyalist beliefs but freed by his wife who brought him a dress to wear to fool the guards.[13]

Titus Fights for a Loyalist Regiment

Simons escaped sometime after his July 1777 trial and could have fled to Canada but he decided to follow the example of some of his relatives and enlist in the militia. With this decision, he joined about 19,000 loyalists who served in loyalist militia regiments. As with his move to Vermont,

---

11. Mary Greene Nye, ed., *State Papers of Vermont, Volume Six: Sequestration, Confiscation and Sale of Estate* (1941), 209–210.
12. Corbett, *No Turning Point*, 280.
13. H. H. Robertson, "Major Titus Gear Simons at Lundy's Lane," *Journal and Transactions of the Wentworth Historical Society* 2 (1899): 49–54 at 53. Apparently, this method of escape was not unusual. Margaret Brush used a similar tactic to free her husband Crean from a Boston jail in November 1777 (Haas, Westminster, 114).

we can only speculate about his motives to enlist. Clearly, as a merchant Titus preferred trade within rather than from without the British Empire. Such trade would be under the protection of the British fleet. He also may have had a conservative nature like his Puritan ancestors or simply felt loyal to his country and king. Perhaps he was simply angry with his intolerant neighbors for condemning him and seizing his property because of his personal political beliefs. In any event enlisting was the most direct way to fight in order to regain his Vermont property. At that time, loyalists generally believed the British would triumph in this struggle.

But for Titus Simons, husband and father, enlisting held high risk. It meant leaving his wife and children in Vermont hoping the safety committee would leave enough resources for them to survive (which it generally did). Titus Geer Simons was about twelve years old so he could do chores on the farm and hopefully avoid being inducted by the rebel army. As we shall see in the next chapter, the family did survive but survival must have been a worry for Titus at the time he enlisted.

In addition to his personal feelings, Titus probably was encouraged to enlist by his loyalist friends. He was a member of Rev. Samuel Peters' parish in Vermont and had been married by Hartland Justice of the Peace and loyalist Zadock Wright so it not surprising he was recruited by the latter to join Rev. Peters' nephew John Peters' provincial regiment, known officially as the Queen's Loyal Rangers (QLR). Even though he was a loyalist, John Peters was a community leader and had been elected as one of Vermont's representatives to the Continental Congress. In May 1777, John Peters was encouraged to raise a loyalist provincial regiment that he would command as a lieutenant colonel. The following month, General Burgoyne ordered Peters' QLR to join his army. Although Peters had raised 643 men, at the first official muster on July 23 at Skenesborough, N.Y., Colonel Peters mustered only 262 men.[14] Titus Simons probably had not yet joined and there was certainly pressure for QLR officers to keep recruiting. Zadock Wright, Simons' neighbor and friend joined the unit as a captain (but was soon promoted to major) in August 1777.[15]

Simons presumably traveled to Stillwater, N.Y., where the QLR was

---

14. Edmond Frank Peters and Eleanor Bradley Peters, *Peters of New England: A Genealogy, and Family History* (New York: The Knickerbocker Press, 1903), 372–73.
15. LAC War Office Papers, W.O. 28, Vol 10, Part 2, p. 268; C-10862, image 69.

headquartered to enlist but his exact date of enlistment is not clear.[16] A December 1780 letter from Colonel John Peters to General Guy Carlton indicates that on August 14, 1777 Simons' neighbor Zadock Wright was promoted to major (and captured less than a week later) and Simons enlisted as quartermaster. Elijah Grout was recruited as an ensign after serving as acting quartermaster since July 15. Several other officers were enlisted at this time to satisfy Wright's recruitment goals in order for him to be promoted to major.[17] Another source indicates that Simons enlisted in August 1777 as a lieutenant.[18] One source indicates that nearly 200 loyalists joined Peters after his July muster of 263 men but before the Battle of Bennington.[19] However, some of these may have been rebel spies who rejoined the rebels at the battle.[20]

Other sources indicate Simons joined the QLR sometime between September 4 and October 1. Family legend says he enlisted on September 4 and was posted as a lieutenant in Major Wright's company.[21] He was reportedly assigned to be regimental quartermaster on September 13, 1777.[22] Another source says he did not officially become quartermaster until October 1. In all cases, sources agree Titus replaced Lieutenant Elijah Grout as quartermaster. Grout was first appointed acting quar-

16. The statement of Captain Justus Sherwood dated 1796 says Titus joined Peter's Corp. at Stillwater in 1777 (Upper Canada Law Petitions LAC vol. 448A, "S" Bundle 2, petition Number 107, p. 107a). A subsistence muster roll dated October 24, 1777 in the John Peters papers in the New York State Archives indicates Simons joined on the unlikely date of June 25, 1777 and served 122 days at 4/8 per diem for a total of £28/9 shillings/4 pence. The pay rate of 4 shillings and 8 pence was consistent through 1783. It is possible he joined this early and perhaps did not attend his July 25 Council of Safety trial or perhaps after joining he was captured and did attend. However, a review of these rolls suggests June 25 was the default date listed for most people unless the compiler knew or learned of a different date.
17. LAC War Office Papers, W.O. 28, Vol 10, Part 2, p. 268; C-10862, image 69.
18. J. F. Pringle, *Lunenburgh, or the Old Eastern District* (1890), Appendix A; Extracts from the Haldimand Papers in the Canadian Archives, Series B, vol. 167, 322, available at http://my.tbaytel.net/bmartin/aid.htm.
19. Thomas C. Lamper, "The Missisquoi Loyalists," *Proceedings of the Vermont Historical Society* 6, no. 2 (June 1938): 81–97 at 87.
20. Mary Beacock Fryer, *Buckskin Pimpernel: The Exploits of Justus Sherwood, Loyalist Spy* (Toronto: Dundurn Press, 1981), 58.
21. This return is reproduced in Hamilton Vaughn Bail, "Zadock Wright: That 'Devilish' Tory of Hartland," *Vermont History* 36 (Autumn 1968): 186–203 at 193.
22. John Robinson Simons, "The Fortunes of a United Empire Loyalist Family," *Ontario Historical Society Papers and Records* 23 (1926): 470–483 at 470. H.H. Robertson does not list an enlistment date, but agrees with the appointment to Quartermaster on September 13, 1777. See H.H. Robertson, *Titus Simons, Quarter Master, Peters' Corps of "Queen's Loyal Rangers," Burgoyne's Campaign 1777–1812* (Hamilton, ON: H.H. Robertson, 1903). This work was previously published in the 1901–1902 *Annual Transactions of the United Empire Loyalists of Ontario*, 36–46.

termaster in July 1777 and presumably was not very good at it since he lasted as quartermaster for about two months.

Simons' background as a merchant qualified him to take inventory of regimental supplies and order what was needed through liaison with the Quartermaster General and Commissariat Department and other supply sources.[23] As quartermaster Titus Simons was responsible for provisioning his regiment with supplies (rations, uniforms, etc.) including ammunition before battle. During battle, Simons fought with his unit.

British Plan of Attack

As noted in the previous chapter, the British developed a straightforward plan for dealing with the rebellion—separate the most troublesome New England colonies from the other colonies by seizing control of the Hudson River in New York. General Burgoyne's plan was to head south from Canada in order to meet General Howe, coming north from New York City, in Albany. Burgoyne wanted to "win the hearts and minds" of the people as he traveled, offering protection to loyalists and encouraging those who could do so to enlist. When he left Canada, he had only 83 loyalists. At the peak of his recruiting efforts, loyalists numbered about 800 including Titus Simons—nearly ten times the number at the beginning.[24]

At the beginning of August 1777, Burgoyne was encamped south of Fort Edward with his headquarters at Fort Miller. He decided to send a foray into Vermont to obtain supplies and recruits. The expedition was led by German Colonel Baum, accompanied by the QLR because Peters was believed to be well known in the area and could use this foray to recruit. At the last minute the expedition was diverted from loyalist-friendly Arlington to rebel-held Bennington, Vermont. These troops left Fort Miller on August 11 and engaged the rebels on August 16 at the Battle of Bennington (Walloomsac).[25] Even if Simons had arrived in Stillwater as early as August 14, he probably would have been too late to join in this battle. Alternatively, perhaps he was one of the loyalists who joined up with Peters' corps while it moved through the area.

23. Ron W. Shaw, *First We Were Soldiers: The Long March to Perth* (Victoria, BC: FriesenPress, 2015), 5. Perhaps Lieutenant Grout was replaced as quartermaster as part of a general review of the existing regimental quartermasters after s a "failure in the management of ammunition" during the Battle of Bennington British defeat in August 1777 (Haas, *Westminster*, 94. See also Gabriel, *Battle of Bennington*, 106).
24. Corbett, *No Turning Point*, 137.
25. Ibid., 183–199.

Peters commanded about 280 loyalists at the August 16, 1777 Battle of Bennington. After a full day of fighting, they were forced to retreat having lost more than half the men (but only one lieutenant killed and one captured).[26] Despite this loss at Bennington, recruiting of loyalists continued. By September 1, there were 682 loyalists with Burgoyne including those with Peters.[27] This is another time when Simons may have joined Peters' unit to be appointed quartermaster on September 13. In a report dated October 1, Colonel Peters noted he had only received three new recruits since September 19 so it is likely Titus Simons joined before that date.[28]

During this time, the QLR retreated back toward Stillwater, fighting the rebels on September 7. From September 13 to 15, Burgoyne moved his army closer to Albany, occupying Schuler's plantation without resistance. Peters' QLR and other loyalist units served as scouts during this movement. They also manned and protected the supply boats (bateaux) on the Hudson River.[29]

The Battles at Saratoga

As discussed above, Titus Simons had likely joined the QLR before September 19 when Burgoyne engaged the enemy at the first battle of Saratoga at Freeman's Farm. Burgoyne sent three columns of 2,000 soldiers each toward the farm where they ran across and attacked the rebel's light infantry. Some of the QLRs were in the right flank and they responded when ordered to protect Burgoyne's men in the center.[30] Others were back in the redoubt where Colonel Breymen was killed by his own German soldiers as he used his sabre on them to encourage them to fight.[31] The rebels were forced back, but in pursuit, the British became too spread out. The battle went back and forth until Burgoyne's third column of German troops finally counter-attacked, driving the rebels from the field. Fifty-seven QLRs were killed that day and in total Burgoyne lost

---

26. Wilbur H. Siebert, "The American Loyalists in the Eastern Seigniories and Townships of the Province of Quebec," *Transactions of the Royal Society of Canada* (3rd series) 7 (1913): 3–41 at 9.
27. Corbett, *No Turning Point*, 205.
28. Mary Beacock Fryer, *King's Men: The Soldier Founders of Ontario*, Toronto, ON: Dundurn Press (1980), pp. 220–222.
29. Corbett, *No Turning Point*, 217–218.
30. Fryer, *Buckskin Pimpernel*, 68; Corbett, *No Turning Point*, 219.
31. Robertson, *Titus Simons, Quarter Master*, 7.

600 men compared to just 65 rebel deaths with 300 rebels wounded.[32]

Within days, some of Burgoyne's staff was urging a second attack before the rebels fully fortified their position but Burgoyne heard that General Clinton was moving north from New York City and he hoped to soon have the rebels caught between the two armies, so he decided not to attack.[33] On September 21, Burgoyne did integrate 120 loyalists into his regular units to bolster their ranks. However, these were men of proven loyalty and since Simons was a relative newcomer, he likely remained with QLR.[34]

On October 6, when all sources agree Simons had joined, loyalists and natives skirmished with rebels for two hours, driving them back to their pickets with only slight losses to the loyalists. The next day, Burgoyne led 1,700 men in a reconnaissance party including a group of Germans led by loyalists and natives. Unexpectedly, he engaged the entire rebel army (about 8,000) at Bemis Heights. After a day of fighting, Burgoyne's force withdrew back to the safety of its encampment.[35] Eighty more of Peters' provincials had been caught or captured. The QLR now had only 62 men of all ranks.[36]

Burgoyne decided to retreat on October 9, 1777. Burgoyne continued to hope to unite with General Clinton's forces from the south. Burgoyne began construction of a temporary bridge at Fort Edward and Captain McKay was put in charge of loyalists assigned to guard the workers. However, they were attacked by rebels and McKay and the loyalists retreated toward Ticonderoga (followed by the bridge workers). They arrived at Ticonderoga on October 17, the same day Burgoyne surrendered after his escape route had been cut off by the rebels.[37] Meanwhile on October 9, a group of loyalists and bateaux men led by Edward Jessup, Daniel McAlpin and Hugh Monro recaptured 18 bateaux (boats) from the rebels.[38] During all of these various skirmishes, the precise involvement of Titus Simons is not known beyond the fact that he survived apparently uninjured.

Peters was concerned about treatment of loyalist prisoners whom

32. Fryer, *King's Men*, 220.
33. Corbett, *No Turning Point*, 219–223.
34. Ibid., 224.
35. Ibid., 231–233.
36. Fryer, *Buckskin Pimpernel*, 73.
37. Corbett, *No Turning Point*, 246–248.
38. Ibid., 242.

the rebels considered traitors rather than prisoners of war. General Burgoyne shared those concerns so on October 14, 1777 Peters received written orders to take as many QLRs as he could and flee to Canada. That night, 35 loyalists left the camp. It is not clear if Titus Simons was in this group or had left earlier, but it was later reported that only 11 loyalists (wounded Captain Sherwood and 10 privates) were with Burgoyne when he surrendered. Five hundred and sixty-two loyalists safely arrived in Canada including 77 loyalists reported safe with Peters. This included Peters' quartermaster—presumably Simons.[39] Peters' group narrowly avoided capture by a group of rebels and eventually made their way to Fort Ticonderoga where they stayed under the command of General Henry Watson Powell until the fort was evacuated. They helped destroy the fortifications preparing the fort for its abandonment on November 8 when all troops headed for St. Johns, as pictured below.[40]

Figure 4.1. A South-West View of St. Johns, James Peachey, c. 1784.

Retreat to St. Johns, Quebec

Peters went from St. Johns to Quebec to meet with General Carleton and lobby for the pay he had never received for his service.[41] Burgoyne had decided that Peters had not satisfied his recruiting goal to be paid as a lieutenant colonel, while Peters argued that he did reach the goal but

---

39. Fryer, *King's Men*, 223.
40. Corbett, *No Turning Point*, 250–251.
41. Edmond Frank Peters and Eleanor Bradley Peters, *Peters of New England: A Genealogy, and Family History* (New York: The Knickerbocker Press, 1903), 375–78.

his unit was decimated shortly thereafter. Over the winter (1777–78), the remaining men of the QLR including Simons were posted to Fort St. Johns under the command of Sir John Johnson. In the spring of 1778, some of the men were sent on scouting/recruiting missions as far south as the Connecticut River Valley. A monthly return dated June 1, 1778 at Busherville (Boucherville, Quebec) indicated Simon(d)s had been absent since April 20 upon leave or under orders from General Powell.[42] Also on June 1, Sir Frederick Haldimand, the newly appointed governor of the Province of Quebec, ordered all troops bound by the Saratoga Convention not to fight for the British to return to duty because the rebels had broken other Convention surrender terms.[43] He estimated that he had 2,500 British and German regulars and about 3,400 loyalists spread across the frontier to the Great Lakes. Since loyalists were the largest group, Haldimand re-emphasized their importance and gradually took responsibility for loyalist family settlements.[44]

In 1778, the British used loyalists for raiding/foraging/scouting parties. Titus Simons was captured in late August 1778.[45] This most likely occurred at some point when Peters led a raiding party (200 provincials and 100 natives) to destroy the settlement at Cohoes, N.Y., on the Connecticut River. The trip was arduous and many abandoned it so the final 34 provincials were redirected to the head of the Onion (now Winooski) River and destroyed the block house at Fort Frederick and all buildings within 30 miles, returning to St. Johns on August 23, 1778 with all 34 men.[46] Haldimand was pleased with the captured loot and prisoners but disappointed with the limited scope of destruction.[47] The next month, the uncaptured members of the QLR were ordered to Sorel with other below-strength loyalist units (except Butler's Rangers) to construct winter fortifications to prevent a repeat of the rebel invasion in spring 1776.[48] Meanwhile, captured Titus Simons faced trial for being disloyal to Vermont and the United States.

42. The March 1 and April 1, 1778, monthly returns checked the quartermaster as present but did not name the quartermaster because only officers of captain's rank and above were named.
43. Fryer, *King's Men*, 224.
44. Corbett, *No Turning Point*, 261–263.
45. John Robinson Simons, "The Fortunes of a United Empire Loyalist Family," *Ontario Historical Society Papers and Records* 23 (1926): 470–483 at 470.
46. Peters and Peters, *Peters of New England*, 378–79.
47. Corbett, *No Turning Point*, 297.
48. Fryer, *King's Men*, 225; Fryer, *Buckskin Pimpernel*, 95.

CHAPTER FIVE

Titus Simons and Family become Refugees in Canada

As a prisoner, Titus Simons (Symonds) appeared before Benjamin Emmons, Commissioner of Confiscation, who billed Vermont for one day's fee at a rate of 1 pound, 1 shilling in late August 1778. Paul Spooner also billed the same amount for a journey to Captain Abel Marsh's house for a trial of Titus Simons and others around the same time.[1] Simons and Wright faced trial sometime after March 1778 by Marsh, Spooner and Emmons but the court lacked a quorum and took no action.[2] Simons was then billeted at Windsor, Vermont, under hard labor with the threat of flogging—"40 stripes on the naked back."[3] According to billing records, he was boarded with a John Benjamin from September 8, 1778 to February 17, 1779. John Burnum, Jr., the state attorney, charged Simons with "inimical conduct" toward Vermont and the United States before superior court in Bennington on December 10, 1778. Simons was charged with going "over to the enemy" on September 4, 1777.[4]

In February 1779, the execution of his sentence of banishment was suspended until June 1779. On February 29, 1779, Sheriff John Benjamin reported that he had confiscated promissory notes in favor of Titus Simons totaling 48 pounds, 16 shillings, and 6 pence.[5] An "Order of Court of Confiscation" dated June 3, 1779 noted that the court had heard

1. Mary Greene Nye, ed., *State Papers of Vermont, Volume 6: Sequestration, Confiscation and Sale of Estate* (1941), 290, 305.
2. Sarah V. Kalinoski, "Sequestration, Confiscation and the 'Tory' in the Vermont Revolution," *Vermont History* 45, no. 2 (1977): 236–246 at 241.
3. *Records of the Council of Safety and Governor and Council of the State of Vermont to Which are Prepared the Records of General Conventions from July 1775 to Dec. 1777, Vol. 1* (Montpelier: Steam Press of J&J Poland, 1873), 291.
4. Vermont Bar Association, *Acts of Incorporation, Constitution, Members, and Papers and Addresses Read* 1878–1881 (Montpelier, VT: Argus and Patriot Steam Book Press, 1882), 82–83.
5. Nye, ed., *State Papers of Vermont, Volume 6*, 333.

evidence concerning "Titus Simonds" and several others and had found that they had joined the "enimies of this & the United States." The court ordered confiscation of both real and personal property and empowered the local Commissioners for Sale of Confiscated Estates in each district to sell the estates to raise money for the state.[6] In the case of Titus Simons, the local commissioner was Captain William Gallup who sold a large amount of tory lands totaling 1,118 pounds, 13 shillings, 6 pence according to a report filed in February 1781.[7]

Migration to Canada—At Last

Vermont loyalists began to migrate to Canada after Burgoyne's defeat in the fall of 1777.[8] One and half years later, the Simons family finally migrated. On June 4, 1779, Captain John "Simonds" Jr. of the Andover, Vermont, militia was directed to transport the wife and family of his brother Titus Simons to Rutland, Vermont, and consult with the commanding officer there to transport the Simons family to Canada.[9] As noted above, John Simons was Titus' eldest brother, being 19 years older. John was appointed as an ensign in Enfield by at least March 1771, according to Enfield town records. After founding Andover, Vermont, with his father and other settlers from Enfield in June 1776, John Simons' militia was assigned to confiscate loyalist property. Andover was only about 40 miles from Hartland.

In the summer of 1779, John Jr. performed the bittersweet duty of escorting his baby brother and family to Canada.[10] The brothers likely realized they would not see each other again and Titus would probably never return to visit relatives in New England. Titus' father reportedly moved to Andover as well, so perhaps he joined his John to escort

---

6. Ibid., 27–28.
7. E. P. Walton, *Records of the Governor and Council of the State of Vermont, Volume 2* (Montpelier: Steam Press of J & J M. Poland, 1871), 76.
8. Theodore Corbett, *No Turning Point: The Saratoga Campaign in Perspective* (Norman, OK: University of Oklahoma Press, 2012), 274–276.
9. *Records of the Council of Safety, Vol. 1*, 291, 304.
10. Dennis Flower, *Hartland in the Revolutionary War with Associated History* (Hartland: Solitarian Press, 1914), 38; Henry P. Johnston, ed., *Record of Service of Connecticut Men in the War of the Revolution* (Hartford: Case, Lockwood and Brainard Co., 1889), 10, 381. The more famous father and son duo from this era, the John Adamses, also left the country at this time spending 14 months in France. See Nancy Isenberg and Andrew Burstein, *The Problem of Democracy: The Presidents Adams Confront the Cult of Personality* (New York: Viking 2019), 36.

Titus and family into exile.[11] John Simons Sr. passed away in January 1781 and was buried in Enfield.[12] We don't know if Titus ever heard this news since he was a refugee at the time. Captain John Simons Jr. had a grandson named Titus Simons (1783–1833), showing Titus was neither forgotten nor condemned for his loyalty by his New England relatives.

John Benjamin transported Titus Simons to Bennington, Vermont, and conducted other business according to an account he submitted on June 5, 1779.[13] Similarly, on July 7, 1779, Thomas Hale of Rutland billed the state of Vermont for boarding Mrs. Simons and two children (Titus Geer, age 14, and Jerusha, 4) for three weeks.[14] Ebenezer Curtis was commissioned as Commissioner for Sale of Confiscated Lands on July 16, 1779 (recorded October 2, 1779) to sell the land of Titus "Simonds," Zadock Wright of the QLR and Titus' friend and neighbor in Hartland, and three others. Titus Simons and family now had no property to return to in Vermont, had they ever wanted to return.

Once the Simons family reached the Vermont border, they then traveled by boat with other loyalist refugees to Montreal.[15] A July 19, 1779 subsistence list indicated that Peters had only 61 men at that time.[16] They were under the command of Captain Daniel McAlpin from June 1, 1778 until McAlpin's death in July 1780. Simons and family joined an estimated 1,000 refugees and an additional 2,000 loyalist troops in the area. They stayed at several different settlements in in the Montreal area for the next five years as illustrated by the map on the next page (Figure 4.1)

Refugee Camps

Records find the family billeted in Machiche on August 24 and October 24, 1779.[17] In October 1779, the number of refugees at Machiche peaked at 462.[18] The previous year, troops and able-bodied refugees at Machiche

---

11. Lewis C. Aldrich and Frank R. Holmes, *The History of Windsor County, Vermont*, transcribed by Jan Grant (1891).
12. John Simons, Find A Grave, https://www.findagrave.com/memorial/32603282/john-simons.
13. State of Vermont, Rolls of Men Engaged in the War of the Revolution, p. 791, available on Ancestry.com.
14. Nye, ed. (1941), *State Papers of Vermont, Volume 6*, 340.
15. John Robinson Simons, "The Fortunes of a United Empire Loyalist Family," *Ontario Historical Society Papers and Records* 23 (1926), 470–483 at 470.
16. Fryer, *King's Men*, 225.
17. Gavin K. Watt, *Loyalist Refugees: Non-military Refugees in Quebec 1776-1784* (Milton, ON: Global Heritage Press, 2014), 49–50.
18. Corbett, *No Turning Point*, 345.

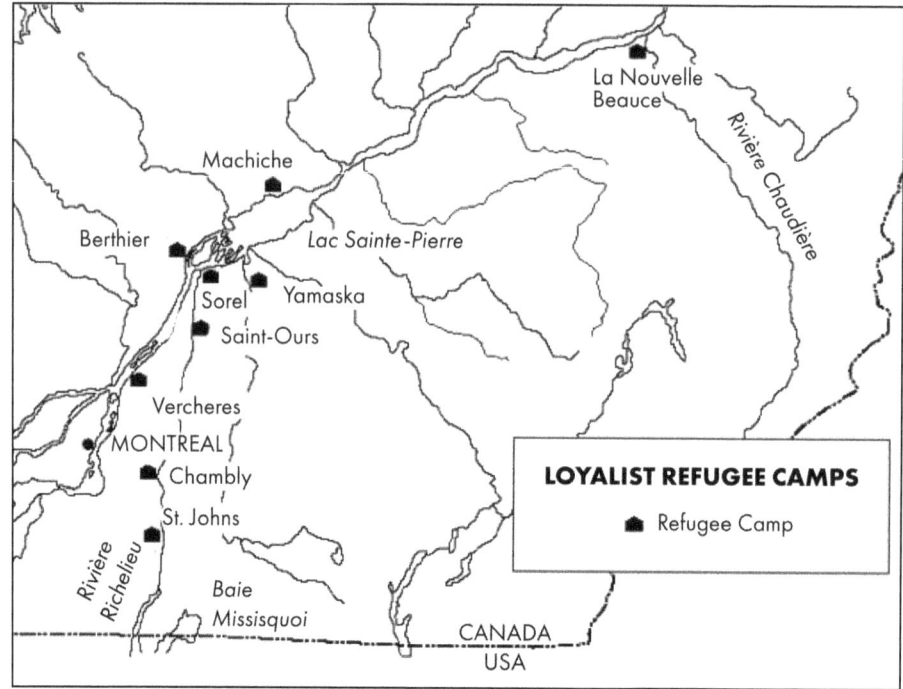

Figure 5.1. Loyalist Refugee Camps

had built twelve houses for refugees each measuring 18 feet by 40 feet. Collectively, these buildings could house 300 troops or 240 women and children, so 200 beds and sufficient household utensils were ordered.[19] Reports on conditions suggest that loyalist officers lived in these houses with their families.[20] The earlier inhabitants themselves agreed that 10 people could occupy one room suggesting that each building had just two rooms.[21] There were complaints of poor conditions at Machiche for the refugees.[22] But there also was a school at Machiche.[23] Perhaps young Jerusha attended as well as Titus Geer if he had not already received a basic education. We know Titus Geer could read and write since one of his first jobs was as a newspaper editor. If his education started in refugee camps, he also may have learned about the aristocratic beliefs of some loyalists who would become tories in Canada. Titus Geer also

---

19. William H. Siebert, "The Temporary Settlement of Loyalists at Machiche," *Proceedings and Transactions of the Royal Society of Canada* (3rd series) 8 (1915): 407–414 at 408.
20. Corbett, *No Turning Point*, 344.
21. Watt, *Loyalist Refugees*, 45–48.
22. http://www.canadiangenealogy.net/chronicles/loyalists_quebec.htm.
23. Siebert, "Temporary Settlement": 408.

probably worked with his father's unit when he was 14 in order to be treated as an adult refugee receiving a full ration.

Conditions at the refugee camps were challenging. One report suggested that the children at Machiche were severely malnourished and many mothers were depriving themselves of their own food in an effort to keep their children alive.[24] To alleviate this problem, loyalists were encouraged to grow or secure their own food. To assist in this venture, the government established a pasture for 50 cows and a garden for growing vegetables at Machiche.[25] Unfortunately, in 1778 the refugees at Machiche were only issued 24 kettles and eight frying pans.[26] These efforts to establish self-sufficiency among the loyalists failed miserably. By 1780, more than 262 men, 308 women, and 798 children at various refugee camps outside of Montreal alone were receiving public assistance in the form of food supplies from the government.[27]

By November 1780, the Simons family had moved south to St. Johns in what is now Quebec.[28] The following month on December 5, all loyalists at Vercheres were placed under the command of Major John Naire and Titus Simons again was appointed quartermaster.[29] Titus Simons was paid £14 for each day he was mustered to duty.[30] Muster rolls place Simons on December 5, 1780 at Vercheres but on QLR regimental returns dated December 14, 1780, Titus Simons was listed as quartermaster but was located at St. Johns. On the QLR muster roles from June 24 through December 25, 1780, Simons was listed as a lieutenant at Vercheres.[31] He was listed at Vercheres from December 25, 1780 through June 25, 1781.[32] The family moved to Vercheres by April 1781 and they were listed there in September 1781 as well.[33] Their daughter Eliza-

---

24. Major John Ross to Sir John Johnson, September 11, 1780, HP 21,824. Daniel McAlpin also would complain about the state of loyalist children and families under his care. "All are in a state of distress … and are in urgent need of help" (Daniel McAlpin to Haldimand, July 1, 1779, HP 21,819).
25. Haldimand to Germain, October 15, 1778, HP 21,819.
26. Gugy to Haldimand, November 16, 1778, HP 21,824.
27. Janice Potter-MacKinnon, *Women Only Wept: Loyalist Refugee Women in Eastern Ontario* (Montreal: McGill-Queen's University Press, 1993), 107–110.
28. Watt, *Loyalist Refugees*, 273.
29. H. H. Robertson, *Titus Simons, Quarter Master, Peters' Corps of "Queen's Loyal Rangers," Burgoyne's Campaign 1777–1812* (Hamilton, ON: H.H. Robertson, 1903), 8.
30. Watt, *Loyalist Refugees*, 273.
31. John Peters Papers.
32. According to a muster roll in the John Peters Papers collection dated July 14, 1781.
33. Watt, *Loyalist Refugees*, 273.

Figure 5.2. Loyalist Encampment in Johnstown on the banks of the St. Lawrence River in Canada West, June 6, 1784, by J. R. Simpson, after James Peachey

beth was presumably born there in August 1781 according to her grave marker.

Loyalist Militia Work

In a December 14, 1780 letter to General Guy Carleton, Colonel John Peters explained what had happened to some of his officers that caused his low current staffing. He noted:

> Mr. Simons was forbid doing duty as an Officer by Major McAlpin in 1779, the other officers of the corps having refused to do duty with him as he had in the most patient, submissive and good natured manner received a decent cudgeling from Major [James] Rogers.[34]

Despite this setback, Titus Simons recovered at least his reputation by January 4, 1781, when William Fraser's company was ordered to the post of Yamaska as soon as possible after they obtained new uniforms. According to Regimental Orders in Jessup's Orderly Book at Vercheres:

---

34. LAC, Naire fonds, MMG23, GIII3, v. 3, pp. 269-270; C-10862, image 71. Fryer, *King's Men*, 239, indicates this was Henry rather than Titus Simons in 1779. She seems to be referring to Lieutenant Henry Simmons in Jessup's King's Loyal Rangers. See Mark Jodoin, *Shadow Soldiers of the American Revolution: Loyalist Tales from New York to Canada* (Charleston: The History Press, 2009), 97–107. Watt, *Loyalist Refugees,* 274, reports that a private Henry Simmons also of the Rangers was discharged in 1778 to support his large family. While these others are possibilities, there would be no reason for Colonel Peters to discuss this incident if it were not related to one of his soldiers.

Mr. Titus Simons is Required to over look the Taylors belonging to the Corps of Royalists and Take Perticular Care that They Shall on No Pretences Do Any Other Work Till the Clothing of Mr. William Frasers Company is finished.[35]

On May 1, 1781, Simons was listed as a lieutenant in the Queen's Loyal Rangers under John Peters with no quartermaster listed. On August 25, 1781, he was listed as acting quartermaster under Major Naire. Two days earlier, Major Naire had posted orders that loyalist officers were to send Simons "an exact provision return, weekly etc."[36]

At this time Titus Simons was located in Vercheres with one male child over six (Titus Geer Simons, born 1765), one female child over six (Jersusha, born 1775) and two female children under six (newborn Elizabeth born August 20, 1781 in Vercheres/Montreal. The second daughter under six appears to be a mistake. His next daughter, Sophia, is believed to have been born in 1782 in Montreal).[37] In November 1781, Major Naire's loyalists were subsumed under the Loyal Rangers with Major Edward Jessup commanding. At this point, Simons was receiving half pay, £7 per muster, which would continue through 1783.[38] John Ferguson was appointed quartermaster, but Lieutenant Simons served until the Loyal Rangers were disbanded the day before Christmas in 1783 when he would become a half-pay officer receiving a half-pay stipend for the rest of his life.[39]

During this time, the Loyal Rangers supported the British war efforts by foraging for supplies and constructing fortifications.[40] Family legend holds that young Titus Geer Simons "carried a musket" with his father.[41] One undocumented source claims the younger Simons enlisted in 1778

---

35. A: *Clothing Provincials in the Canadian Department*, 2007, p. 32, available at http://royalyorkers.ca/documents/A-MILITARYCLOTHINGQUEBEC.pdf, accessed July 31, 2015.
36. Simons, "Fortunes": 471. See also Robertson, *Titus Simons*, 8.
37. Watt, *Loyalist Refugees*, 273. For Elizabeth's exact birthdate in Montreal, see William D. Reid, *The Loyalists in Ontario* (1993), 291.
38. Watt, *Loyalist Refugees*, 273.
39. Simons, "Fortunes": 470–483; Mary Beacock Fryer, *Buckskin Pimpernel: The Exploits of Justus Sherwood, Loyalist Spy* (Toronto: Dundurn Press, 1981), 201.
40. Fryer, *King's Men*, ch. 9.
41. Hamilton UEL, *Loyalist Ancestors: Some Families of the Hamilton Area* Toronto: Familia Genealogical Services (1986), 225; Simons, "Fortunes": 473; Robertson, *Titus Simons*, 8.

when he was 13 years old.[42] Enlistment this early seems unlikely because it was before the rest of the family migrated to Canada (Titus Geer was lodged with his mother and sister for three weeks in Vermont before they left for Canada). Furthermore, Titus Geer himself never asserted any such official service when seeking government rewards for his service. Over time, rations diminished so boys over twelve who had not enlisted might have been removed from the ration roll in order to encourage them to work.[43] Perhaps Titus Geer received rations informally for working with his father. This still was better than having Titus Geer remain in Vermont where he might have been compelled to join patriot forces, as was common for boys over twelve regardless of their political leanings.[44]

The family continued in the Montreal area, first at Riviere-du-Chene in March and July 1783 and then Coteau-du-Law by January 1784. Titus' daughter Mary was born in 1783. By September 1784, Titus Simons' family is listed in a return of loyalists and disbanded troops in and about the Montreal area. The survey is inaccurate, not listing any adult males, listing one male under 10 when Titus Jr. was 19, and only listing two females under 10 when there actually were four young daughters.[45] The following month Lieutenant Simons is listed with more than 400 other settlers in the Ernestown settlement; the listing includes the two parents, three females, one male over 10 years old and one female under 10. Perhaps three of the daughters were reported as over 10 in order to get a full ration for each of them. They had cleared five acres of land and collectively received six and one half rations.[46] Many of Jessup's Loyal Rangers settled in Ernestown with the bulk of them settling in Edwardsburgh, Augusta, and Elizabethtown.

The road (or more accurately the St. Lawrence River) to settlement at Cataraqui (now Kingston) was not easy. Governor Haldimand had ordered all those refugees who were going to settle in the Cataraqui area

42. The Dundas Museum houses the Woodhouse Family History Collection which consists of unsourced notes on the family history of various Dundas-area families and people.
43. Potter-MacKinnon, *Women*, 120.
44. Ibid., 86, 117. Loyalist returns for 1780 and 1781 suggest that some 50 to 60 boys (about 20 percent of the total number of boys over 12) above the age of 12 were not receiving provisions as refugees and therefore had joined regiments for provisions.
45. Watt, *Loyalist Refugees*, 273.
46. Ibid., 273; Norman K. Crowder, *Early Ontario Settlers: A Source Book* (Baltimore: Genealogical Publishing Co., 1993), 65.

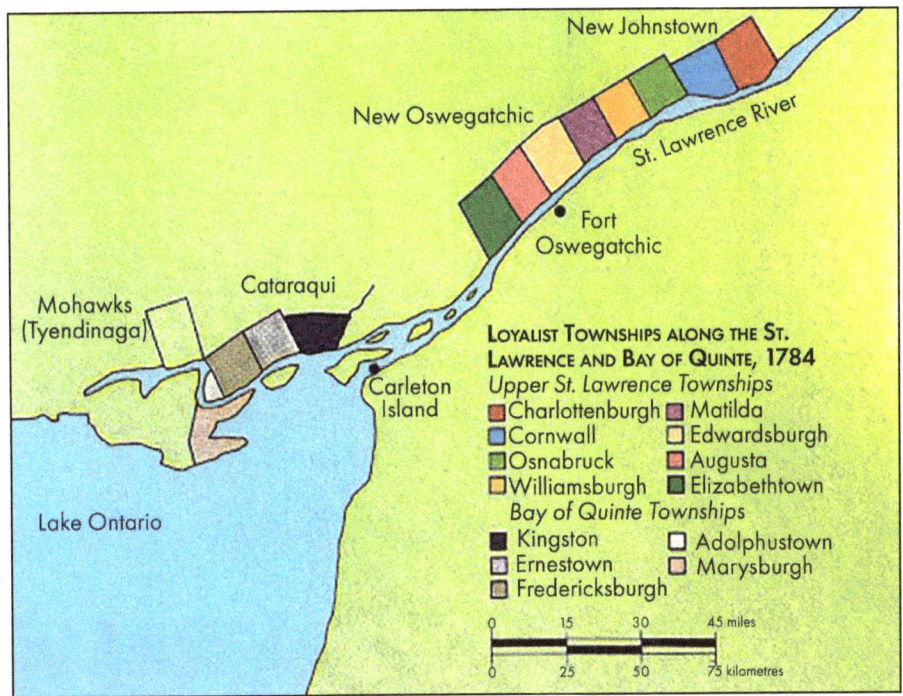

Figure 5.3. Loyalist Townships, 1784

to assemble in Sorel, which was the only location continuing to supply loyalists after May 10, 1784. Each man and boy over 10 was issued a coat, waistcoat, breeches, hat, shirt, blanket, shoes, show soles, leggings and stockings. Women and girls over 10 received ten yards of woolen cloth, four yards of linen, one pair of stockings, a blanket and shoe soles. Younger children received one yard of wool, two yards of linen, stockings, shoe soles, and half a blanket. The Simons family would have received one tent to share and a cooking kettle. Titus would be entitled to 500 acres provided he cleared and cultivated a specified portion of the land and built a dwelling greater of a specified size, after which he could request the issuance of a deed for the property.

The families were loaded onto flat-bottomed bateaux boats during the month of June for the twelve-day river journey. Each bateaux held four or five families and was about two tons in weight.[47] Each night the settlers would steer the bateaux ashore and pitch tents to spend the night. Like most loyalists in the new community, they arrived too late in 1784

---

47. Potter-MacKinnon, *Women*, 128–129; Bruce Wilson, *As She Began: An Illustrated Introduction to Loyalist Ontario* (Toronto: Dundurn Press, 1981), 70–78.

to plant crops. The government provided provisions until 1785. The government also built a school in Cataraqui in 1786 and hired a teacher.[48] However, settlers endured several years of hardship through the famine of 1788.[49] Nonetheless, as the painting below (Figure 5.4) suggests, the town grew rapidly.

Figure 5.4. A South-East View of Cataraqui-Kingston by James Peachey (1785).

---

48. Potter-MacKinnon, *Women*, 139.
49. George M. Wrong and H. H. Langton, eds., *The Chronicles of Canada, Vol. IV: The Beginnings of British Canada* (Tucson, AZ: Fireship Press, 2009), 148.

CHAPTER SIX

From Kingston to Flamboro

Given the difficult life of refugees, the first mission was simple survival. Titus employed several strategies for survival including working as a deputy sheriff or bailiff, merchant, and innkeeper, and he requested additional land beyond his refugee grant in the Kingston area. His land petitions confirm that he moved around during this period from Kingston to Newark (Niagara) to York (Toronto) and eventually to West Flamboro where he was granted land.

Deputy Sheriff of Montreal

Edward William Gray served as Sheriff of Montreal from 1765 to 1810. Titus Simons appears to be one of about six deputies or bailiffs who assisted the sheriff by serving civil process and even pursuing and arresting criminal defendants. About one third of the bailiffs in Montreal and Quebec were English rather than French. Most were middle-aged and about one third were ex-soldiers. Some bailiffs served in rural areas, supporting the possibility that Titus was a bailiff for Montreal while residing in and serving the Cataraqui/Kingston area. Donald Fyson notes that Titus, like some of the other bailiffs, was a merchant in Kingston in 1789. He also says most bailiffs served for five years or more but that Titus Simons was an exception, having acted as a bailiff only in 1785.[50]

Fyson is, however, incorrect in stating that Titus only served for one year. He served as a bailiff at least until September 1786 when he seized the personal property of an Indigenous trader and explorer of the Great Lakes in Canada named John Long, who first published a description of his travels in 1791. His account of Long's property was used in a law-

---

50. Donald Fyson, *Magistrates, Police, and People: Everyday Criminal Justice in Quebec and Lower Canada, 1764–1837* (Toronto: University of Toronto Press, 2008), 144–153. Fyson also says Titus was only 20 years old, clearly confusing Titus with his son Titus Geer Simons (147).

suit against Long brought by a London watchmaker named John Brookbank.⁵¹ Other sources indicate Titus was appointed a deputy sheriff in 1783 when the family was in the Montreal-area refugee camps of Rivière-du-Chene and Coteau-du-Law.⁵² It would have been more convenient to meet the Montreal sheriff from one of these area camps than from Cataraqui, which is more than 150 miles from Montreal. Thus, Titus may have been recruited as a deputy while in a Montreal-area refugee camp with an understanding he would relocate to the Cataraqui/Kingston area and continue as a deputy.

However, in his first land petition, dated in 1796, Titus Simons claimed he settled in Quebec (presumably Montreal-area refugee camps) in 1777 and Upper Canada (presumably Cataraqui) in 1788 rather than 1784, apparently forgetting or ignoring that he and his family appeared on the October 1784 Cataraqui settlers' list.⁵³ This is consistent with a biography by his great grandson that Titus Geer Simons was educated in Montreal.⁵⁴ While it is possible Titus and family left Cataraqui shortly after arriving and settled in Montreal for a few years for him to serve as bailiff, it seems more likely Titus was mistaken about arriving in Kingston in 1788. Further support for this idea is the reported birth of Titus' second son, John Kingsley Simons, in Kingston on February 20, 1786.

In any case, sources seem to agree that Titus and family were in the Kingston area after Cataraqui's name change to Kingston in 1788. Fyson identifies Simons as a merchant in Kingston in 1789. Court records, as discussed below, begin in Kingston for Titus Simons in 1790 and explicitly identify him as being from Kingston starting in January 1791. Furthermore, Titus subscribed £1, 15 shillings toward construction of St. George's Anglican Church of Kingston around that time. The church was then built in 1792.⁵⁵

---

51. Michael Blanar, "Long's *Voyages and Travels*: Fact and Fictions," in *The Fur Trade Revisited*, ed. Jennifer S.H. Brown, W.J. Eccles and Donald P. Heldman (East Lansing: Michigan State University Press, 1994), 447–463 at 456.
52. Gavin K. Watt, *Loyalist Refugees: Non-military Refugees in Quebec 1776–1784* (Milton, ON: Global Heritage Press, 2014), 273; John Robinson Simons, "The Fortunes of a United Empire Loyalist Family," *Ontario Historical Society Papers and Records* 23 (1926): 470–483 at 471.
53. Upper Canada Law Petitions LAC vol. 448A, "S" Bundle 2, petition Number 107, petition of Titus Simons.
54. H. H. Robertson, "Major Titus Gear Simons at Lundy's Lane," *Transactions of the Wentworth Historical Society*, 2 (1899): 54.
55. Simons, "Fortunes," p. 473.

Private Lawsuits

While in Kingston, Titus Simons was involved in a series of lawsuits from 1790 to 1793 according to surviving records of the Court of Common Pleas in the District of Mecklenburg that begin in March 1789.[56] Many of these actions involve commercial disputes that seem related to him operating as a merchant rather than as a farmer. As deputy sheriff, he appears to have learned about courts and litigation, something which assisted him in his own lawsuits. None of these documents indicate the names of jurors and whether Titus Simons ever served or was even eligible to serve on a jury.

According to these records, Titus first appeared in the Kingston court on March 16, 1790, to deny he was indebted to Joseph Allen.[57] This and related proceedings would drag on for months. On March 27, Titus personally appeared in court to successfully defend a lawsuit brought by Joseph Allen before a jury. The jury was requested to consider a verdict three times but couldn't agree on a verdict involving a contested promissory note for £23. Despite the deadlocked jury, the case continued. It was initially dismissed when the plaintiff failed to appear with costs that were to be paid by him. However, on July 1, 1790, the court ordered trial to occur in September 1790 to give the plaintiff enough time to collect subpoenaed evidence. The trial was later initially scheduled for September 23, 1790, and actually held on September 27. Based on the jury verdict, the court ordered that Allen should recover £23, 3 shillings, 4 pence and also recover the costs of the suit at 16/13/3.[58]

Meanwhile, on July 8, 1790, Simons filed a case against Allen. Because the defendant Allen was not prepared, trial was postponed to the next term. In January 1791, the trial of *Simons v. Allen* was ordered for later in the year because of the "badness" of the roads between the court and Titus's home in Kingston. In March, the trial was delayed again due to the poor health of the defendant. Finally, on July 7, 1791, the *Simons v. Allen* trial was held with Simons alleging that he was owed £150, 19 shillings, 6 pence. The court recalled Simons' defense in the prior case was that a settlement had been reached between the two

---

56. Alexander Fraser, *14th Report of the Bureau of the Archives for the Province of Ontario* (Toronto: A. T. Wilgress, 1917), 190.
57. Ibid.; *Joseph Allen v. Titus Simons*, Upper Canada Court Records 210 (March 16, 1790).
58. Fraser, *14th Report*, *Joseph Allen v. Titus Simons*, Upper Canada Court Records 230 (September 27, 1790).

parties on October 3, 1789 for all amounts that Simons owed Allen, so the court only awarded Simons £4, 9 shillings, 26 pence plus 22 shillings and 2 pence in costs for debts incurred after the settlement. On July 15, 1791, the court dismissed the defendant after charging him additional costs of £14, 6 shillings but allowing deduction of the amounts previously paid.[59]

This rather neutral description of this litigation is tempered by a later report in *The Canadian Law Times* noting that defendant Allen requested receipts from the first case that showed that at least part of the debt had been paid and apparently some of the ordered rum was not delivered. Since Simons' defense when he was defendant was that the dispute had been settled, the court chastised him as plaintiff for now arguing he was still owed money for debts incurred before the settlement: "the plaintiff's demand for monies … is a most impudent attempt to pervert the forms of law to the Purposes of Knavery and Injustice."[60]

Other Titus Simons Kingston court cases were more succinct. For example, on March 23, 1790, Titus was sued by James Clark who claimed some promissory notes from Simons payable to George Peter Hoyle had been endorsed over to Clark. Simons initially failed to appear and defaulted but they agreed to trial in July. However, the case was dismissed on March 27 for several reasons. First, the promissory notes were endorsed to James Clark *Esq.* not James Clark *Jr.*, the plaintiff of the suit. Second, after the plaintiff produced a document allegedly granting power of attorney from James Clark Esq. to Clark Jr., Simons showed the document was flawed. It wasn't witnessed as required nor was it endorsed by the correct James Clark. Finally, the declaration in the lawsuit should have named the principal as the plaintiff rather than the agent.[61]

The shortest possible lawsuit is one in which a party defaults. This occurred just over a year later when Titus Simons sued William Sherriff claiming he owed £3, 18 shillings on a promissory note. When the defendant, who was duly called, failed to appear, the court awarded Simons the full damages he requested plus 11 shillings, 2 pence for the costs of bringing the lawsuit.[62]

---

59. Fraser, *14th Report, Titus Simons v. Joseph Allen,* Upper Canada Court Records 253, 254, 258 (July 1, 7, 8, 1791).
60. *The Canadian Law Times,* 35 (1915): 976–77.
61. Fraser, *14th Report, James Clark vs. Titus Simons,* Upper Canada Court Records 213 (March 27, 1790).
62. Fraser, *14th Report, Titus Simons v. William Sherriff,* Upper Canada Court Records 326

Another relatively short proceeding occurred in January 1792. Terrence Hunt, a private in the 60th Regiment of Foot based in Kingston, sued Titus Simons for assault. Simons initially was held in default on January 3 for not appearing and not having his excuse supported by an affidavit. Simons did appear on January 10 and paid court costs to remove the default judgement against him. The trial before a jury occurred on Friday, January 13. The jury initially decided that Simons should pay damages of 10 shillings to the plaintiff and that each side should cover its own costs, but when told it could not decide costs, the jury reconsidered and ordered only 5 shillings and 6 pence in damages. The following day, the court held that costs would be awarded because an actual battery occurred as opposed to merely assault (threatened violence), where damages only would be awarded with no costs.[63]

Perhaps Titus paid this amount or settled the case because there are no further reported court decisions. As discussed above, more than a decade earlier Quartermaster Simons was shunned by his fellow officers for not resisting a beating from a higher-ranking officer. The 1792 lawsuit (and his fighting in the battles of Saratoga) suggest he may not have been a coward (at least towards lower-rank individuals) as had been presumed by his fellow officers.

This period of litigation ended with two concise proceedings in 1792 and 1793. Titus sued John Howard in 1792 for non-payment of a £5 note. Although the defendant did not appear to defend, the court noticed there was no proof of signature and ordered the case dismissed with Titus paying costs.[64] The following year (1793) at the end of December, Simons sued Neil McLean, a judge of the court, apparently in a rental dispute. Simons admitted to paying the defendant money but claimed it was not rent, that he didn't get a receipt for rent, and he did not know the defendant had any right or title to the premises—the defendant never showed him the title. But the court held the Titus should have pled and proven the defendant did not have good title or that there was no overdue rent. Because he did not allege, much less prove, these details, the defendant did not have to prove title, merely request rent.

(May 14, 1791).
63. Fraser, *14th Report, Terrence Hunt v. Titus Simons,* Upper Canada Court Records 266, 273–275, (3,10, 13–14 Jan. 1792).
64. Fraser, *14th Report, Titus Simons v. John Howard,* Upper Canada Court Records 352 (November 3, 1792).

Therefore, McLean would "have a return of said goods."[65] This case is the first to identify Titus Simons *Senior* of Kingston, implicitly acknowledging that Titus' eldest son, Titus Geer Simons, sometimes known as Titus Simons Jr., was nearly 30 years old and living in Kingston, perhaps with his father at the newly licensed inn as discussed below.

The year 1791, when the infamous *Simons vs. Allen* trial was held, also saw Vermont admitted as the fourteenth state in the United States of America. Vermont now would allow loyalists to return and purchase property but the return of confiscated land, personal property, or payment of Vermont reparations for such losses would never occur because that property had been sold and Vermont faced large debts from the war.[66]

Titus was better off taking his chances with another opportunity created in 1791—settling in what was now to be called Upper Canada. The British Parliament passed the 1791 Constitution Act, dividing what was then the province of Quebec into Lower Canada (now Quebec) to the east, containing 145,000 French speakers, and Upper Canada (now Ontario) in the west to accommodate loyalists and future English-speaking settlers from Britain and the U.S.

Like others living in Kingston at the time, Titus probably hoped this leading community in Upper Canada would become its capital. Indeed, as if to tease Kingston residents, on July 8, 1792, newly-appointed Lieutenant-Governor John Graves Simcoe was inaugurated and proclaimed his new government in the recently completed St. George's Anglican Church of Kingston—the same church Titus Simons (and many others) pledged money to construct a few years earlier. For the next two weeks, Simcoe held Executive Council meetings in the Council Chamber of Kingston. Unfortunately for Kingston and its inhabitants, Simcoe decided to establish the capital of Upper Canada at Newark in Niagara.[67] Simcoe thought Kingston was too close to the United States, was favored by his political rival Lord Dorchester, and lacked affordable land for purchase by members of the government relocating to the city.[68]

---

65. Fraser, *14th Report*, *Titus Simons v. Neil McLean*, Upper Canada Court Records 310, 311 (December 20, 24, 1793). Neil McLean did not sit in judgement of his own case but Hector McLean was one of the two presiding judges.
66. Jennifer S. H. Brown and Wilson B. Brown, *Col. William Marsh: Vermont Patriot and Loyalist* (Denver: Tiger Rock Press, 2013), 247.
67. Richard A. Preston, ed., *Kingston Before the War of 1812: A Collection of Documents* (Toronto: University of Toronto Press, 1959), cvi–cx.
68. John Andre, *Infant Toronto as Simcoe's Folly* (Toronto: Centennial Press, 1971), 152.

Titus Simons, Innkeeper

Although not the seat of the government, Kingston remained a bustling commercial center. The township of Kingston, including the town of Kingston itself, had an estimated population of 625 in 1794 and the neighboring township of Ernestown added another 1036.[69] Thus in 1793, rather than follow the seat of the government, Titus Simons decided to stay at Kingston and applied for an innkeeper's license. In 1801, the first year that statistics are available, the 34,600 people in Upper Canada were served by 108 inns or taverns.[70] He likely continued his work as a merchant, something which we know was not uncommon for innkeepers. His wife probably ran the inn while Simons worked on merchant business. The inn may have housed periodic business transactions. It does appear that Titus stopped appearing in court at the time. Litigation would tend to alienate potential inn customers.

Inns or taverns typically were private homes open all hours to provide lodging to travelers with at least three or four beds in one or more rooms. They often would have multiple rooms for customers such as a parlor, sitting room, dining room, and bar room. They also provided food and stabling for horses and were licensed to serve spirituous liquor in small containers (as opposed to liquor shops that were licensed to sell liquor in large containers). Locals, including men, women and families, also gathered at taverns to socialize and enjoy games and often gambling. They were joined by equally diverse travellers.

Inns also offered acceptable chores for daughters who would be taught domestic duties by working in the family inn.[71] Seven out of nine of Titus and Jerusha's children were daughters so operating an inn was a good fit for this family. Apparently, the innkeeper's license was granted because the stables for Simons' inn along with those for the nearby inn of William Wallace were destroyed in a 1797 fire.[72]

---

69. Preston, *Kingston Before the War of 1812*, cxiii.
70. Julia Roberts, *In Mixed Company: Taverns and Public Life in Upper Canada* (Vancouver: UBC Press, 2009), 59.
71. Ibid., pp. 142-143, 160. In contrast, a family with a large number of sons would tend to use them as field hands on a family farm.
72. Richard D. Merritt, "Early Inns and Taverns," in *The Capital Years: Niagara-on-the-Lake 1792-1796*, ed. Richard Merritt, Nancy Butler and Michael Power (Toronto: Dundurn Press, 1991), 187-222 at 215.

Land Grant Petitions

At first glance, it would seem reasonable to assume that Titus remained with his inn at Kingston at least through the stable fire of 1797 even though innkeeping called for long hours and produced little profit. However, land grant applications once again create some ambiguity. Grants indicate that Titus Simons lived in Niagara from at least 1796 to 1797. From Niagara on June 1796, Titus petitioned for a land grant based on his militia experience in the war.[73] He included statements from various officers verifying he had served from 1777 through 1781.[74]

In a second land petition dated July 1797, also from Niagara, he noted that pursuant to his previous petition, he had "received 410 acres of land in the Eastern District covered by warrant of survey [?] for 850 acres, 350 of which are allowed for his family lands."[75] He requested the complement of lands owed to quartermasters. Ultimately, he received land in West Flamboro where the family would settle in 1801–1802—roughly five years after the first settlers in that area.[76]

Titus Simons' relocation to Niagara by 1796, if not earlier, is consistent with the fact that his name did not appear on a list of loyalists in the township of Kingston compiled in October and November 1796.[77] However, the names of both senior and junior did appear on the Loyalist Rolls of October 1797 for Newark, Niagara, in the Home District. Both therefore had taken an oath of loyalty in front of a magistrate before that time. Titus Sr. also was listed on a second Home District roll also subscribed in October/November 1797.[78]

Perhaps Simons moved to Niagara with his son and presumably his entire family to avoid paying a quit-rent of one-half penny per acre on his original 1784 land grant.[79] A more likely motive is the pursuit of opportunity in the provincial capital of Newark in Niagara after Kingston was passed over for this honor. The town of Newark was not that large,

---

73. Upper Canada Law Petitions LAC vol. 448A, "S" Bundle 2, petition Number 107.
74. Hamilton UEL, *Loyalist Ancestors: Some Families of the Hamilton Area* (Toronto: Familia Genealogical Services, 1986), 228.
75. Upper Canada Law Petitions, LAC vol. 450, Bundle S3 Number 126.
76. Hamilton UEL, *Loyalist Ancestors*, 226, 228.
77. Preston, *Kingston Before the War of 1812*, 348–350.
78. E. Keith Fitzgerald, *Ontario People: 1796–1803* (Baltimore: Genealogical Publishing Co., 1993), 188, 203.
79. Mary Beacock Fryer, *King's Men: The Soldier Founders of Ontario* (Toronto: Dundurn Press, 1980), 329.

having about 70 buildings at that time.[80] But it would grow larger if it remained the seat of government. As a merchant, Titus Simons could have been seeking to broaden his opportunity for trade with the west and with the provincial government.

Figure 6.1. Edward Walsh, "A View of Fort George, Navy Hall and New Niagara" (1804) (Newark is pictured in the upper right corner).

If this was his goal, Titus Sr. soon would be disappointed to see the capital begin to move again from Newark to York (now Toronto) in February 1996. The Upper Canada Parliament would hold its first session in York on June 1797. While Newark was small, York was both smaller and less settled. By the end of 1797, York had about 40 completed houses with several more under construction. These structures accommodated 241 registered inhabitants and its total population was estimated as 600 people in 1796.[81] The unsettled nature of "Muddy York" did provide inexpensive land for new government-related settlers who moved to York.

If the move of the capital of Upper Canada from Newark to York was a setback for the Simons family, they quickly recovered. At least by July 1796, Titus Jr. was living in York when he followed his father's example

---

80. William R. Wilson, "Simcoe's Arrival at Niagara," in *Historical Narratives of Early Canada*, available at http://www.uppercanadahistory.ca/simcoe/simcoe3.html.
81. Andre, *Infant Toronto*, 91.

and filed a land petition from there. Titus Geer's petition was based solely on his promise to settle and develop the land (and being Christian). One month later the Executive Council recommended Titus Geer be granted 300 acres if he had none before.[82]

If, as seems likely, father and son were seeking benefit from government largesse including land grants, then Titus Geer Simons was successful in York even beyond his grant. Lieutenant-Governor John Graves Simcoe appointed to his executive and legislative councils men, such as loyalists, who shared his conservative aristocratic values. As discussed in the next chapter, Titus Geer was selected to be the official government printer beginning in July 1797 primarily because he was the son of a loyalist. However, the printing business he took over was still located in Niagara. So Titus Geer would move to Niagara (perhaps staying with his father) by July 1797 to become the official printer and then would move the printing business to York in the summer of 1798.

Titus Geer also must have spent enough time in Niagara to meet and court his first wife, Elizabeth Green, whom he married in Newark, Niagara, on June 3, 1798—the month before they moved to York.[83] The urgency of Titus Jr.'s marriage may have increased after the reported death of his stepmother Jerusha Kingsley Simons in February 1798.[84] Titus Jr. would marry just four months later. His marriage provided the extended family with a new mother figure, particularly for Titus Sr.'s youngest daughters aged 3 and 5 years old.

"Lizzie" Green was born in New Jersey in 1781, reportedly the daughter of John Green and medical practitioner Mary Davis. John Green was born in Greenwich, Morris County, New Jersey, the son of Samuel Green Sr. by his third wife, Hannah Wright. Samuel Green Sr. may have been the son of Richard Green who arrived in Burlington Harbor, New Jersey, in 1678 on the ship *The Shield* from Hull. John Green operated several grist and saw mills first in New Jersey and then in the Flamboro area where he settled in 1796, just two years before his daughter married. John Green died in 1830 at the age of 80 years,

---

82. Upper Canada Law Petitions LAC vol. 448A, "S" Bundle 2, Petition Number 112. Titus Geer Simons was not included on a July 1796 draft list of 31 male inhabitants capable of bearing arms developed by Commander William Berczy (Andre, *Infant Toronto*, 88–89).
83. Ontario Historical Society Papers and Records, 3 (1901): 7–73, records of St. Marks and St. Andrews of Niagara by Rev. Robert Addison at 54.
84. William D. Reid, *The Loyalists in Ontario: The Sons and Daughters of the American Loyalists in Upper Canada* (Baltimore: Genealogical Publishing Co., 1973), 291.

Figure 6.2. Edward Walsh, "York … as It appeared in the Autumn of 1803."

one year after the death of his wife. Greensville was named after them in 1846.[85]

By 1800, widower Titus Simons Sr. had joined the newlyweds in York. In the census of 1799 it was reported that the household of "Simons Titus" in York had one male and two females. I assume this is Titus Geer and that the reference is to his wife and daughter Charlotte, who was born that year. In the following year, 1800, the household of "Simons Titus G." continued to report one male and two females and his father "Simons Titus" had four males and five females in his household. This would include sons Walter Williams and John Kingsley Simons and five of his daughters. In 1801 there is reported "Simons Titus Sen'r" with two males and four females, while "Simons Titus G. Jun'r" had two males and four females. Perhaps two female servants were added, or the two next-oldest daughters of Titus Sr. were essentially acting as servants, as only Jerusha, the eldest daughter of Titus Sr., was married before 1801.[86]

---

85. Waterdown-East Flamborough Heritage Society, *Connecting the Dots: Snapshots of Flamborough Communities* (Waterdown: Waterdown-East Flamborough Heritage Society, 2017), 50.
86. Christine Mosser, *York: Upper Canada Minutes of Town Meetings and List of Inhabitants 1797–1823* (Toronto: Metropolitan Library Board, 1984), 14, 22, 29.

Jury Duty

The land grants received by Titus Sr. and Titus Jr. qualified them for jury duty as land owners. Jury duty records generally are consistent with their move to Niagara and then to York. For example, according to a modern transcription of judicial records, both father and son were fined 5 shillings by the Newark court of Niagara in the Home District for not appearing on juries in January 1798.[87] As noted above, a land grant petition places Titus Sr. in Niagara in July 1797 and Titus Jr. was the government printer in Niagara in January 1798. This is the first time they are mentioned for jury duty in the surviving judicial records that date back to the fall of 1792. There is no record of whether they paid the fines, but Titus Sr.'s wife may have been sick since she died the next month and taking care of her may have been a sufficient excuse to avoid the fines.[88]

As noted above, in January 1800, both father and son were living in York. This continued at least through 1801.[89] On January 20, 1800, Titus Sr. was sworn into the grand jury in the York courthouse but he was not selected for the petit jury that heard an interesting murder trial on that same day.[90] Major John Small was charged with murder for killing John White, the first Attorney-General of Upper Canada, in a gentlemen's duel. Major Small challenged White to a duel to defend his wife's honor and reputation against scandalous remarks about her made by Mrs. White. The duelists met with their seconds and conducted a fair duel where in the first exchange of gunfire, only Mr. White was hit, unfortunately shattering his spine. He suffered a painful death 36 hours later.

Although there was no question that Small killed White, the jury trial and deliberations lasted eight hours, ending with a unanimous verdict of not guilty of murder. It seems likely that the presiding judge, Justice Henry Allcock, believed the duel was conducted honorably and instructed the jury in a manner that urged the not guilty verdict.[91]

---

87. Linda Corupe, *Upper Canada Justice: Early Assize Court Records (Court of Oyer & Terminer) of Ontario*, Vol. 1 1792–1809, 51.
88. Reid, *The Loyalists in Ontario*, 291.
89. Martha Hemphill reports that Titus Simons owned property (number 13, corner of Duke and Caroline St.) in York as late as 1807.
90. Linda Corupe, *Upper Canada Justice*, Vol. 1, 72.
91. Hugh A. Halliday, *Murder Among Gentlemen: A History of Dueling in Canada* (Toronto: Robin Brass Studio, 1999), 42–47.

Two days after Major Small was acquitted of murder after killing John White, Titus Geer Simons was listed as the first member of a petit jury in a forgery case in York. This may mean he was the jury foreman—a reasonable choice given his prior experience with courts and litigation, and his growing stature in the community. The jury found a transient Irishman, Humphrey Sullivan, guilty of one count of knowingly passing a forged note. The presiding judge, Chief Justice Elmsley, then sentenced Sullivan to death by hanging. The *Upper Canada Gazette* reported on this case with apparent satisfaction as to the result.[92] At this time in Upper Canada, fraud amounting to larceny by a lowly transient worker was punishable by death whereas murder by gentlemen's fair duel was not punishable at all. Social class was clearly an important factor in Upper Canadian society.

The younger Simons appeared again on a grand jury in York in March 1800 (when the grand jury released some prisoners for various reasons) and there again in February 1801. In March 1809, when Titus Geer would have been living in West Flamboro, he sat with a grand jury that heard evidence of possible future cases.[93] Jury duty was tedious, and could also be expensive if lodging and food had to be purchased in York and jurors were taken away from their normal business activities. The fee paid to jurors was only about 20–25 cents per sitting, so jurors might bring their own food and stay with friends, or camp out overnight to save money.[94]

---

92. Corupe, *Upper Canada Justice*, Vol. 1, 73; Andre, *Infant Toronto*, 159–160.
93. Corupe, *Upper Canada Justice*, Vol. 1, 51, 72, 73, 88, 237.
94. Frederick H. Armstrong, *The Forest City: An Illustrated History of London, Canada* (N.p.: Windsor Publications, 1986), 39–41.

Part Three

The Life and Times of Titus Geer Simons

CHAPTER SEVEN

Titus Geer Simons, Government Printer and Public Citizen

Since the British blamed the American Revolution in part on unregulated and seditious colonial newspapers, it is not surprising that Upper Canada had only one newspaper until 1799. The newspaper was subject to both prior censorship and lawsuits claiming published articles constituted seditious libel.[95] Because of his loyalist heritage (and presumably basic education and writing skills), Titus Geer Simons was appointed as the third official government printer and newspaper editor for Upper Canada.

The first printer was Frenchman Louis Roy who began publishing the *Upper Canada Gazette, or American Oracle* in April 1793. He had been apprenticed to the proprietor of the *Quebec Gazette* when he was recruited by Lieutenant-Governor Simcoe to be the first government printer for Upper Canada. Unfortunately, according to Mrs. Simcoe, Roy could not "write good English."[96] He also was criticized for failing to print the statutes of the first parliament on time. Not surprisingly, Roy soon left the relative isolation of Upper Canada in 1794 and returned to Montreal to establish the *Montreal Gazette* the following year.[97]

Roy was replaced by two American printers: Gideon Tiffany in 1794 and in 1796 his brother Silvester, who was appointed assistant printer.[98] They changed the format to place American news on the front pages and

---

95. Alan Taylor, "The Late Loyalists: Northern Reflections of the Early American Republic," *Journal of the Early Republic* 27, no. 1 (2007): 1–34 at 16.
96. J. Ross Robertson (ed.), *The Diary of Mrs. John Graves Simcoe* (Toronto: William Briggs, 1911), 161.
97. Brian Tobin, *The Upper Canada Gazette and its Printers, 1793–1849* (Toronto: Ontario Legislative Library, 1993), 4–7.
98. For biographies of Gideon and Silvester Tiffany, see the *Dictionary of Canadian Biography* at http://www.biographi.ca/en/bio/tiffany_gideon_8E.html and http://www.biographi.ca/en/bio/tiffany_silvester_5E.html, respectively.

Upper Canada government proclamations and stories on the back pages with occasional local news stories. If news was light, they would print literary material.[99] Gideon Tiffany ceased to be government printer on July 5, 1797 when he was disqualified from any public office by law after pleading guilty of blasphemy, paying a fine of £20, and being confined to the Newark jail for one month.[100]

Later that month, Titus Geer Simons' search for a government appointment paid off. Despite his lack of printing or newspaper experience, Titus Geer Simons was hired to be the third Upper Canada government printer at an annual salary of £50.[101] His only apparent qualification was that he was the son of an American Revolution loyalist militia lieutenant. It seems fair to assume that Simons had some interest in public affairs and publishing as well as a basic education and some skill at writing. But Simons had neither experience nor a printing press, so Silvester Tiffany continued as Simons' assistant until May 1, 1798. They published their first issue on September 20, 1797.[102] Below is a copy of the original masthead and a sketch of the wood screw printing press used by the *Upper Canada Gazette:*[103]

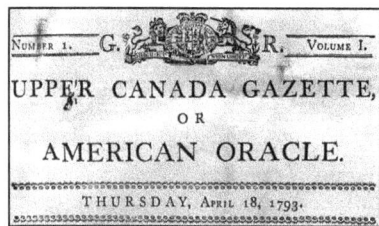
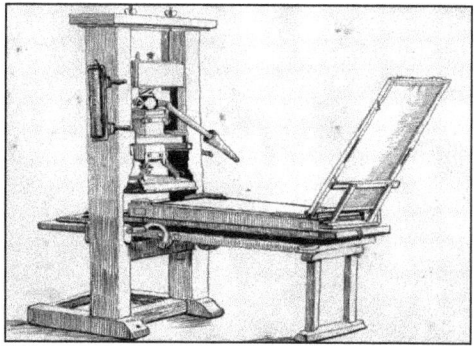

Figures 7.1 and 7.2. Upper Canada Gazette *Masthead and Press*

Simons reorganized the weekly *Gazette* to appear less cluttered. The first page was devoted to government of Upper Canada news as later

---

99. Tobin, *The Upper Canada Gazette and its Printers,* 7–9.
100. Patricia Kennedy, "What Marie Tremaine Did Not Find: An Exploration of Archival Back Rooms," *Papers of the Bibliographic Society of Canada* 30, no.1 (1992): 27–46 at 45, 46.
101. Gideon Tiffany was paid £50. Patricia Kennedy, "What Marie Tremaine Did Not Find," 46.
102. Frederick H. Armstrong, *Handbook of Upper Canadian Chronology* (Toronto: Dundurn Press, 1985), 45.
103. The actual printing press believed to have been used for the initial issues of the *Upper Canada Gazette* is currently on display at the Macenzie Printery in Niagara-on-the-Lake, Ontario. See http://www.niagaraparks.com/niagara-falls-attractions/roy-press.html.

required by an April 25, 1798 resolution of the Executive Council. The second and third pages contained foreign news and articles from other newspapers. Advertising and local news appeared on the fourth and final page.

The Executive Council continued to have concerns that the news was slanted toward the United States rather than Canada—"every trifle related to the damn'd States in printed in large character."[104] At this time Upper Canadians traded and interacted with merchants in the United States and were interested in news from that country. Moreover, the French Revolution had occurred and U.S. federalists in particular agreed with Upper Canadians that the French "had to be guarded against." However in 1800, republicans under Thomas Jefferson, took control of the U.S. government causing Upper Canadians to worry about being overcome by republicanism.[105]

Despite this interest in American news, to address the concern of U.S. bias Silvester Tiffany was fired at the end of April 1798 and replaced by William Waters who was appointed co-printer and partner of Titus Geer Simons in July 1798.[106] They were equal partners, sharing profits and losses. Besides their government salaries, they earned money from government print jobs, selling newspapers and placing classified ads in their paper. Presumably they earned a profit after covering their cost of printing. Although second to be appointed, Waters was listed first because he was older, Titus Geer Simons explained when a reader (perhaps one of the Tiffany brothers) snidely raised the issue, wondering if Waters was the "master" of Simons.[107]

The April 25 resolution of the Executive Council also required that Simons move the printing business to York (the Legislature had already moved from Niagara to the new capital of York two years earlier in 1796).[108] Moving the business was no easy task. According to expense receipts submitted by Titus Geer, on June 23, he paid a carpenter more

104. Tobin, *The Upper Canada Gazette and its Printers*, 9–11.
105. Jane Errington, *The Lion, the Eagle, and Upper Canada: A Developing Colonial Ideology*, 2nd ed. (Montreal: McGill-Queen's University Press, 2012), pp. 62–63
106. W. Stewart Wallace, "The First Journalists in Upper Canada," *The Canadian Historical Review* 26, no. 40 (1945): 372–381 at p. 376.
107. W. George Eakins, "The Bibliography of Canadian Statute Law," *Index to Legal Periodicals and Law Library Journal* 1, no. 3 (1908): 65–66.
108. The capital of Upper Canada was moved from Niagara to York after Fort Niagara was ceded to the Americans, making the town of Niagara vulnerable to bombardment and attack from the fort.

than £4 to refurbish the press by devising a set of folio size galleys and press furniture and reglets to hold the lines of type in place. He also acquired a press stone and six boxes in which to pack printing materials. The move began on September 6 by transferring the materials to Newark from which they were shipped to York, arriving on September 12. They were then moved on land to their final destination, with the entire bill for shipping amounting to £8 settled on September 13. Within a month Waters and Simons had the press up and running, publishing their first issue from York on October 4, 1798.[109] They managed to print the Statutory Laws of 1797 in Niagara before the move but did not print the 1798 Statutory Laws until 1799.[110]

A year later on September 24, 1799, Titus Geer Simons and William Waters were officially proclaimed as "Printers to the King's Most Excellent Majesty" by the new Lieutenant Governor Peter Hunter.[111] When requested, they printed a variety of government forms including marriage licenses, land grants, nomination forms for election candidates, militia commissions, and various handbills.[112] Meanwhile, in July 1799, the Tiffany brothers established the *Canada Constitution*—the first nonofficial newspaper in the province. They soon dissolved their partnership and Silvester Tiffany continued in the newspaper business by starting the *Niagara Herald* in January 1801.[113]

To address the nascent competition from private newspapers, Waters and Simons published a notice in every issue of the *Upper Canada Gazette* of the month of January 1801 explaining the improvements they had made including increased dimensions and the occasional use of small type for "occurrences of the week" resulting in a "very material augmentation of size and contents, without any augmentation of price."[114]

In the January 17, 1801 issue of the *Upper Canada Gazette,* Simons published "An Ode on Her Majesty's Birthday that began:

109. Patricia Fleming, "Toronto in Print: To Work and Back," *The Halcyon*, no. 21 (June 1998): 8–9.
110. W. George Eakins, "The Bibliography of Canadian Statute Law," 65.
111. For a biography of Peter Hunter, see *Dictionary of Canadian Biography* at http://www.biographi.ca/en/bio/hunter_peter_5E.html.
112. Patricia Lockhart Fleming and Sandra Alston, *Early Canadian Printing: A Supplement to Marie Tremaine's A Bibliography of Canadian Imprints 1751–1800* (Toronto: University of Toronto Press, 1999), 375, 376, 411.
113. Wallace, "The First Journalists in Upper Canada," 377.
114. Tobin, *The Upper Canada Gazette and its Printers*, 11.

Bring me an harp from Heav'n, ye sacred nine,
And fill each string with harmony divine.

Silvester Tiffany suggested in his new *Niagara Herald* that this poem was sufficiently bad that it might have been written by Simons' dog Sancho. Simons, ever loyal to the Queen (and loyal to his dog as well), responded in the January 31 issue. He called Tiffany a scavenger who constantly groveled amongst filth. He further suggested Tiffany was an exile, alien, atheist and a democrat who had sought asylum in Canada. Tiffany responded that he was a cripple and not pretty like the dog Sancho but was grateful he was not Sancho with his poetry. He angrily asserted that he was not an alien, exile, or atheist and had been attached to the province for a long time. The next year in the summer of 1802, he stopped publishing the *Herald* and returned to the U.S.[115] Without a government salary and profits from government printing jobs, publishing a newspaper in Upper Canada was not profitable at this time.

Still, Tiffany outlasted Waters and Simons in the newspaper business, which had political risks. During the election of 1800, the *Gazette* reported that William Allan would become a candidate for the York riding in an article signed by "A Farmer." Allan was furious and demanded that Titus Geer Simons and William Waters be fired, according to the March 25, 1800, minutes of the Executive Council. He complained to the government that if the assertion reached his commercial connections in Lower Canada uncontradicted, it would "very materially affect his Interests."[116] Two days later, the King's Printers petitioned the Lieutenant Governor, acknowledging their error in printing the article and requesting clemency. Initially, they were pardoned with a reprimand, but in July 1801, they were fired for similar (or perhaps belatedly for the same) misconduct. They were replaced by John Bennett, an experienced printer who served a significantly longer tenure of 1801–1807.[117]

Titus Geer Simons' four-year tenure as a newspaper publisher seemed

---

115. Wallace, "The First Journalists in Upper Canada," 377–378.
116. "Allan, William," in *Dictionary of Canadian Biography*, vol. 8 (University of Toronto/Université Laval, 2003–), accessed March 30, 2014, http://www.biographi.ca/en/bio/allan_william_8E.html.
117. Edith G. Firth, *The Town of York, 1793–1815: A Collection of Documents of Early Toronto* (Toronto: University of Toronto Press, 1962), 160–161; Tobin, *The Upper Canada Gazette and its Printers*, 11–12. July 1807 also marks the first issue of Joseph Willcocks' independent newspaper, *Upper Canada Guardian or Freeman's Journal*.

sufficient to stimulate an interest in politics and government affairs that would continue the rest of his life. He would continue to be loyal to the crown and the British aristocratic life style as it was adapted to Canada and of course he would continue to seek acceptance and support from the leaders of Upper Canada.

Becoming Known

Although they may not have met him in person, members of the Executive Council who advised the Lieutenant Governor certainly knew Titus Geer Simons by reputation as the former government printer. They also came to know him as a frequent land petitioner. As noted above, when living in York in 1796, Titus Geer first applied for land and was granted 300 acres if he had none before.[118] This was when he chose West Flamboro as the place he wished to settle.[119]

As the government printer in York he petitioned in July 1799 for additional land to augment Lot 13, which he had already obtained in York. His request was denied because he did not fit any of the grounds for granting such a request.[120] This denial did not stop petitioning by Titus Geer and his siblings. On June 10, 1800, Titus Geer Simons petitioned from West Flamboro to lease two sections of land that were contiguous to his land in West Flamboro. It seems he was maintaining residences on land he owned in both West Flamboro and in York as evidenced by York censuses through 1801 that were discussed above. His request to lease the lot from the clergy reserve was denied, but his request to lease the Crown reserve next to his existing property was granted.[121]

In 1801, Titus Geer petitioned D.W. Smith, the Surveyor General of Upper Canada, seeking land to operate a business as a butcher and victualer. He described himself as a poor man with large family. In April 1811, Titus Geer again petitioned from West Flamboro for additional land. He noted that as the son of a loyalist, he had received 150 acres of land in 1798, now cultivated, and requested additional land of whatever amount was thought appropriate. He was recommended for 400 acres for which he paid more than £16.[122]

118. Upper Canada Law Petitions LAC vol. 448A, "S" Bundle 2, Petition Number 112.
119. Waterdown-East Flamborough Heritage Society, *Connecting the Dots: Snapshots of Flamborough Communities* (Waterdown, ON: Waterdown-East Flamborough Heritage Society, 2017), 110.
120. Upper Canada Law Petitions LAC vol. 451, "S" Bundle 4, petition Number 129.
121. Upper Canada Law Petitions LAC vol. 490, "S" Leases 1797-1808, petition Number 24.
122. Upper Canada Law Petitions LAC vol. 456, "S" Bundle 10, petition Number 36.

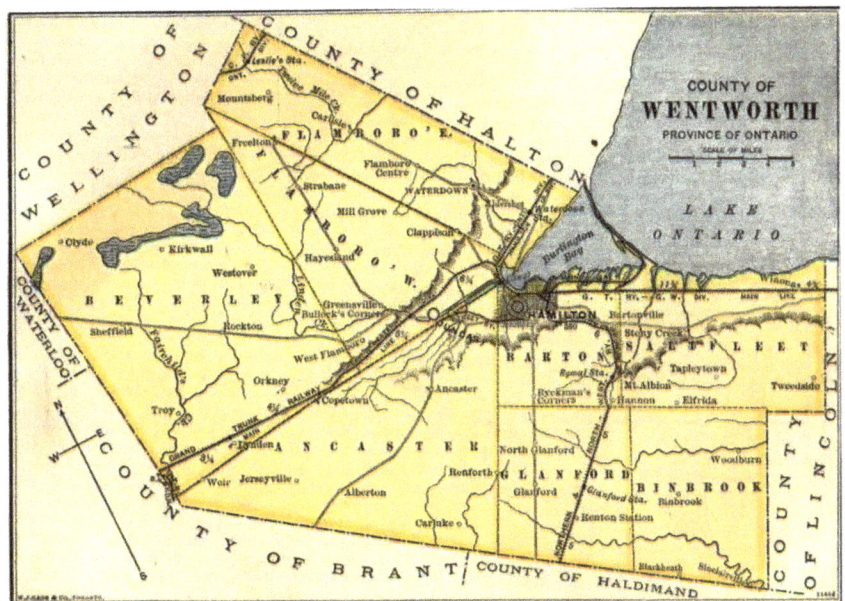

Figure 7.3. Map of County of Wentworth, showing location of West Flamboro and Ancaster townships.

He also purchased land when it suited his needs, such as Lot 45 in Concession 1 of Ancaster, which he purchased in 1812 from Mrs. Eleanor Hanes who had acquired this parcel as a United Empire Loyalist daughter. After the war, he petitioned to retain this property because his war service prevented him from settling upon and improving the land as required to perfect title.[123] Thus, his continued acquisition of land paid off for him, his father, and five of his siblings who petitioned for land between 1801 and 1809, as detailed in Appendix Two.

At this time West Flamboro was growing with an influx of settlers. From 1805 to 1809, it saw an increase of over 300 settlers, two-thirds of which were children under the age of sixteen. In contrast, the population of the town of York increased by 577 inhabitants, of which only 220 were below the age of sixteen.[124] In a history of Dundas, Titus Geer Simons was listed as a shop keeper but not a mill owner in the decade from 1810–1819.[125]

---

123. LAC Upper Canada Sundries, RG 5 A 1, January–March 1818, Vol. 38, pp. 17579–18120 at C-4601, pp. 17893–17895, 17934–17935.
124. John Andre, *Infant Toronto as Simcoe's Folly* (Toronto: Centennial Press, 1971), 156–157.
125. T. Roy Woodhouse, *The History of the Town of Dundas, Part I* (Dundas, ON: Dundas Historical Society, 1965), 29.

Titus Geer Simons became known not only because of his petitioning for land grants but also for his other activities after being a printer. In 1792, newly appointed Lieutenant Governor Simcoe established the Agricultural Society of Upper Canada, which was devoted to the scientific improvement of agriculture. The following year, the society was renamed the Niagara Agricultural Society but it closed its doors in 1805. The next year (1806), Titus Geer Simons co-founded the Burlington Board of Agriculture, pursuing his interest in encouraging agriculture generally. He was the society's first secretary and wrote its bylaws in his own hand. The bylaws proclaim that the Burlington Board sought to promote "the science of Agriculture and carrying into effect the improved art of husbandry."[126]

Thus, it would seem the Burlington Board was one of the earliest agricultural societies to be inspired by Simcoe and his original society of 1792. There are no further records of meetings by the Board but there is mention of a Burlington and Nelson Agricultural Society in the early 1900s.[127] Taylor argues that civic culture, including such societies, outside the government barely existed before 1820, but Titus Geer Simons formed this society in 1806 and joined the Masons in 1810, as discussed in Chapter Ten.[128]

On November 27, 1806, Titus Geer Simons and several others attended a dinner party on Yonge Street in York at the home of John Mills Jackson. Apparently such trips to York were not unusual for Titus Geer since we know he served on a grand jury in York in March 1809. At this dinner, the subject of politics was raised by Joseph Willcocks, Sheriff of the Home (York) District since 1804,[129] even though some attendees

126. H. H. Robertson, "The First Agricultural Society within the Limits of Wentworth—1806," *Journal of Transactions of the Wentworth Historical Society*, 4 (1905): 93–95. Retired U.S. President John Adams was president of the Massachusetts Society for Promoting Agriculture from 1805 to 1812 suggesting that such societies were common on both sides of the border. Nancy Isenberg and Andrew Burstein, *The Problem of Democracy: The Presidents Adams Confront the Cult of Personality* (New York: Viking, 2019), 271.

127. *Souvenir Booklet of Burlington the Beautiful: Diamond Jubilee of Confederation 1867–1927* (Burlington, ON: Gazette Print, 1927), 15, available at http://images.ourontario.ca/Partners/Burlington/BHS0027970101T.PDF. Some twenty years later, several prominent men in Ancaster founded the Upper Canada Agricultural Society, but Titus Geer Simons was not listed among them according to the *Gore Gazette*, August 23, 1828, p. 103.

128. Taylor, "The Late Loyalists," p. 33.

129. Elwood H. Jones, "Willcocks, Joseph," in *Dictionary of Canadian Biography*, vol. 5 (University of Toronto/Université Laval, 2003–), accessed September 20, 2021, http://www.biographi.ca/en/bio/willcocks_joseph_5E.html.

sought to avoid the topic. Several witnesses reported that the sheriff used "abusive language" against the government, calling it "tyrannical and oppressive." He further noted that he expected he would be dismissed as sheriff because he supported the rights of the people. He offered to reveal official correspondence to support his claims. The host, John Mills Jackson, supported the sheriff's views, calling the government a "set of rascals" that had "plundered the country." Such hostility toward the government led to fisticuffs.[130]

A couple of weeks after the dinner party, Lieutenant Besserer swore an affidavit outlining this occurrence. Titus Geer Simons and three other attendee-witnesses swore affidavits in February of 1807. Titus Geer's affidavit was by far the most detailed, being about three times the size of the others. Simons was paid £3 to cover his expenses from reporting the details of this incident.[131] Willcocks should have known better than to criticize the government in front of a former government printer and several officers in the militia—all could be presumed to be loyal to the crown.

The affidavits were sent to Lieutenant Governor Francis Gore presumably with the intention of causing exactly what happened—Willcocks was dismissed as sheriff in April 1807.[132] Three months later, Willcocks began operating a reformist newspaper and was soon elected to the Canadian Parliament, where he was tried and convicted of sedition that following year.[133] On February 20, 1808, the Legislative Assembly voted unanimously to issue a warrant for Willcocks' arrest for contempt and to have him committed to the "Common Gaol [jail]."[134]

Speaking of gaols, two years later in 1810, Titus Geer Simons promised to contribute £100 towards the building of a gaol and courthouse in Dundas if the government approved the proposal. This proposal was sent to the Legislative Assembly on February 16, 1810 but was ultimately

---

130. Harry H. Guest, "Upper Canada's First Political Party," *Ontario History* 54 (1962, December): 275–296 at 287.
131. *The Journals of the Legislative Assembly of Upper Canada for the Years 1805, 1806, 1807, 1808, 1810, 1811, Volume Two* (Toronto: Ontario Archives, 1911), 250.
132. Douglas Brymner, *Report of Canadian Archives 1892* (Ottawa: S.E. Dawson, 1893), 76–80. He was later replaced by Miles MacDonell, who would later become the first governor of Assiniboia in 1811.
133. Guest, "Upper Canada's First Political Party," 289–290.
134. *Journals of the Legislative Assembly of Upper Canada, Volume Two*, 225–228. Barry Wright, "Sedition in Upper Canada: Contested Legality," *Labour/Le Travail* 29 (Spring 1992), 7–57 at 27.

rejected.[135] Simons would champion a Dundas gaol-courthouse for more than a decade. Contrary to the political interest demonstrated by the gaol-courthouse subscription agreement, Dundas and West Flamboro did not elect any public officials in 1810 so no taxes were collected. This changed in 1811, when the magistrates in York appointed Titus Geer Simons and John Sutton as tax assessors and several other local men to other positions.[136]

These incidents and activities allowed Titus Geer Simons to increase his visibility with the leaders of Upper Canada as a loyalist tory in his own right. While he was not appointed as sheriff of the Home District replacing Willcocks, he would continue to ingratiate himself with the politically powerful. After the War of 1812, he would be successful in obtaining government appointments. Sadly, as he was developing a name for himself, Elizabeth Green Simons, Titus Geer Simons' first wife, passed away. He had to once again quickly address family concerns.

The Death of Titus Geer Simons' First Wife and his Second Marriage

After marrying Titus Geer Simons in 1798 and having at least three children with him (see Appendix Three), Elizabeth Green Simons died at some point in the early 1800s. Titus Geer was left with at least three young children who had neither a mother nor grandmother since Jerusha Kingsley Simons had died four months before his marriage to Elizabeth Green in 1798. At that time, Titus Senior had two young teenage daughters who could help with household duties, but a new mother was needed.

The most obvious choice for Titus Geer's replacement wife and mother to his children was Hannah Coon Van Every. Hannah had just given birth to her daughter Elizabeth in 1804 when her husband Samuel passed away sometime after signing a will in November 1805 and its being filed in court in February 1806. With this death and her own young children to raise, new widow Hannah also would be interested in finding a new husband quickly. The Simons and Van Everys were likely not just neighbors but also friends. Not only did Titus Geer Simons serve as a co-executor to Samuel's estate and Titus Senior as a witness to the will, but the Van Everys named a daughter Elizabeth.

---

135. *Journals of the Legislative Assembly of Upper Canada, Volume Two*, 316–317.
136. Woodhouse, *The History of the Town of Dundas*, 20–21.

Hannah was the daughter of John Coon who, according to his 1787 memorial claiming losses from the rebellion, was born in America and leased some undivided property with his father from the "Rencellor's [Rennselaer's] patent" with at least 100 acres cleared. His share was about 40 acres of cleared land with a separate house. The commissioners valued his claim for losses at £180, 4 shillings, and allowed payment of £67. John Coon joined Butler's Rangers as a private in 1777.[137] According to payroll records, he served at least from May 1, 1778 to October 24, 1778. He also gathered intelligence near Albany in May 1781.[138] A November 1783 survey of Niagara lists Sergeant John Coon with five children, the eldest being "Hanney" Coon who was twelve years old (receiving a full ration) indicating she was born about 1771. According to the return, Hanney had four siblings ranging in age from three to ten.[139]

Unfortunately, no known records document the date of the passing of Titus Geer Simons' first wife Elizabeth Green or his subsequent second marriage to Hannah Coon Van Every. We have a few pieces of conflicting evidence that indicate possible timeframes. There is a report that Elizabeth Green as the wife of Titus Geer Simons was living in York in 1814.[140] Inconsistently, there is a land sale record dated March 3, 1812, for the sale of land belonging to Hannah Van Every by Titus Geer Simons and Hannah, "his wife."[141]

George Hill Detlor, the son of one of Titus Geer Simons' half-sisters, started a diary in 1851. He reports that Titus Geer and Elizabeth Green had Charlotte, Alexander and Jane Elizabeth and then Titus married the widow of James (actually Samuel) Van Every and they had Matilda, Hannah and Arabella Gore.[142] Matilda was born on August 26, 1808[143] but not

---

137. Claims for Revolutionary War Losses Heard by Commissioners of Claims at Niagara on August 23, 1787, Archives of Ontario, 12, Vol. 28, pp. 1–3, summarized in Alexander Fraser (1905), *Second Report of the Bureau of Archives for the Province of Ontario 1904, Part II*, 962–963.
138. William A. Smy, *An Annotated Nominal Roll of Butler's Rangers 1777–1784 with Documentary Sources* (2004), 70–71.
139. Norman K. Crowder, *Early Ontario Settlers: A Source Book* (Baltimore: Genealogical Publishing Co., 1993), 1.
140. A reference from the Canadian Genealogy Index, 1600s–1900s, about Elizabeth Simons suggests she was living in 1814 according to page 18 of Richard Feltoe, *Redcoated Ploughboys* (extracts of the Incorporated Militia Muster Listings from 1813–1815), 1994. Apparently, there also is a similar reference in the Upper Canada Sundries materials.
141. E-mail from Martha Hemphill to Ross Petty, December 27, 2012.
142. George Hill Detlor, *Journal of Diary of George Hill Detlor (commencing 25 Sept. 1851)* on page 5 or 685 of part 2.
143. Francis Beverley Robertson Family Bible. The gravestone in Maitland Cemetery, Goderich

baptized until October 29, 1815, when Hannah was listed as her mother.[144] If Detlor is correct about the identity of Matilda's mother then Titus and Hannah were married after early 1806 when Hannah's first husband's estate was processed but before the year end of 1807 when Matilda was conceived. Alternatively, perhaps Elizabeth Green died giving birth to Matilda or soon thereafter and Simons married Hannah Van Every before 1812 when they sold land as husband and wife. Detlor's recollection of this family some 40 years after these events may not have been as mistaken about this detail as it was mistaken about Van Every's first name.

Whenever Simons' second marriage occurred, Hannah Coon Van Every would have brought her young children to live in the Simons household. This probably would include her son William (born 1796) and two daughters Mary (born 1798) and Elizabeth (born 1804). Her eldest two sons, James (born 1792) and Peter (born 1793-4) may have been old enough to be living on their own. Interestingly, Titus ignores these stepchildren in his will (beyond noting that he raised and educated them), despite having been raised by a stepmother himself from when he was nine years old. In contrast, Titus was generous to his own half-siblings and their children in his will and even recognized his namesake Titus Geer Simons Nevills, who was not a blood relative.

Militia Activation

Starting in 1793, Upper Canadians were subject to various militia acts that required all men between the ages of 16 and 50 years (increased to 60 years in 1794) to report annually for a parade that theoretically constituted military training but typically was a celebration of the king's birthday that ended "in excess" celebration at the local tavern.[145] Britain wanted local militia help if hostilities broke out between Britain and the U.S. Companies of 20 to 50 enlisted men were to be formed under a captain, lieutenant and ensign. Captains were required to call out their companies two to four times per year for inspection and exercise. In large

---

indicates that Matilda Robertson died on August 1, 1855 at age 47 which is consistent with August 25, 1808. This birth date also is indicated in Emma Siggins White (1916), *The Kinnears and their Kin*, 136.

144. Ontario Historical Society Papers and Records, 3 (1901): 7-73, Records of St. Marks and St. Andrews of Niagara by Rev. Robert Addison at 34.

145. James W. Paxton, "Merrymaking and Militia Musters: Mohawks, Loyalists and the (Re)Construction of Community and Identity in Upper Canada," *Ontario History*, 102, no. 2 (2010): 218-238.

districts, eight to ten companies would be amalgamated into a regiment (or battalion) under a colonel and major.¹⁴⁶

As tensions between the U.S. and Britain increased over Atlantic shipping rights during the long Napoleonic war between Britain and France in the early 1800s, General Isaac Brock, the commanding officer of British forces in Upper Canada, sought to strengthen militia requirements. In the larger districts, two companies of 20 to 100 enlisted men below the age of 50 years were to be formed and designated flank companies. These were subject to initial training of six times per month until fully trained and then they received further training once per month. The intent was to have these better trained militia units "flank" British companies in battle.¹⁴⁷

When the U.S. with its 7.5 million people declared war on Britain in June 1812, General Brock had less than 2000 British regulars to defend the 1200-mile border with the United States. Upper Canada had about 75,000 settlers (up from 14,000 in 1791), not including the Indigenous peoples, and about 13,300 militia men in 30 regiments of which about 1800 received flank company training.¹⁴⁸ More than half of Upper Canadian settlers, so called "late loyalists," were born in America so their loyalties were uncertain.¹⁴⁹ Many of these settlers preferred to remain home rather than join the Canadian militia. No more than a few hundred of them fought for the U.S. invaders.¹⁵⁰

Americans (and others) had been encouraged to settle in Upper Canada settlers by low land prices. They could purchase 200 acres of land for just nominal fees (and an oath of allegiance). In contrast, the American Revolution left the states in debt causing them to sell land to speculators for immediate cash who in turn would sell to settlers for a premium. In addition, real estate taxes in Upper Canada were one-fifth of those in New

---

146. William Gray, *Soldiers of the King: The Upper Canadian Militia 1812-1815* (Erin, ON: Boston Mills Press, 1995), 25-28.
147. Richard Feltoe, *Redcoated Ploughboys: The Volunteer Battalion of Incorporated Militia of Upper Canada 1813-1815* (Toronto: Dundurn, 2012), 31; George Sheppard, *Plunder, Profit, and Paroles: A Social History of the War of 1812 in Upper Canada* (Montreal: McGill-Queen's University Press, 1994), 42-43.
148. Robert Malcomson, *A Very Brilliant Affair: The Battle of Queenston Heights, 1812* (Annapolis: Naval Institute Press, 2003), 268.
149. Sheppard, *Plunder, Profit, and Paroles*, 13, 18, 35, 43. Taylor estimates that two-thirds of Upper Canada residents were "late loyalists," i.e., born in America but living in Canada by 1812. Alan Taylor, "The Late Loyalists," 19.
150. Ibid., 30-31.

York, because Britain subsidized colonial operations and expenses.[151]

The four years or so that Titus Geer Simons spent as a refugee with his father's militia unit undoubtedly prepared him for the harsh conditions of militia field service as an adult. He would have observed the lifestyles of both officers (his father was a lieutenant) and enlisted men. But unlike his father who fought for the crown against rebels, causing him to lose all his property in Vermont, Titus Geer Simons was fighting to retain his property ownership in Canada. Not surprisingly, as a landowner and business man, Titus Geer Simons sought the more comfortable and more prestigious officer status—the higher the rank the better. Such an officer's rank was consistent with Simons' belief in a social hierarchy and his desire to be in the aristocracy. This was a belief shared by many Canadian tories and by American leaders in the Revolution.[152]

One source indicates that in 1803, Titus Geer Simons was appointed lieutenant in the Second West Riding Regiment of Lincoln.[153] The following year, he is still listed as a lieutenant in both that regiment and in the Second York.[154] "Titus Simons" also was listed as adjutant in the First Regiment of the West Lincoln militia.[155] The adjutant was responsible for unit administration such as managing training and enforcing discipline.[156] The lack of a middle initial suggests this would be Titus Senior, though he would have been 61 years old at this time when the age limit for militia service was 60 years. However, some over-age men still reported for militia duty.[157] Alternatively, the adjunct appointment may have been the fourth listing for Titus Geer Simons in 1804. In either event, by 1812, Titus Senior was no longer listed in the militia and pre-

---

151. Alan Taylor, *The Civil War of 1812: American Citizens, British Subjects, Irish Rebels and Indian Allies* (New York: Vintage Books, 2010), 37–38. However, transportation costs (and winter stoppages) were higher in Canada than in the U.S. for both exporting wheat and importing consumer goods (Taylor, 61).
152. Many Americans also rejected the French idea of political equality in favor of a hierarchical society. For example, both Presidents John Adams held such beliefs. See Isenberg and Burstein, *The Problem of Democracy*, 195. See also Tom Cutterham, *Gentlemen Revolutionaries: Power and Justice in the New American Republic* (Princeton: Princeton University Press, 2017).
153. L. Homfray Irving, *Officers of the British Forces in Canada During the War of 1812-15* (Welland, ON: Welland Tribune Print, 1908), 65–66.
154. Robertson, *The Gore District Militia*, 13, 17, 23.
155. Simons, 470–483; and Robertson, *The Gore District Militia*, 26.
156. Ron W. Shaw, *First We Were Soldiers: The Long March to Perth* (Victoria, BC: Friesen Press, 2015), 5.
157. Fred Blair, https://warof1812cdnstories.blogspot.com/p/introduction-to-stories.html (visited March 6, 2021).

sumably stayed home to run the family farm and other businesses.

These various appointments suggest Titus Geer was seeking the highest possible rank.[158] Ultimately, the younger Simons joined the Second York on June 4, 1811.[159] He took his oath of allegiance as a captain in front of his commander Colonel Richard Beasley on March 25, 1812. Simons was officially commissioned as a major in the Second York Militia less than three months later on June 4, 1812.[160] This may have been based on his recruitment of additional soldiers to the Second York. As a major, he would be paid 16 shillings per day plus 2 shillings 6 pence per day for a horse.[161]

Titus Geer Simons' half-brothers also served in the Second York. Walter William Simons (1784–1834) was an ensign in the Second York until he joined his brother's Incorporated Militia Battalion (discussed in the next chapter) as a sergeant major. John Kingsley Simons (1786–1832) served as adjutant after enlisting on December 25, 1812.[162] Walter William Simons was promoted back to the rank of ensign in the Incorporated Militia by November 1813.[163] By 1821, the Gore district had been created and the Second Gore militia included Major Titus Geer Simons, Captain John K. Simons and Lieutenant/Adjutant Walter William Simons.[164]

---

158. One source incorrectly suggests that Titus Geer Simons left the Second York for the Second West Lincoln in order to get a promotion (presumably to captain) but then returned to Second York as a major. David Richard Beasley, *From Bloody Beginnings: Richard Beasley's Upper Canada*, Simcoe: Davus Publishing, 2008, 237 (this work is labeled as "creative non-fiction").
159. Homfray Irving, *Officers of the British Forces in Canada*, 65.
160. LAC, RG 9 I-B-1, May 11, 1818, Returns of Second Gore.
161. Fred Blair, Transcripts of Documents of the Second Regiment of York Militia During the War of 1812 Taken from Library and Archives Canada R1022-11-6-E, Upper Canada Militia Records, Volume 16, revised January 26, 2017, available at http://images.ourontario.ca/TrafalgarTownship/3327290/page/3?n=
162. Homfray Irving, *Officers of the British Forces in Canada*, 37, 65; National Archives of Canada, Militia and Defense, Monthly Muster Roll and Pay List, Major Titus Simons Company, RG 9 IB7, vol. 2, 100, 104; Microfilm t-10379, 608, 613.
163. National Archives of Canada, Militia and Defense, Monthly Muster Roll and Pay List, Major Titus Simons Company, RG 9 IB7, vol. 2, 106, 114, 118, 120; Microfilm t-10379, 618, 621, 624, 626.
164. H.H. Robertson, "The Gore District Militia and the Militia of West Lincoln and West York," *Journal and Transactions of the Wentworth Historical Society* 4 (1905): 34–35.

CHAPTER EIGHT

Initial Militia Service and the Incorporated Militia

The Second York militia was large enough to have two flank companies (elite units trained monthly rather than just yearly) under Captains Chisholm and Applegarth.[165] One of Titus Geer Simons' first assignments after war was declared in June 1812 was to march with 60 men in these two flank companies to Queenston on the Niagara frontier. The Orderly Book of the First Lincoln Militia under the date of July 6, 1812 noted that "Captain [recently appointed Major] Simons of the Second York arrived this day with sixty men and will march to Queenston in the cool of the evenings to join the flank company of the same regiment, now quartered there."[166] The arrival of the Second York allowed General Brock to grant leave to members of the Lincoln militia to return home for the July harvest.[167]

Simons' 1826 Memorial of Service simply notes that he "commanded the flank companies of the Second Regiment of York Militia on the Niagara frontier."[168] In the earlier version he adds that documents which would show the particular nature of his service on the Niagara frontier "down to May 13th," were lost with the capture of Fort George on May

---

165. William Gray, *Soldiers of the King: The Upper Canada Militia 1812-1815* (Erin, ON: Boston Mills Press, 1995).
166. H. H. Robertson, *Titus Simons, Quarter Master, Peters' Corps of "Queen's Loyal Rangers," Burgoyne's Campaign 1777-1812* (Hamilton, ON: H.H. Robertson, 1903), 9. This work was previously published in the 1901-1902 *Annual Transactions of the United Empire Loyalists of Ontario*: 36-46.
167. Robert Malcomson, *A Very Brilliant Affair: The Battle of Queenston Heights, 1812* (Annapolis: Naval Institute Press, 2003), 73-74. Malcomson indicates the two flank companies totaled about 90 men.
168. Titus Geer Simons, "Memorial of Colonel Titus Geer Simons," *The Documentary History of the Campaigns Upon on the Niagara Frontier in 1812-1814* [E.A. Cruikshank] (Welland, ON: Tribune Office, 1908), 85-86.

27, 1813.¹⁶⁹ These vague statements suggest Simons sought some credit for his early activities on the Niagara frontier but did not want to explicitly claim credit for battles in which he did not participate. As illustrated below, Titus Geer Simons was not shy about identifying later battles in which he did participate.

Repelling Western Invasions

The availability of the York militia units in Niagara allowed General Brock to respond quickly when he received reports in the third week of July that U.S. forces from Detroit had invaded Canada. He first recalled the units on leave to Niagara in case the western attack was a diversion from a larger attack in the Niagara region. He then organized an expedition to Detroit including the two Second York flank companies that had been led by Major Simons to Niagara. These two units were placed under command of Captain Stephen Hatt of the Fifth Lincoln. Had Simons remained in Niagara, as the highest-ranking militia officer he should have led the militia at Detroit.

Brock led 300 militia and 50 regulars (British soldiers) to Detroit, adding another 350 troops and 600 Indigenous warriors when he arrived, and invaded Detroit on August 16, 1812. He proposed to General William Hull, Governor of the Michigan Territory and veteran of the American Rebellion, that the Americans should surrender to avoid a fight that could lead to a massacre by the Indigenous troops. To everyone's surprise, General Hull unconditionally surrendered, ceding the entire Michigan territory to Great Britain.¹⁷⁰ Brock captured 2200 U.S. troops, 33 artillery, and a vast supply of stores that he valued at £30,000. He was awarded a knighthood of the Order of the Bath.

This almost bloodless victory was a huge boost to morale and arguably the beginning of the "militia myth" that the Canadian militia fought off the American invaders with the assistance of a few regiments of British regular troops.¹⁷¹ The myth would be further advanced by stories of militia participation in the next major battle—Queenston.¹⁷² General Brock was right to be suspicious of an attack on Niagara. Such an at-

---

169. Letter to Colonel Coffin from Titus Geer Simons, August 8, 1826, LAC, RG9 I-B-1, vol. 13.
170. Graves, *Where Right and Glory Lead*, 14.
171. Donald R. Hickey, *Don't Give Up the Ship: Myths of the War of 1812* (Urbana, IL: University of Illinois Press, 2006), 165–168.
172. Malcomson, *A Very Brilliant Affair*, 73–79.

tack occurred on October 13, 1812 when American boats landed troops at Queenston Heights. The Second York flank company under Captain George Chisholm was engaged early in the battle.[173] Meanwhile General Brock left Fort George to travel to Queenston and ordered the Light Company 49th to reinforce the village and for reinforcements to be dispatched from Fort George.

The Americans in Queenston outflanked the British, appearing on the high ground behind them, and spiked a number of British cannon. As day broke, Brock raised a small force including the Second York and personally led the force to retake the high ground, but he was an easy target and quickly was shot. The militia myth was further advanced by Brock's alleged final words encouraging the York volunteers to "push on." This story placed the York militia fighting heroically alongside the general in battle. It is more likely Brock encouraged his troops generally.[174]

Brock's aide, Lieutenant Colonel John Macdonell, led a second assault on the hill with the remnants of the 49th Regiment and York militia, but after initial success, he too was shot and the British forces retreated carrying their wounded leader once again. It remained for General Roger Sheaffe when he arrived from Fort George with reinforcements to take the high ground, by flanking rather than a direct assault. This effort was ultimately successful, driving the Americans back into the water.[175]

The York militia supported this effort rather than led it. Their overall casualties from the battle were relatively small: four deaths and three wounded. The militia came away from the battle "with a pride in having fought in a victorious major battle," and the knowledge they had successfully assisted in the defense of "their families and homes." In the community of York, citizens were dazzled by "the exploits of the militia flank companies which had accompanied Brock," and who had selflessly "fought as auxiliaries at Queenston Heights," reports that "were soon exaggerated by local patriotism."[176] The militia myth of the War of 1812 continued to grow.

---

173. E. A. Cruikshank, "Record of Services of Canadian Regiments in the War of 1812, Part XII, The York Militia," in *Selected Papers from the Transactions of the Canadian Military Institute* 16, no. 6 (1908): 31–49 at 36–37.
174. Hickey, *The War of 1812*, 58; Malcomson, *A Very Brilliant Affair*, 231–33.
175. Richard Feltoe, *Redcoated Ploughboys: The Volunteer Battalion of Incorporated Militia of Upper Canada 1813–1815* (Toronto: Dundurn Press, 2012), 45–50.
176. Steven D. Bennett, "The Militia Myth in the War of 1812" available at http://stevendbennett.wordpress.com/essays/the-militia-myth-in-the-war-of-1812/.

After the battle on October 13, the two opposing generals at Queenston agreed to a three-day armistice after the battle to treat the wounded and exchange prisoners. The ceasefire ended up lasting until November 20.[177] The two Second York flank companies continued on duty at Queenston until December 13, 1812, when they began a period of rotating leaves to visit family.[178]

Developing the Incorporated Militia

Second York pay records indicate that Major Simons was paid from October 25 through December 24, 1812.[179] During this time period, Simons may have been supervising one or more of the routine duties performed by militia such as transport of goods and supplies, guard duty, and road maintenance. At some point during this quiet time, Major Simons suggested to General Sheaffe that two or three battalions be formed to create a longer-term militia service. Canadian residents would be induced to join this group through the promise of Canadian land grants after the war. Simons volunteered to raise 200 to 300 men from the York area and suggested another group of about the same size could be raised from other parts of the province. General Sheaffe wrote on January 6, 1813, to Sir George Prevost recommending this idea that he credited as a proposition from Major Titus Geer Simons. Prevost approved the idea under the designation "Incorporated Militia" on January 21.[180]

The legislature agreed with this perceived need to strengthen the militia and passed a law in March 1813 to create a full-time provincial militia

---

177. Malcomson, *A Very Brilliant Affair*, 200.
178. Cruikshank, "Record of Services," 39. Malcomson, *A Very Brilliant Affair*, 270, lists Colonel Beasley in an appendix as commanding the Second York at Queenston Heights with no mention of Simons even though Malcomson listed Major William Allan of the First York under Colonel William Graham commanding. However, in his discussion of the battle, the Second York flank companies seem to be reporting only to their captains and were assigned to report to Captain Dennis (Malcomson, *A Very Brilliant Affair*, 74, 135). This suggests neither Beasley nor Simons were involved in the Battle of Queenston Heights.
179. Fred Blair, "Transcripts of Documents of the Second Regiment of York Militia During the War of 1812 Taken from Library and Archives Canada R1022-11-6-E, Upper Canada Militia Records, Volume 16," revised January 26, 2017, available at http://images.ourontario.ca/TrafalgarTownship/3327290/page/3?n=.
180. E.A. Cruikshank (ed.), *Records of Niagara: A Collection of Contemporary Letters and Documents January to July 1813* (Niagara-on-the-Lake, ON: Niagara Historical Society, 1939). Richard Feltoe credits one of Sheaffe's senior officers, Lieutenant Colonel Thomas Pearson, with developing the idea in a January memorandum (*Redcoated Ploughboys*, 59). However, given the fact that Sheaffe proposed the idea in a January 6 letter, it seems likely that the original idea came from Simons and then Sheaffe asked Pearson to develop a formal proposal based on Simons' idea.

to be known as the Incorporated Militia. Eager to join the new unit he had proposed, Major Simons submitted a list of officers from his own regiment that had satisfied the recruiting quotas for units of the Incorporated Militia on March 4. This timing was remarkable given that the recruiting quotas were not officially printed and released until March 10. Since this was his idea, Simons appears to have been informed about its progress as it went forward. He was the first Canadian to join the Incorporated Militia with pay starting March 25, 1813.[181]

The new quotas called for a regiment consisting of one lieutenant colonel (with 40 recruits), one major (with 30 recruits), ten captains (each with 20 recruits), ten lieutenants (each with 10 recruits) and ten ensigns (each with 50 recruits), for a total of 32 officers and 420 of enlisted men.[182] Although his soldiers had already seen action, by April Major Simons led his unit through an intensive drill instruction and by May 1813, they were stationed at Burlington Heights.[183]

When the Americans captured Fort George on May 27, 1813, the British troops retreated to Burlington Heights. British General (and area commander) John Vincent met Major Simons there. Vincent called out the sedentary militia and they were placed under Simons' command along with the Incorporated Militia. Simons' initial command of the entire militia at Burlington Heights lasted less than one week. On June 3, 1813, General Vincent ordered Simons to leave his newly formed unit and report to headquarters in part because of his "local knowledge and other qualities not necessary to enumerate." He requested that some other officer take charge of the militia going to Stoney Creek.[184]

The next day, Simons, as the officer commanding the Incorporated Militia at Burlington was sent a Militia District General Order from Lieutenant-Colonel John Harvey, Deputy Adjunct General to John Vincent. The order praised the rallying of the militia in response to the attack on Fort George but also asked that militia soldiers be patient as

---

181. Gray, *Soldiers of the King*, 189; L. Homfray Irving, *Officers of the British Forces in Canada During the War of 1812-15* (Welland, ON: Welland Tribune Print, 1908), 37. Titus Geer Simons' memorial states simply that "in March 1813, he received orders to recruit for a majority in the Incorporated Militia, and completed his quota of men forthwith" (85).
182. Feltoe, *Redcoated Ploughboys*, 63.
183. Ibid., 91, 93.
184. E.A. Cruikshank, *The Documentary History of the Campaign upon the Niagara Frontier in the Year 1813, Part I (1813)* (Welland, ON: Tribune Office, 1902), 294; Feltoe, *Redcoated Ploughboys*, 106–107.

plans were prepared to retake lost territories. The "gallant" militia would then be asked to join the armed forces to implement those plans.[185]

Stoney Creek

The Lincoln and York militias were soon called to join the Incorporated Militia to participate in what became the Battle of Stoney Creek on June 5-6, 1813.[186] Vincent's June 3 letter suggests that Simons should leave his newly formed Incorporated Militia units that were currently traveling to Stoney Creek, so Simons seems not to have commanded the militia at the Battle of Stoney Creek. He likely was among the staff officers of General Vincent who followed the light infantry and cheered them on. This eliminated the element of surprise but also encouraged the troops.[187] After 45 minutes of nighttime fighting, the British managed to capture two U.S. cannon and disable two more. The fighting reportedly was heard back in the Simons' Flamboro cottage causing Major Simons' wife to ride to Burlington Heights for news at dawn. She was reassured by Simons' prior commanding officer of the Second York, Colonel Beasley, that the British had won.[188]

Also as dawn broke, both sides withdrew from the battlefield with the Americans later pulling back to Forty Mile Creek where they met reinforcements. However, the appearance of the British fleet on Lake Ontario caused the Americans to retreat to Fort George, which they would occupy until December when they returned to American territory. The British harassed the retreating Americans for several days, capturing both prisoners and supplies.[189]

On June 22, 1813, General Vincent wrote to Simons who was back at Burlington Bay. Vincent ordered Simons to form and lead a committee of paymasters at Burlington Bay so that the mustered militia companies could be listed and paid.[190] Two days later, the British decided to

---

185. Cruikshank, *Documentary History*, 301–302.
186. Richard Feltoe, *The Pendulum of War: The Fight for Upper Canada January–June 1813* (Toronto: Dundurn, 2013), 118, lists the Lincoln and York militia as participating but under an unknown commander.
187. James E. Elliott, *Strange Fatality: The Battle of Stoney Creek, 1813* (Toronto: Robin Brass Studio, 2009), 119.
188. H.H. Robertson, "Major Titus Gear Simons at Lundy's Lane," *Transactions of the Wentworth Historical Society*, 2 (1899): 53.
189. Elliott, *Strange Fatality*, 121–176.
190. John Robinson Simons, "The Fortunes of a United Empire Loyalist Family," *Ontario Historical Society Papers and Records*, 23 (1926): 470–483 at 474.

attack the American encampments and they began to lay siege to American-controlled Fort George. According to a District General Order issued July 14, 1813, Major Simons "would remain at the headquarters of the army and take charge of all the militia. All requests for bateau [boats used to transport troops]"[191] crews were to be addressed to Major Simons by the Quartermaster General's or Commissary's Department.[192] Simons and the militia became proficient at organizing boat crews and ferrying supplies across the various waterways.[193]

On July 29, 1813 after two months' duty at headquarters, Simons, as the senior militia officer at Twelve Mile Creek, received orders to return to the field. He returned to his unit that was reorganized into three companies.[194] He was ordered to proceed immediately to Head-of-the-Lake, collecting all regular troops he might find on the way to fortify the British supply depot at Burlington *"which we must not lose"* (emphasis in the original).[195] Simons led this group in a 30-mile forced march through the night and arrived with 320 men in 48 hours. Simons then saw the arrival of Indigenous warriors from Grand River and two companies of the Glengarry Light Infantry. He stationed all these troops in strong defensive positions causing American Colonel Winfield Scott to call off his attack.[196] Had Scott been able to seize Burlington, he would have cut off all supplies to Niagara, likely causing the British to withdraw from the area.[197] After participating in such a display of bravado, Simons' Incorporated Militia unit could only muster 40 out of 82 enlisted men by the end of August and was pulled off the front line to convalesce at Twelve Mile Creek.[198]

The Americans continued their withdrawal from Canadian territory after being defeated on November 11, 1813, at the Battle of Crysler's

---

191. Robert Malcomson, "'Nothing more uncomfortable than our flat-bottomed boats': Batteaux in the British Service during the War of 1812," *The Northern Mariner/Le marin du nord* 13, no. 4 (2003): 17–28.
192. E.A. Cruikshank, *The Documentary History of the Campaigns Upon on the Niagara Frontier in the Year 1813, Part II* (Welland, ON: Tribune Office, 1902), 234.
193. Robert Smol, "The Wartime Service of Titus Geer Simons, 2nd York Militia, Part 1," *Heritage News*, 27, no. 2 (Spring 2014): 12–13. Recall Simons' father was a quartermaster during the American Revolution.
194. Gray, *Soldiers of the King*, p. 190.
195. Richard Feltoe, *The Flames of War: The Fight for Upper Canada July–December 1813* (Toronto: Dundurn, 2013), 29–31; Cruikshank, *Documentary History*, 291.
196. Cruikshank, "Record of Services," 31–49 at 43; Feltoe, *Flames of War*, 29–31.
197. Smol, "Wartime Service of Titus Geer Simons": 12–13.
198. Feltoe, *Redcoated Ploughboys*, 106–120.

Farm. Late in November 1813, Simons' unit learned that Joseph Willcocks and his Canadian Volunteers, much hated because they fought for the Americans, were pillaging near Forty Mile Creek, where their families lived. An "impromptu sortie" was formed to attack and capture these traitors but after a brief skirmish, Willcocks and his unit fled. When they arrived back at the American position, Willcocks reported that they had engaged the entire advancing British army. This caused the Americans to withdraw toward the Niagara River, in turn inspiring the Canadians to slowly advance. Before withdrawing from the Canadian capital of Newark, the Americans set fire to the town on December 10. This infuriated the Canadians. Shortly thereafter, the Incorporated Militia re-took abandoned Fort Erie and Major Simons led the re-occupation of Fort George.[199] Many Canadians and British now wanted to take the fight to the Americans on the American side of the river.[200]

Fort Niagara and Black Rock (Buffalo)

The first step of revenge for the burning of Newark by American forces was the British surprise attack against U.S.-held Fort Niagara on December 19, 1813, using boats manned by boat crews and guides from the Incorporated and Lincoln militias to cross the river at night. Simons was consulted before the battle and placed in charge of the entire armed militia in the area.[201] He likely continued his previous charge of the bateau boats (from July 1813) making sure the boats were manned and transported the troops needed for the battle expeditiously.[202] He may have recalled similar transportation efforts from his childhood when boats were mustered to move refugees to new settlements. He also must have realized that if the boat crews were not properly instructed and experienced with the Niagara River, that boats could go off course as experi-

---

199. Richard Feltoe, "Redcoated Ploughboys: A History of the Volunteer Battalion of Incorporated Militia, 1813-1815," http://www.warof1812.ca/imuc.htm, visited January 2, 2021.
200. Feltoe, *Redcoated Ploughboys*, 123.
201. John Robinson Simons, "The Fortunes of a United Empire Loyalist Family," *Ontario Historical Society Papers and Records* 23 (1926): 470–483 at 475.
202. Simons was known by General Vincent to know the area and Major Gleg requested to see Simons on December 13, 1813 because "The General wishes to consult with you on some points of considerable moment." E. Cruikshank, *The Documentary History of the Campaign upon the Niagara Frontier in the Year 1813, Part IV (1813)* (Welland, ON: Tribune Office, 1907), 277–278. Feltoe says that "Once again, Major Simons was required to assume crucial responsibilities in the attack."

enced by the Americans at Queenston Heights.²⁰³ Under his direction, after the first wave of troops landed, the boats and crews returned for two more runs. Within an hour, the fort was surprised, fell to the British, and many Americans were captured.²⁰⁴ Two paintings representing the capture of Fort Niagara are reproduced below.

Figures 8.1 and 8.2.
The Capture of Fort Niagara

After this success, Simons was ordered with volunteers from the Lincoln militia to collect the group of boats used in the Fort Niagara raid and transport them over land more than 30 miles in secret to Fort Erie for a proposed attack on Buffalo. After successfully accomplishing this difficult mission, on December 28, 1813, Simons was again appointed to command the armed militia.²⁰⁵ The next day Simons and his militia were in charge of embarkation of each wave of troops for the attack in the dark. Simons himself joined the fourth and final wave of the attack in charge of remaining militia volunteers and some Indigenous troops.²⁰⁶ This second attack on Buffalo on December 30, which came to be known as the Battle of Black Rock, was successful, forcing the Americans to retreat and destroying several ships moored there.²⁰⁷ At this point, the Americans had been completely expelled from the Canadian side of the Niagara frontier. In January, General Drummond wrote to the Governor General, describing Simons as being "useful and indefatigable in em-

---

203. Malcomson, *A Very Brilliant Affair*, 140, 148.
204. Feltoe, *Redcoated Ploughboys*, 127–130.
205. Letter from Chippawa, December 29, 1813, from J. H. Holland, Capt. A.D.C. noting that "Major Simons of the Incorporated Militia is appointed to command the armed militia and volunteers" (Cruikshank, *The Documentary History of the Campaigns*, 63).
206. Feltoe, *Flames of War*, 144
207. L. Hamfray, *Officers of the British Forces in Canada during the War of 1812-15* (Welland, ON: Canadian Military Institute, 1908), 66. Simons' Memorial notes he "commanded all the volunteer armed militia in the successful attack on Black Rock and Buffalo in December" (85). Feltoe says that "Once again, Major Simons was required to assume crucial responsibilities in the attack" (*Redcoated Ploughboys*, 132).

barking the troops" and recognizing the difficulty of the task because of the "great rapidity" of the current.²⁰⁸

Figure 8.3. The Burning of Buffalo during the War of 1812, an engraving from Pictorial History of America, *by Samuel G. Goodrich (1847).*

After these two successes transporting attacking army units over the water, on January 1, 1814, Simons' unit was detailed to act as guards for 279 American prisoners of war, marching them to York and then returning to the Niagara frontier.²⁰⁹ The Incorporated Militia, including Simons' company, was rewarded with extended furloughs that allowed them to return home in January and February of 1814. They then reported to Fort York for training so that by the summer they would ready to fight as a full military unit.²¹⁰ In May, Major Simons relinquished his company command in favor of becoming second in command of the entire Incorporated Militia regiment reporting to Captain William Robinson of the King's 8th Regiment (regular British Army), who was given the militia rank of Lieutenant Colonel.²¹¹ Simons was the highest-ranking Canadian in the Incorporated Militia; after his promotion, his militia unit was dissolved and his men were transferred to Captain Rapelje's company.²¹²

208. Feltoe, *Redcoated Ploughboys*, 133.
209. Titus Geer Simons, 86; Feltoe, *Redcoated Ploughboys*, 133.
210. Feltoe, *Redcoated Ploughboys*, 206–208.
211. Ibid., 32–34, 193.
212. Regimental Order, York, May 2, 1814: The officers, non-commissioned officer and privates of Major Simon's Company are transferred to Captain Rajelje's Company from the last 24th. Source: LAC, Clark Papers.

CHAPTER NINE

Messing with his Militia Record through the Battle of Lundy's Lane

Up to this point, Simons' actions as a militia major had been successful and praised. He had just become second in command on the staff of William Robinson, the British commander in charge of the Canadian militia. He also had been placed in command of the entire militia in Niagara on at least three separate occasions, served well at headquarters under General Vincent and performed well in the field. He had proven himself a capable leader of men and administrator. His dispatching of troops in battle by boat called for both skills. Furthermore, the future of the war seemed optimistic because Napoleon had been defeated in Europe and exiled to Elba so that British reinforcements presumably soon would be sent to North America.[213] Simons was well positioned to complete an illustrious militia career through the end of the war.

The Scuffle in the Officers' Mess

Unfortunately, on June 4, 1814 Simons' militia record suffered a setback because he participated in a scuffle inside and outside the Fort York officers' mess. He interceded in a scuffle between two officers inside the mess and attempted to stop it. When an Ensign Charles Short proposed to join the scuffle, he and Simons argued vehemently. Simons invited the junior officer outside to settle their differences, then went outside and waited for the other man. When Short eventually left the mess, Simons attacked him either with his fists or with a piece of wood. Versions of the story vary, but Short may have drawn his sword on the unarmed Simons. In any event, Simons would later learn that a fight inside the officers'

---

213. J. Mackay Hitsman, *The Incredible War of 1812: A Military History* (Toronto, ON: Robin Brass Studio, 1999), 213.

mess was bad but a fight in front of enlisted men was worse since it could damage military discipline. Even though he arguably did not start either part of the dispute, as the senior officer involved Simons would be held accountable.[214] He did not help his situation the next morning when Simons ordered his horse saddled and left the post without orders, permission, or explanation. Pictured below is the Fort York Officers' Mess as it was rebuilt in 1815.

Figure 9.1. The Officers' Barracks and Mess at Fork York, as rebuilt in 1815. A diagram showing the interior layout appears on the next page.

The regimental adjutant waited for Simons to return but finally on June 16 wrote to Simons in Flamboro that he should consider himself under arrest. A court of inquiry was convened six days later. The next day Simons had a letter delivered to the inquiry complaining of a conspiracy against him and asserting that he had only left the post on legitimate urgent business (perhaps the birth of his daughter Hannah).

---

214. As noted in Chapter 5, in 1779, Simons Sr. submissively and good naturedly accepted a beating from a higher ranked officer. This led to his being shunned by his fellow officers. If Simons Jr. knew about this incident, he might have sought to avoid appearing weak, especially to lower ranked officers.

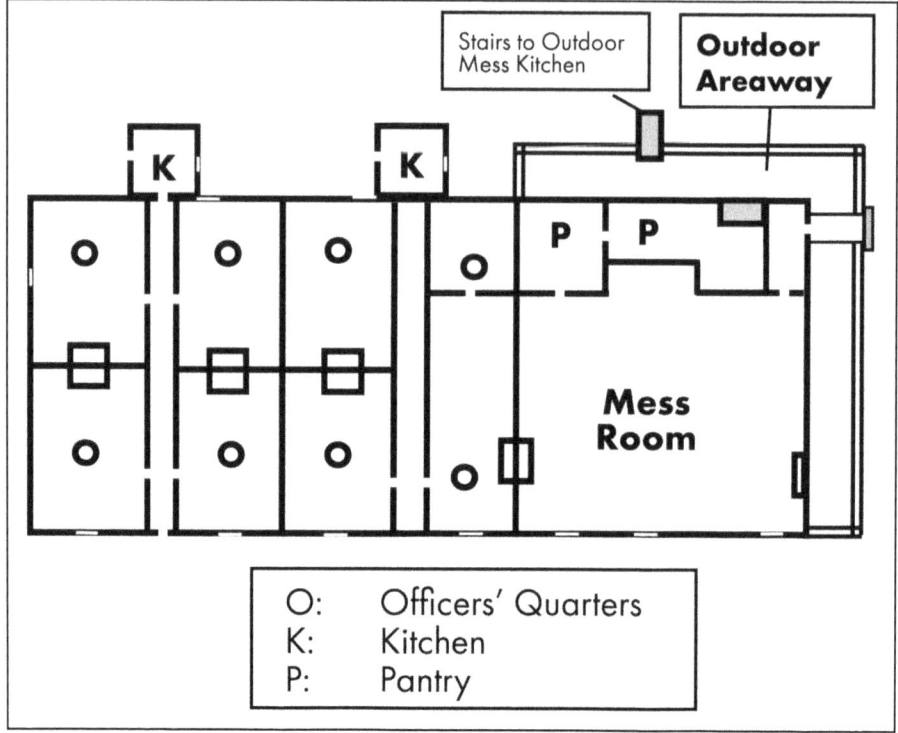

Figure 9.2. Officers' Mess and Barracks at Fort York. This diagram shows the main features of the building interior but is not to scale.

During this time, Simons apparently persuaded several officers to write letters on his behalf explaining that he tried to quell the initial argument and maintain the peace.[215] An official court of inquiry was convened on June 22 and the court took statements from both officers and enlisted soldiers who had witnessed the events. Major Simons was absent.[216]

On June 23, 1814, Simons wrote to Lieutenant Colonel Foster, Adjutant General of the Militia, noting how painful it was for him to have to write in order to vindicate his conduct. He further noted he had never been in this sort of trouble before either in a military or civil capacity and had always showed respect to his commanding officer. However, in this case, he did not know of the trial until he returned from Chippawa, 50 to 60 miles away.[217] Because the trial was held in his absence, he had

---

215. The court martial records and supporting documents are available at Library and Archives Canada, RG 9 1-B-1, vol. 3.
216. Richard Feltoe, *Redcoated Ploughboys: The Volunteer Battalion of Incorporated Militia of Upper Canada 1813-1815* (Toronto: Dundurn, 2012), 213.
217. It is not clear what "urgent business" Titus Geer Simons might have had in Chippawa but

no opportunity to confront his accusers. The inquiry focused entirely on him and his actions and not the conduct of other scuffling officers and the causes of that conduct. He admitted he had enemies but also noted he had an aged father who had served in the militia during the American Revolution and a large family dependent on him. The next day, he wrote to Lieutenant Colonel Robinson requesting an impartial investigation and that Lieutenant McDonnell and Ensign Short also be arrested.

Although Simons initially requested a full court martial so he could vindicate himself and received some support in letters from other officers, he appears to have carefully considered his position in order to decide how best to move forward. Court martials of enlisted soldiers for desertion or dereliction of duty were not uncommon, but a court martial of a militia officer was rare.[218]

Lieutenant Colonel Foster, Adjutant General of the Militia, offered two options to Simons. He could request and receive a full court martial, which would risk his dismissal from the militia (or other punishment such as reduction in rank). Alternatively, Simons could resign his commission in the Incorporated Militia and then return as major with the Second York. Simons chose practicality over principle and selected the resignation option. Thus the man who first proposed the Incorporated Militia, was its first enlistee and for a while was its highest ranking Canadian militia officer, officially tendered his resignation from the Incorporated Militia on June 29, 1814. It was accepted on July 10.[219] He also may have been the first Canadian to resign from the Incorporated Militia.[220]

According to Incorporated Militia pay records, Simons earned nearly £200 from March 1813 through March 1814.[221] On June 20, 1814, he

---

whatever it was, it was not related to militia orders or operations. Perhaps there was a transaction he could accomplish for his father who was running the family business or perhaps his wife had a favorite midwife in Chippawa to assist in the birth of Hannah Simons, who was born sometime in 1813–1814.

218. Feltoe, *Redcoated Ploughboys*, 399–405 lists selected court martial records, all of enlisted men in the Incorporated Militia.

219. Feltoe, *Redcoated Ploughboys*, 208–213. Cruikshank, *Documentary History*, 85 simply indicates that Major Simons served with the Incorporated Militia until June 1814 when he rejoined his former regiment, the Second York Militia.

220. Major James Kerby offered his resignation after being wounded on August 12 but it was not accepted. He was instead granted a one-month furlough in January 1815 and the unit was disbanded in March 1815. Feltoe, *Redcoated Ploughboys*, 335, 338–339, 347.

221. LAC RG 9 I-B-7 vol. 2 on microfilm T-10379 pp. 595-626 available http://www.collection-scanada.gc.ca/microform-digitization/006003-119.01-e.php?q2=35&q3=2840&sqn=628&tt=1244&PHPSESSID=adnvrii1fj04gbsm8uq4p2rli8fu66ervjnobl61umeomtf664h1

was listed with the Second York but with the notation of being with the Incorporated Militia. Second York pay records indicate that he was paid for July 13 to July 24, and was also paid for two horses from July 4 to 24.[222] Curiously, Major Simons' Second York commanding officer, Colonel Beasley, also faced a court of inquiry investigating charges that men of the Third York surrendered voluntarily during the Battle of York. No officers were held liable in that proceeding.[223] Beasley would face another inquiry initiated by Major Simons about five years later as discussed in the next chapter.

Return to the Second York

As Simons was suffering his militia setback so too did Napoleon suffer defeat and exile in Europe, thereby allowing British troops to begin being diverted from Europe to North America. In anticipation of likely peace negotiations, the Americans sought to bolster their negotiating position by invading Canada again. They captured Fort Erie on July 3, 1814, and then met Major General Phineas Riall's forces in battle at Chippawa on July 5, 1814.[224] Major General Phineas Riall, General Vincent's successor as commanding officer of the Niagara Peninsula, mistakenly believed the Americans at Chippawa were only militia and was surprised by their military competence and ultimately forced to retreat. This was the first time Americans defeated a British army in an open battle.[225]

Eager to return to active duty, Simons did not wait for acceptance of his resignation from the Incorporated Militia. Cruikshank reports that Simons along with Colonel Beasley and a good portion of the Second York joined General Riall's Right Division "about" July 5, 1814.[226] Other than this arrival date of "about" July 5 there is no indication that the Second York fought in Chippawa.[227] They presumably arrived after the battle had ceased, as the two forces faced each other across the Chippawa River for three days before the Americans began searching for an

222. Fred Blair, "Transcripts of Documents of the Second Regiment of York Militia During the War of 1812 Taken from Library and Archives Canada R1022-11-6-E, Upper Canada Militia Records, volume 16," revised January 26, 2017, available at http://images.ourontario.ca/TrafalgarTownship/3327290/page/3?n=
223. LAC, RG 9 I-B-1, vol. 3.
224. Hitsman, *The Incredible War of 1812*, 213–223.
225. Graves, *Where Right and Glory Lead*, 92.
226. Cruikshank, "Record of the Services": 48.
227. Donald E. Graves, *Red Coats and Grey Jackets: The Battle of Chippawa, 5 July 1815* (Toronto: Dundurn Press, 1994) (no mention of the Second York or any of its soldiers).

alternate route across the river. On July 12, 1814, Riall fortified the Canadian forts and then withdrew the remainder of the Right Division to Twenty-Mile Creek. Before this withdrawal, Riall surrounded the U.S. forces with a loose line of militia who ambushed small groups of Americans and reported on their movements.[228] Given that the Second Lincoln had suffered 43 casualties in the battle, the Second York assisted in this screening operation. During this action Adjutant John K. Simons and two other officers were captured on July 22.[229]

After Chippawa, Simons and the Second York were part of Right Division, which was stationed near Twenty-Mile Creek. Specifically, they were stationed near St. David's on July 18, 1814, when that town was captured, looted and burned by American militia. The First Lincoln militia was unable to defend the town, but with the help of others that probably included the nearby Second York, the town was retaken the next day after nearly every building had been burnt down.[230]

Other than these skirmishes with the militia, the Americans were frustrated by their inability to draw the British into battle outside of their fortified positions. So on July 22, the Americans decided to retreat back to Queenston where they again skirmished with the militia who had been occupying Queenston Heights. After a day-long battle, the Americans drove the Canadians off into the woods.[231] That evening, General Riall's superior, Lieutenant Governor General Gordon Drummond, arrived at York from Kingston with fresh troops. As they were preparing to attack, the Americans retreated further toward Chippawa.[232]

The Second York was one of several units under the command of Lieutenant Colonel Thomas Pearson, who was assigned the task of shadowing the Americans. Pearson led his troops to the charred remains of St. David's by the morning of July 25, 1814. After making sure the Americans posed no immediate threat, Pearson posted his troops around Wilson's tavern and posted the First Militia Brigade, including the Second

---

228. Graves, *Red Coats*, 147.
229. Cruikshank, "Record of the Services": 48. Official records indicate John Simons was captured on July 25, the day of the battle, and then dispatched to the United States. William Gray, *Soldiers of the King: The Upper Canada Militia 1812-1815* (Erin, ON: Boston Mills Press, 1995), 235, 278.
230. Dorothy Walker, *A Village in The Shadows: The Remarkable Story of St. David's, Ontario* (Victoria, BC: FriesenPress, 2018), 46-48; Graves, *Where Right and Glory Lead*, 100-01.
231. Graves, *Where Right and Glory Lead*, 132; Richard Feltoe, *A Crucible of Fire: The Battle of Lundy's Lane, July 25, 1814* (Toronto: Dundurn 2014), 56.
232. Graves, *Where Right and Glory Lead*, 102-04.

York, in the woods near the junction of Portage Road and Lundy's Lane. There they waited most of the day for other troops to arrive.[233]

Wounded at Lundy's Lane

On July 25, 1814 just before sunset, both sides engaged at Lundy's Lane near Niagara Falls. At some point during this nighttime battle, Major Titus Geer Simons of the Second York was shot off his horse by artillery fire and nearly killed. The battle began just before sunset around 6 p.m. when the Second York as part of the First Militia Brigade moved into position on the far west side of the British troop formation that was centered around the artillery they had placed on the Lundy's Lane hilltop. As the Americans moved out of the surrounding woods, the British artillery opened fire.[234]

Because the British artillery had seized the highest ground and was out of range, the American infantry and artillery could not respond. When American General Winfield Scott managed to move his troops out of British artillery range he had to draw his right flank out of the woods. Seizing the opportunity, the Glengarry Light Infantry supported by the Second York, some other Canadian militia units, and Indigenous warriors attacked the exposed flank. This is likely where and when Simons was shot off his horse by an artillery round.[235] American artillery could not reach the British artillery on the hill but did strike at the attacking enemy troops.

While many Canadians took cover and fought from the ground as they attacked Scott's flank, Simons remained on horseback while leading his men. He may have sought to prove himself again as a courageous soldier. In contrast, Simon's commander, Colonel Richard Beasley, preferred to command from the rear of the unit. While Beasley would later be accused of cowardice, some would argue this was normal procedure.[236] When Beasley countermanded his superior's order to open fire, Simons in turn contradicted Beasley's order, threatening to cut down the first man that ceased firing.[237]

---

233. Graves, *Where Right and Glory Lead,* 107–108.
234. Ibid., 118–125; Feltoe, *Crucible of Fire,* 80–88.
235. Graves, *Where Right and Glory Lead,* 132–134, 145.
236. On page 3 of "Dissension and the Battle of Lundy's Lane" available at http://www.davuspublishing.com/pdf_files/Beasley_and_Lundy_Lane.pdf , David Richard Beasley argues it was standard military procedure for a major to lead the troops from the front while a colonel monitored the battle and planned actions from the rear.
237. Graves, *Where Right and Glory Lead,* pp.132–33. On page 6 of "Dissension," Beasley further

After fierce fighting the unit was ordered to withdraw to their original position. Unfortunately, as the Second York, Glengarries and others moved out, they ran into the just-arriving 103rd and 104th Regiments who were exhausted after a 20-mile forced march. No one informed these British regiments of the fact their comrades were retiring. In the darkness, the newly arrived regiments mistook the retiring British troops as attacking Americans and opened fire. These two regiments were accompanied by three 6-pounder artillery pieces, so if they had time to position these cannons during this mistaken skirmish, it is possible but unlikely that these two new regiments could have fired artillery wounding Simons (so-called "friendly fire") in the unlikely event he had not been hit during the earlier encounter with American artillery.[238]

Simons was shot off his horse by three "partially spent canister bullets." Canisters were tin containers filled with small bullets and fired from artillery as an anti-personnel round.[239] A single salvo of canister from a battery of six 6-pounder canons was calculated to be the equivalent of a musketry volley by an entire infantry battalion.[240] When Simons first fell, he was first treated in the field by Robert Kerr, senior surgeon to the Indian Department. Kerr later described Simons as "severely wounded ... by ... case shot."[241] Fortunately, Kerr managed to suppress the bleeding. Simons also was fortunate not to be treated in a military hospital where amputation would have been commonplace because there was no time for more complex procedures. Furthermore, close to half of all amputees

Figure 9.3. Canister shot (image from the Minnesota Historical Society/Wikimedia Commons)

---

suggests Simons may have been shot in the arm by his own men as a retaliation for ordering them to fire after their colonel ordered them to cease firing. However, this theory is inconsistent with the fact that he was hit by artillery fire. The Second York had no artillery and any "warning shot" of canister balls fired by cannon would hit multiple people.
238. Feltoe, *Crucible of Fire*, 107–109 (claiming the friendly fire incident occurred between 9:30 and 9:50 p.m.); Feltoe, *Redcoated Ploughboys*, 272–274 (claiming the same incident occurred between 8:45 and 9:15 p.m.).
239. Graves, *Where Right and Glory Lead*, p. 36.
240. Graves, *Red Coats and Grey Jackets*, 51.
241. Certification by Robert Kerr, Senior Surgeon, Indian Department, July 30, 1815, Upper Canada Sundries, RG5, A1, vol. 2, 3, p. 10237.

would later die from infection because washing hands and sterilization was not standard procedure.²⁴²

After Simons was stabilized, an Indigenous runner was dispatched to inform Simons' wife. The family legend describes his wife as young but does not indicate if she was his first or second wife. Both would have some training in frontier medicine since physicians were rare. Either would have been in her forties, so perhaps "young" is an altered recollection for "new." Most evidence suggests this was his second wife Hannah Coon Van Every and she reportedly rode on horseback with an infant in her arms (Hannah?) accompanied by one attendant to tend her wounded husband.²⁴³ She met her husband near Drummondville. She had nursed him back to health (except for his disabled right arm) by the end of the war.²⁴⁴

Later, Simons was examined by Alexander Thom, Staff Surgeon for General John Vincent's division, and Thomas Robertson who reported in February 1815 that Simons was deprived for the present of the use of his right arm.²⁴⁵ He had been hit in the right arm and right breast by iron-case shot.²⁴⁶ The report of a medical board dated July 31, 1815, records that he had lost the use of his right arm, a little below the shoulder, by iron canister shot passing through it, "dividing some nerves … [the shot] came out from the auxiliary plexus and finally lodging in his breast from where the ball was extracted." ²⁴⁷ A re-examination occurred in 1821 and found no material change in Simons' disability.²⁴⁸

---

242. Graves, *Where Right and Glory Lead,* 202–203.
243. However, Nathan Tidridge in *The Extraordinary History of Flamborough: East Flamborough, East Flamborough and Waterdown* (Waterdown, ON: The Waterdown-East Flamborough Heritage Society, 2017), 103–104, indicates without discussion that Titus Geer Simons' wife during this adventure was Elizabeth Green, who died in 1844. Tidridge incorrectly states that Titus Geer Simons was an American Revolution veteran under General Burgoyne who was taken prison after the battle of Saratoga.
244. Robertson, "Major Titus Gear [sic] Simons," 49–54. Simons' great grandson Alexander Godfrey Robertson served for eleven years in the Queen's Own Rifles militia unit based in Toronto before joining the Canadian Expeditionary Forces in World War I. He also was discharged from service because of a medical disability.
245. LAC, RG9 I-B-1, February 28, 1815, "Medical Board Report on Titus Geer Simons."
246. Feltoe, *Redcoated Ploughboys,* 272, 396. His memorial describes "a severe wound from a grape shot passing thro' his right arm near the shoulder, which has deprived him of the use of it, and for which he has since received a pension of two hundred pounds per annum." Titus Geer Simons, 86.
247. LAC, RG8 C Series C-3236 p. 273 available at http://data2.archives.ca/microform/data2/dm13/d13/006003/c-3236/pdf/c-3236-00273.pdf.
248. Civil Secretary's Correspondence, Upper Canada Sundries, July-September 1821, RG 5, A1, Vol. 53, pp. 26283–26963 at p. 26299, Microfilm C-4607, image 125.

Shortly after Simons was disabled, the militia brigade that included the Second York was stripped of its ammunition cartridges in order to re-supply the regular troops.[249] The five-hour battle of Lundy's Lane ended with both sides withdrawing from the battlefield. The British had stopped the invasion of Canada and followed the Americans to Fort Erie, which they put under siege. Fortesque describes the battle of Lundy's Lane as the "best contested fight of the whole war." He noted the sides were pretty evenly matched, totaling about four thousand. The British had slightly higher casualties—878 with 84 deaths compared to 860 for the Americans with 71 killed.[250] Simons was one of five officers and four privates of the Second York wounded at Lundy's Lane.[251] Fortesque concludes the battle was "a stout little fight honourable alike to Americans and British."[252] Others describe this five-hour battle as desperately fought but ultimately a draw.[253] A contemporary etching of the battle (also called the Battle of Niagara) is included below.

Figure 9.4. "Battle of Niagara. From a sketch by Major Riddle." Etching by William Strickland, 1815.

249. Graves, *Where Right and Glory Lead,* 147.
250. Ibid., 195–196.
251. Cruikshank, "Record of the Services": 48.
252. J. W. Fortescue, *A History of the British Army, Vol. X* (London: Macmillan and Co. Ltd., 1920), 116.
253. Hickey, *The War of 1812,* 188.

Figure 9.5. Titus Geer Simons' Uniform. It is on display at the Hamilton Military Museum.

Peace negotiations began within two weeks of the Battle of Lundy's Lane but were not concluded until December 24, 1814. One month after Lundy's Lane, the British occupied Washington, D.C., for a day, setting fire to several building including the White House.[254] On November 4, 1814, the Americans abandoned Fort Erie, destroying its entrenchments, and left Canadian soil.[255] While the legend of the Canadian militia would later prove a myth, the War of 1812 did produce that and other patriotic legends that helped cement this collection of various peoples (British- or Canadian-born subjects, French Canadians, loyalists from the American colonies, and post-revolution American migrants) into a nation.[256]

---

254. Graves, *Where Right and Glory Lead*, 224–25.
255. Ibid., 191, 229
256. Hickey, *The War of 1812*, 287–304.

CHAPTER TEN

Post-War Activities

Pension Claims

Muster and payroll records show Simons was paid through July 24, 1814. He then sought a pension for his war service disability. For 1816, he received a pension of £20.[257] After that he was initially awarded £250 per year, which was later reduced to £200.[258] His was one of 326 pensions granted by the Upper Canadian government between 1815 and 1840.[259] On August 8, 1826, he wrote a first "Memorial" of his service in a letter to Colonel Coffin. He had learned that officers of the Incorporated Militia were to receive a pension of half-pay, but was disappointed that his name was not on the list of officers. He asked that his name be placed on the list and that he receive the appropriate pension. He respectfully submitted "a brief statement of his humble, but he trusts, faithful service" in the hope of receiving the pension of a "major commanding."[260]

A revision of this Memorial dated September 25, 1826 is addressed to Lieutenant Governor Maitland.[261] In this revised version, he refers to thirteen supporting documents. For example, instead of referring to his own testimony at the court martial of Colonel Beasley (discussed below) to document his leadership and injury at Lundy's Lane, as in the first version, he refers simply to a District General Order in the second version. He also removes the argument he makes in the first version that his

---

257. Militia Pension Agent's Office, York, September 18, 1816.
258. Johnson notes that pensions were reduced in 1821; see J.K. Johnson, *In Duty Bound: Men, Women, and the State of Upper Canada, 1783–1841* (Montreal: McGill-Queen's University Press, 2014), 116. In 1821, he received two payments of 107/2/10½; see Alexander Fraser, *Tenth Report of the Bureau of Archives for the Province of Ontario,* (Toronto: L. K. Cameron), 307, 313.
259. J. K. Johnson, "Claims of Equity and Justice: Petitions and Petitioners in Upper Canada 1815–1840," *Histoire Sociale/Social History* 27, no. 55 (1995): 219–40 at 224, 227.
260. Letter to Col. Coffin from Titus Geer Simons, October 18, 1827, LAC, RG9 I-B-1, vol. 14.
261. Titus Geer Simons, 85–86.

removal from the Incorporated Militia enabled him to serve his country more efficiently as the commanding officer of the Second York rather than as second-in-command of the Incorporated Militia. In the early version he admits to his "removal" (without further explanation) from the Incorporated Militia to his previous militia unit but in the revised version, he simply says he served in the Incorporated Militia until June 1814 when he rejoined his former regiment. In both versions, he discloses that he was receiving a disability pension of £200.

About one year later, Simons acknowledged in a letter to Colonel Coffin that he will receive a pension for a "Major Commanding in lieu of that which I have been in receipt of [a disability pension]." He further states that it was "honor and good fortune to have fought, and have bled, as my father did before me" and that he had not the "language to express his gratitude" but that those responsible would have the "grateful prayers of a loyalist family."[262] From July through December 1828, his half-year pension was £129, 16 shillings, 13 pence, which annually amounted to nearly £260.[263] It should be noted that Simons, perhaps because of his status as a major, received relatively prompt responses to his requests both for a pension and for a land grant. Other applicants were subject to multiple hearings and delays and some literally waited decades for a pension or land grant.[264]

Post-War Militia Service

Although the war was over, militia service continued. Invasions of Canada by the U.S. during the war established the American interest in acquiring Canada. Canadians were reminded of this truth by the remaining property destruction from these invasions. For this reason, after the war, the British and Canadians prepared defenses for invasions from the south including settling loyalists along the border and enhancing the St. Lawrence River with canals for better transportation of goods and military supplies.[265]

---

262. Letter to Colonel Coffin from Titus Geer Simons, August 8, 1826, LAC, RG9 I-B-1, vol. 13.
263. *Appendix of the Journal of the House Assembly of Upper Canada* (Toronto: F. Collins, 1929), A40
264. Richard Feltoe, *The Ashes of War: The Fight for Upper Canada, August 1814–March 1815* (Toronto: Dundurn, 2014), 202. Others sought reparations for losses that occurred during the war. For example, Titus Geer Simons' brother John K. Simons was captured on July 22, 1814 and made a war loss claim on January 20, 1816, for a saddle and bridle taken by the Americans (https://warof1812cdnstories.blogspot.com/p/canadian-stories.html).
265. Hickey, *Don't Give Up the Ship,* 316–318.

Major Titus Geer Simons had a more limited goal—he simply wanted his own command. His commanding officer in the Second York, Colonel Richard Beasley (commissioned to the Second York in January 1809), was exposed as an advocate for reform rather than a conservative tory like Simons and most militia officers. As a result, reaction by the tory elite including Simons was "an immediate, almost reflexive response."[266] Adjutant General Nathaniel Coffin began corresponding with the ambitious Simons as though Simons commanded the Second York. Of particular interest within that correspondence is a May 5, 1816, letter from Simons to Coffin enclosing the muster roll for the Second York and proposing it be reorganized as the First Gore with entirely new commissioning so that he could drop officers that had left the area or who did not conduct themselves in a loyal manner during the war.[267] When in 1819 Beasley objected to being bypassed for official correspondence,[268] he was stripped of his command and his office as a magistrate. He also was charged with withdrawing from the Battle of Lundy's Lane five years earlier, disobedience, neglect of duty and conduct unbecoming an officer. Coffin placed Simons in temporary command of the Second York.[269]

It seems likely that Simons played an important role in starting the court of inquiry against Beasley because he had court of inquiry experience and had previously reported disloyalty. Remember the dinner party in November 1806 where Joseph Willcocks, Sheriff of the Home District, criticized the government. Simons submitted the most detailed affidavit describing what happened and testified in a later proceeding against Willcocks that led to his dismissal as sheriff.

In the 1819 court of enquiry proceeding against Beasley, Simons was appointed one of the judges. He stepped down temporarily to testify against Beasley for staying in the rear of the Second York during the battle of Lundy's Lane and attempting to overrule Simons' commands for the militia to fire. The court of enquiry upheld these charges and Bea-

266. David Mills, *The Idea of Loyalty in Upper Canada 1784–1850*, (Kingston: McGill-Queens University Press 1988), 13. It is interesting to note that Beasley and Simons initially seemed to be friends; the former recruited the latter and quickly promoted him. Simons also supported Beasley's 1815 claim for war losses (LAC RG 19 E5(a), vol. 3740, file 3).
267. LAC, RG 9 I-B-1, Letter from Simons to General Coffin, May 5, 1816.
268. Letter from Beasley to Maitland, March 31, 1819, LAC, RG9-1-B-1 v. 7. The treatment of Simons as regimental commander may have dated back to 1818 or as early as 1816; see David Richard Beasley, *From Bloody Beginnings: Richard Beasley's Upper Canada* (Simcoe, ON: Davus Publishing, 2008), 329.
269. Letter from Coffin to Simons, December 6, 1819, LAC, RG 9 I-B-1.

sley's dismissal from the militia, so Beasley demanded (twice) a formal court martial. Like Simons when facing a court of inquiry back in 1814, Beasley complained that neither he nor his witnesses were allowed to testify and insisted on a full court martial.[270]

The court martial finally was held in Grimsby in January 1820. The court found Beasley not guilty of all charges except neglect of duty which was declared unintentional. This generous result may have led Simons to regret his decision not to pursue a court martial for himself after the officers' mess incident. Despite this favorable result for Beasley, he was informed in a March 1820 letter of reprimand that his militia services were no longer needed because of his reformist political activities.[271] Major Abraham Nelles was then appointed lieutenant colonel of the Second York.[272]

Simons became the major in the Second Gore (rather than colonel in the First Gore as he had proposed). Major Simons was (finally) promoted to colonel of the Second Gore in April 1822—two years before Titus Simons Sr. passed away.[273] The rank of colonel was the highest and most prestigious in the militia and the entire Simons family was undoubtedly proud of the younger Titus. During the war there had been only a dozen or so militia colonels in Upper Canada.[274]

On July 1, 1826, Colonel Simons hosted a banquet of about one hundred people in honor of Lieutenant Governor Peregrine Maitland's visit to Burlington Heights to commemorate the opening of the Burlington Bay Canal that connected Burlington Bay (later Hamilton) to Lake Ontario, which in turn connected to St. Lawrence River. The Gore militia and the Burlington Canal Commissioners were well represented and celebrated. Several songs were played by the marching band. As presiding officer, Colonel Simons sat next to Maitland. Many others sought introductions to the Lieutenant Governor and many speeches and toasts

---

270. LAC, RG 9 I-B-1, vol. 7.
271. Robert L. Fraser, "Richard Beasley," *Dictionary of Canadian Biography*, vol. 1836–1850(VII), available at http://www.biographi.ca/en/bio.php?id_nbr=3238 and David Richard Beasley, "Dissension and the Battle of Lundy's Lane" available at http://www.davuspublishing.com/pdf_files/Beasley_and_Lundy_Lane.pdf .
272. Beasley, *From Bloody Beginnings*, 333.
273. Bruce Elliott, Dan Walker, and Fawne Stratford Davis, *Men of Upper Canada: Militia Nominal Rolls 1828–29*, 65. After Titus' death, William Chisholm was promoted to colonel of the Second Gore in May 1830.
274. William Gray, *Soldiers of the King: The Upper Canadian Militia 1812–1815* (Erin, ON: Boston Mills Press, 1995), 33.

were made in his honor.²⁷⁵ Fortunately, Maitland survived his arrival by boat—the craft reportedly ran aground and caused the drowning of one of the band members.²⁷⁶

Administrative militia work also consumed a significant amount of Major and then Colonel Simons' time. He submitted an annual return of his unit's members. He corresponded with his superiors about officer departures and resignations as well as recommending officers for promotions. He also submitted special reports, such as a recommendation that the division be subdivided in 1826, and a list of pensioners in the Second Gore District in 1816.²⁷⁷ His correspondence regarding militia business as its colonel continued through June 1829.²⁷⁸

Land, Business, and Community Service

Immediately after the war, Titus Geer Simons resumed his acquisition of land with the 1815 purchase of Lot 7, Concession 1 in West Flamboro. A record book the following year of land grants to militia officers confirmed his 200-acre grant of Lot 4, Concession 2 in West Flamboro.²⁷⁹ In 1819, he also petitioned for clarification of a purchase on Lot 45, Concession 1 in Ancaster township from a daughter of a loyalist that he had received permission for and started before the war. His petition appears to seek clarification of this transaction now that someone else was claiming rights to the land. In the spring of 1818, he erected a house and cleared five acres of land despite the fact the land had been laid waste by "Western Indians."²⁸⁰ In May 1820, he received 1,000 acres on Lots 17 to 19, Concession 4, and Lot 18, Concession 5 and 6, in Eramosa Township (near Flamboro).²⁸¹ In June 1821, Simons received a Crown patent on Lot 14, Concession 1 in Beverly Township and then October 1821, he received a patent on Lot 12.²⁸² In his final land petition dated April 1823

---

275. John Robinson Simons, "The Fortunes of a United Empire Loyalist Family," *Ontario Historical Society Papers and Records* 23 (1926), 479480; Mary Weeks-Mifflin and Ray Mifflin, *Harbour Lights Burlington Bay* (Erin, ON: Boston Mills Press, 1989), 16.
276. Lois C. Evans, *Hamilton: The Story of a City* (Toronto: Ryerson Press, 1970), 96
277. Militia correspondence is generally available at LAC RG9 I B-1.
278. Robertson, "Gore District Militia": 34, 36; LAC, RG9, 1B5 vol. 1.
279. LAC, Upper Canada Sundries, April–May 1819, RG 5, A1, vol. 43, 20749–21234 at 20971.
280. Upper Canada Law Petitions, LAC, vol. 458, "S" Bundle 12, petition Number 65, C-2812, 886–888.
281. Land Book Register of Grants to Militia Veterans of the War of 1812, Ontario Archives, Microfilm 693, Reel 140, vol. 132, grant 276.
282. Fred Blair, "Major Titus Geer Simons (1765–1829)," January 2014.

and originating from York, he noted he was a disabled war veteran, but thanked Governor Maitland for his generous land grants to him of Lots 3 and 4 in the Second Concession of West Flamboro in the past. He noted that he had developed the West Flamboro property and built a grist mill and saw mill. He requested that he be granted a patent for this property.[283] These mills allowed Simons to trade in Upper Canada's most important goods at that time: wheat and flour produced by the grist mill, and lumber and potash from the saw mill.[284]

The war stimulated trade as did immigration, primarily from the British Isles after the war. Upper Canada's population increased from 83,300 in 1817 to 118,200 in 1821 to 237,000 in 1831. These new residents typically bought land which they cleared to grow wheat that could be sold or bartered. Clearing the land would involve using some lumber for firewood or personal building construction as well as making potash for fertilizer. Surplus lumber or potash could be sold or bartered.[285] The amount of land under cultivation rose from 325,000 acres in 1817 to 818,000 in 1831.[286]

Simons was described as a shop keeper in Dundas but not a mill owner in 1819.[287] Such merchants at this time in Upper Canada were the intermediaries between wheat farmers and their need for goods they could not produce on the farm, particularly imported goods like tea, sugar, tobacco, salt as well as hardware, textiles, clothing and footwear. The annual value of imports arriving in Quebec to be shipped to Upper and Lower Canada increased from less than £200,000 in 1813 to over

283. Upper Canada Land Petitions, LAC, vol. 462, "S" Bundle 13, petition no. 138; Waterdown-East Flamborough Heritage Society, *Connecting the Dots: Snapshots of Flamborough Communities* (Waterdown, ON: Waterdown-East Flamborough Heritage Society, 2017), 110.
284. Harold A. Innis, *Essays in Canadian Economic History* (Toronto: University of Toronto Press, 2017), 114–119. There is some disagreement about when Simons' saw mill started operating. The Waterdown-East Flamborough Heritage Society's book *Connecting the Dots: Snapshots of Flamborough Communities* says it began in 1825, five years after his grist mill started production (110). However, Simons' 1823 land petition says he had built both mills by that date.
285. Gerald M. Craig, *Upper Canada: The Formative Years, 1784–1841* (Oxford: Oxford University Press, 1963), 146. Douglas McCalla, *Consumers in the Bush: Shopping in Rural Upper Canada* (Montreal: McGill-Queen's University Press, 2015), 26, reports that according to tax records about 200,000 acres of land were under cultivation in 1808; that tripled in 1828 to 18 percent of 3.6 million acres assigned to owners, or about 650,000 acres under cultivation.
286. Douglas McCalla, *Planting the Province: The Economic History of Upper Canada 1784–1870* (Toronto: University of Toronto Press, 1993), 32–69, 249, 253.
287. T. Roy Woodhouse, *The History of the Town of Dundas: Part 1* (Dundas, ON: Dundas Historical Society, 1965), 29. Simons opened his general store in 1819 according to Waterdown-East Flamborough Heritage Society, *Connecting the Dots*, 110.

£1 million in 1814 and 1816.[288] Textiles, particularly cotton, were the most commonly purchased goods, mostly for home sewing but also with some purchases of completed textile products. Spirits, both imported like rum or locally produced like whiskey, also were popular purchases. Other popular locally produced products sold by shopkeepers included boards, flour, pork and butter.[289] While most local shopkeeper customers were farmers, store owners also sold products to lumber operators, villagers, artisans, and laborers.

Merchants would normally sell goods to farmers on credit until the crop was harvested and sold.[290] Similarly, lumber operators, who may have been farmers as well, also purchased needed supplies in the fall and paid off their debts the following summer. Merchants would often barter and accept wheat or more likely flour as payment on farmers' accounts. Similarly, they would accept boards as payment from lumber operators.[291] Thus, merchants through the offering of credit were actually financing the expansion of agriculture and development generally.[292]

One historian said of merchants in Northampton, Massachusetts:

> They were economic and cultural innovators, the central agents of social transformation in their communities. They represented the human link to the wider world of export and exchange, the main conduit for commodities, credit and consumer goods. Thus, they had considerable influence on the emergence of new consumption patterns and market oriented activities among their neighbors.[293]

Like many merchants, Simons with the help of his father and other family members developed and operated many businesses. By 1825, the year after his father had died, Titus Geer Simons and family had built an industrial empire on the third lot of the Second Concession in West

---

288. McCalla, *Planting the Province*, 32.
289. McCalla, *Consumers in the Bush*, 37–57, 68–82, 194.
290. Douglas McCalla, "Retailing in the Countryside: Upper Canadian General Stores in the Mid-Nineteenth Century," *Business and Economic History* 26, no. 2 (1997): 393–403.
291. Douglas McCalla, "The Internal Economy of Upper Canada: New Evidence on Agricultural Marketing Before 1850" in *Historical Essays on Upper Canada* (J. K. Johnson and Bruce G. Wilson, eds.; 1999), 237–260.
292. Beatrice Craig, *Backwoods Consumers and Homespun Capitalists: The Rise of a Market Culture in Eastern Canada* (Toronto: University of Toronto Press 2009), 114.
293. Gregory Nobles, "The Rise of the Merchants in Rural Market Towns: A Case Study of Eighteenth Century Northampton, Mass.," *Journal of Social History*, 43 (1990): 5–23 at 5.

Flamboro that consisted of a sawmill (one of 422 in the province) and a grist mill (one of 250 in Upper Canada), both previously mentioned in his April 1823 land petition, as well as a distillery, ashery, cooperage, stables, hog pens and 13 dwellings for his employees.[294] In January 1820, Titus Geer and his half-brother John K. Simons were licensed for a year as shopkeepers to retail "spirituous liquors." They distilled 230 gallons of liquor that year—the fourth-highest amount among 15 distillers in Gore.[295] Licensed distillery capacity province wide was nearly 13,600 gallons. Five years later there were just over 100 licensed distilleries in Upper Canada.[296]

The grist mill, which might have taken up to two years and more than £1,000 to construct, produced flour from wheat for local consumption and perhaps for export. The flour could be packaged in barrels assembled from staves cut at the sawmill (which in Simons' case operated until 1906)[297] and assembled at the cooperage. Barrels also could be made to package potash made from burned wood too small for or left over from the sawmill. Potash could be used as fertilizer both locally and for export.

Simons' industrial complex appears to have modeled after that of his friend and neighbor James Crooks, who had an even bigger complex at nearby Crooks' Hollow. Crooks' businesses started with a grist mill in 1813, supplying the British during the war.[298] His complex grew to include most of what Simons would later develop as well as an axe, hoe and scythe factory, a tannery and woolen mill and eventually in 1826 the first paper mill in Upper Canada to produce white paper.[299]

Presumably Simons was no longer poor as he had described himself in an 1801 letter as a new settler in West Flamboro. In fact, according to 1819 tax assessments, Titus Geer Simons had amassed 670 acres of land making him one of the largest landowners in the West Flamboro township. He was assessed the second highest amount of tax—47 shillings

---

294. Adam Elsebroek, "From the Vault: Titus Geer Simons" (2013); Waterdown-East Flamborough Heritage Society, *Connecting the Dots*, 110.
295. Fraser (1914), *Tenth Report of the Bureau of Archives*, 293, 299.
296. McCalla, *Planting the Province*, 99, 279.
297. Waterdown-East Flamborough Heritage Society, *Connecting the Dots*, 110.
298. This pattern of development from sawmill to grist mill to others businesses was fairly typical; see Craig, *Upper Canada*, 146.
299. Waterdown-East Flamborough Heritage Society, *Connecting the Dots*; Nathan Tidridge, *The Extraordinary History of Flamborough: East Flamborough, West Flamborough and Waterdown* (Waterdown, ON: Waterdown-East Flamborough Heritage Society, 2017), 105–109.

and 6 pence.[300] He could easily pay his taxes with the income from his various activities plus his then £200 annual disability pension.

Simons' business interests were not confined to the Flamboro/Dundas locality. According to the Library and Archives of Quebec, Notarial Records 1637–1935, he often did some business in Montreal. In June 1820 he was given a power of attorney by another party, whose name in the records is illegible. In October 1826, Simons received a notarized engagement letter to David Finlayson. Finally, in October 1828, Simons received an engagement letter from Francois Lemontagne. Unfortunately, we lack details of these engagements but they probably involved exporting flour after the fall wheat harvest and lumber in exchange for British manufactured goods such as textiles. We do know that his need to visit Montreal for business was a point of friction with respect to his serving as sheriff of Gore, as discussed below.

Simons' businesses prospered and stimulated town growth.[301] Industrial and commercial initiatives sprung up near mills such as those operated by Simons and his neighbor James Crooks in West Flamboro and others in Dundas, Ancaster, and Burlington Bay/Hamilton. These areas competed to see which would be the district town of Gore District and therefore the home of district government offices. They also competed for Lake Ontario trade by developing canals and port facilities.

Initially Dundas enjoyed brisk trade but by Titus Geer Simons' death in 1829, it was being overshadowed by the newly developed town of Hamilton. Hamilton had a locational advantage with direct access to Lake Ontario through the Burlington Canal completed in 1827. That same year construction started on the cut-stone jail and courthouse that would open in 1832, ensuring Hamilton's dominance after that time.[302]

Freemasonry

Colonel Simons also was a Freemason. Freemasonry is a fraternal organization that evolved from the guilds of stonemasons and cathedral builders of the Middle Ages. With the decline of cathedral building, some lodges of operative (working) masons began to accept honorary members to bolster their declining membership. From these honorary

---

300. Woodhouse, *The History of the Town of Dundas: Part 1*, 28.
301. Craig, *Upper Canada*, 146.
302. John C. Weaver, *The History of Canadian Cities—Hamilton: An Illustrated History* (Toronto: James Lorimer & Co., 1982), 16–20.

members evolved lodges that developed modern symbolic or speculative Freemasonry. This form of Freemasonry, particularly in the 17th and 18th centuries, adopted the rites and trappings of ancient religious orders and of chivalric brotherhoods. In time these became more important than masonry skills.

Simons first showed an interest in Freemasonry when, as the co-editor of the *Upper Canada Gazette*, he published a description of a Masonic funeral ceremony.[303] When Union Lodge No. 24 was formed in West Flamboro in 1810, he soon joined. Officers were elected every six months and Simons was one of the "names in the old records" suggesting he served as an officer.[304] Simons followed the lodge as it moved from West Flamboro to Ancaster in 1820. One of the last acts of this now defunct lodge (it only had 21 members in 1821) occurred in July 1824 when Simons laid the cornerstone for the Free Church of Ancaster with masonic honors. As marshall that day, he co-hosted a public dinner at Rousseaux's Hotel. Over 200 invitations had been issued and over a hundred people attended. The attendees enjoyed several performances by the military band of the 76th Regiment and numerous toasts.

Figures 10.1 and 10.2. Old Free Church; Simons' scroll.

THE SCROLL.
ON THE SEVENTH DAY OF JULY,
IN THE YEAR OF OUR LORD
1824
AND OF MASONRY,
5824
IN THE FIFTH YEAR OF THE REIGN
OF HIS MAJESTY,
KING GEORGE IV.
THE CORNER STONE OF THE
ANCASTER FREE CHURCH.
WAS LAID WITH MASONIC HONORS.
BY
TITUS G. SIMMONS ESQR.
MARSHALL OF THE DAY.
ACTING IN THE NAME AND BY THE APPOINTMENT OF THE
UNION LODGE OF FREE AND ACCEPTED MASONS
OF ANCASTER.
SIMON McGILLIVRAY, ESQR., GRAND MASTER AND JAMES FITZ-GIBBON, ESQR., DEPUTY GRAND MASTER.
LIEUTENANT GENERAL, THE RT. HON. GEORGE, EARL OF DALHOUSIE, G. C. B. GOVERNOR GENERAL OF THE BRITISH PROVINCE IN UPPER CANADA.

The president and vice president retired at 11 o'clock while the festivities continued into the night.[305] Simons may have been given such a prominent role because he had been a leading member of

---

303. J. Ross Robertson, *The History of Freemasonry in Canada from its Introduction in 1749* (Toronto: George Morang & Co., 1900), 610.
304. Ibid., 957.
305. Ibid., 973–974; John Robinson Simons, "The Fortunes of a United Empire Loyalist Family," *Ontario Historical Society Papers and Records* 23: 470–483 (1926) at 478.

the subscription committee for the church. To the left are pictures of the Free Church of Ancaster (1824–1866) and the text of the scroll that Simons placed beneath its cornerstone in the 1824 ceremony.

Civic Service

At this time, Upper Canada had two, often overlapping, roads for individuals to become prominent in their community.[306] The first was through military appointment. As discussed above, Simons eventually was appointed colonel in 1822—the highest and most prestigious militia rank possible. Prior to that, then Major Simons was appointed the first sheriff of the newly created Gore District in April 1816.[307] Each district had only one sheriff but a sheriff may have deputies. Titus Jr. probably knew something of his father's activities as a Montreal deputy sheriff some thirty years earlier. Simons would serve for as long as the Crown wished.[308] Sheriffs were empowered to make arrests, keep the jails, conduct hangings and sell land for non-payment of taxes or debts.[309]

The sheriff position was both prestigious and lucrative. For example, in 1819 and 1822, Sheriff Simons seized and sold land belonging to Hector MacKay and received fees for doing so.[310] Simons earned £50 in salary as sheriff and £210 in fees in 1821.[311] As noted above, in that same year his disability pension was reduced from £250 to £200. As sheriff, Simons also felt he had the political substance to recommend others for (part-time) government positions such as flour inspector.[312]

However, Simons needed to pursue his merchant businesses and was reluctant to share his authority with an appointed deputy. This led to controversy. In July 1819, Simons wrote to Lieutenant Governor Peregrine Maitland saying he wished to go to Montreal for four weeks but promised to return before the Assizes courts and to "regularly appoint

---

306. J. K. Johnson, *Becoming Prominent: Regional Leadership in Upper Canada, 1791–1841* (Kingston, ON: McGill-Queen's University Press, 1989), 61.
307. LAC, RG 5 A-1, vol. 46, p. 22485, microfilm reel C-4604; Armstrong, *Handbook of Upper Canadian Chronology*, 170.
308. David Murray, *Colonial Justice: Justice, Morality, and Crime in the Niagara District 1791–1849* (Toronto: University of Toronto Press 2003), 42–43.
309. Johnson, *Becoming Prominent*, 81.
310. Woodhouse, *History of the Town of Dundas: Part 1*, 18.
311. Charles K. Talbot, *Justice in Early Ontario 1791–1840* (Ottawa: Crimecare Pub., 1983), 34.
312. For example, letter to Hillier from Simons, August 19, 1822, Civil Secretary's Correspondence, Upper Canada Sundries, July–September 1822, RG 5, A1, vol. 57, 292224–29894 at 29589, microfilm C-4609, image 430. Simons recommends Jordan Davis for the post of flour inspector.

a deputy to act in my absence."³¹³ In December 1819, Maitland received a complaint from William Campbell regarding the fact that Simons had not appointed a permanent deputy. Instead, he would appoint his brother Walter William Simons as the temporary sheriff when he was away and then accept or disavow his brother's actions upon his return.

This left the public with no confidence in the brother's decisions. Campbell was careful to note that he had been asked by the grand jury to send this complaint without a judicial proceeding to determine the accuracy of the allegations.³¹⁴ The grand jury was chaired by Richard Beasley, who knew at this time that Simons was acting against him within the militia and that Simons had essentially obtained de facto command of the Second York.³¹⁵

As with his own threatened court martial, Simons' response was swift and multipronged. First, he wrote a letter to Major George Hillier, civil secretary to Maitland, arguing that a sheriff like him who did his duty was inevitably found at fault by some. He further asserted he had support of the majority within the district. He vaguely referred to his efforts to give satisfaction to all and the make "the situation respectable." He further asserted the complaint was from "Gourlay-ites" (reformers) who were jealous of his community standing and his command of the Second York. He closed by asserting he had always tried for the faithful discharge of his duties and any failure here was a "mistake in judgment not in will."³¹⁶

Second, since Simons often seemed to believe the best defense was to take the offense, he reviewed the commission of peace—the list of Gore district magistrates—and discovered that three current magistrates were either no longer living in the district or living closer to other districts. Indeed, one magistrate could not attend the quarter session court because he had left the district four years earlier, and another actually lived outside the district.³¹⁷ In a bold move, he therefore "detained" all

---

313. Letter from Titus G. Simons to Maitland, July 16, 1819, *Upper Canada Sundries*, vol. 44, microfilm C-4603, 21545.
314. Letter from William Campbell to Maitland, December 7, 1819, *Upper Canada Sundries*, vol. 44, microfilm C-4604, private manuscript, 22277–22279.
315. Beasley, 332.
316. Letter from Simons to Hillier, January 3, 1820 *Upper Canada Sundries*, vol. 46, microfilm C-4604, 22481–22484.
317. John C. Weaver, *Crimes, Constables, and Courts: Order and Transgression in a Canadian City* (Montreal: McGill-Queen's University Press, 1995), 39.

of the magistrates until this situation could be resolved.[318] (Perhaps he was hoping for a magistrate appointment). Finally in July 1820 while in York, Simons appointed his youngest brother Walter W. Simons as deputy sheriff while he was out of town dealing with business affairs in Montreal in September 1820. He promised to return in time to perform his official duties in the Assizes court.[319] The Assizes court typically conducted about six criminal trials each lasting between three to seven days and the sheriff had to select jurors from the juror list for the trials.[320] As noted above, Simons seemed to have ongoing business to attend to in Montreal.

Simons wrote again two years later in June in response to the provincial parliament's interest in "incapacitating" merchants from being sheriffs. Sheriffs were in charge of seizing and selling property for the payment of a debt. Many felt that the ranks of sheriffs were dominated by merchants who favored creditors over debtors, sometimes selling properties to a small group of bidders rather than a public auction and obtaining a below market price.[321] In Simons' case there also was a concern about his absences from the district to conduct merchant business. Simons sought reassurances that the Lieutenant Governor was pleased to have him continue in office. He admitted that he had "often erred in the execution" of his duties, but again asserted those were errors "of the judgment not of the will."[322] One month later in July 1822, he wrote requesting three weeks leave to settle up his mercantile transactions in Montreal before the fall Assizes. He assured the secretary to the Lieutenant Governor that he had sold out his stock in trade and leased out warehouses and other storage areas for a term of years so this would be the last time he would have to ask for a similar favor.[323] However, we

---

318. Letter from Simons to Hillier, February 9, 1820, *Upper Canada Sundries*, vol. 46, microfilm C-4604, 22756–22758.
319. Letter from Simons to Hillier, July 7, 1820, *Upper Canada Sundries*, vol. 46, 23598–23599, microfilm C-4605, images 371–372.
320. John C. Weaver, *Crimes, Constables, and Courts*, 26, 28.
321. Paul Romney, "Upper Canada (Ontario): The Administration of Justice, 1784–1850," *Manitoba Law Journal* 23 (1995): 183, 190–191.
322. Letter to Hillier from Simons, June 16, 1822, Civil Secretary's Correspondence, *Upper Canada Sundries*, April–June 1822, RG 5, A1, vol. 56, 28346–29223 at 29094–29096, microfilm C-4608, images 1444–1446.
323. Letter to Hillier from Simons, July 22, 1822, Civil Secretary's Correspondence, *Upper Canada Sundries*, July–September 1822, RG 5, A1, vol. 57, 292224–29894, at 29382–29384, microfilm C-4609, images 225–227.

know his business conducted in Montreal outlasted his appointment as sheriff.

Unfortunately, while the appointment of his brother as deputy appeared to resolve the immediate controversy, mistakes made by Walter led to Simons' dismissal as sheriff two years later.[324] The details of these mistakes are not documented. Simons' April 19, 1824 resignation letter only mentions the desire of the officers of his regiment for him to run in the general election of 1824. He states it would be inappropriate for him to run for election while holding public office of sheriff.[325] However, this appears to be just an excuse since his former commanding officer and current rival Richard Beasley was elected to Parliament in the election of 1824 while holding the public office of magistrate.[326] Curiously, the *Colonial Advocate* newspaper reported in June 1826 about a previous case in the Gore Assize in the prior September (1825) when Sheriff Simons offered to protect Justice Bolton from injury.[327] The date is hard to read so perhaps this occurred in September 1824, but even that date was after Simons' resignation and the appointment of his successor.

Simons also sent a "Memorial" to Lieutenant Governor Maitland in April 1824 expressing his gratitude for allowing him to continue in office despite various complaints directed against him. However, he noted the complaints appeared in a more favorable light after they were investigated by the attorney general. John Willard joined Simons in recommending Simons' brother Walter W. Simons for sheriff. However, William M. Jarvis, son of Provincial Secretary William Jarvis, apparently was politically better connected than Walter Simons and was appointed sheriff in May 1824.[328]

Despite being removed as sheriff in 1824, Titus Geer Simons was ap-

---

324. Beasley, 332–33, suggests that Simons was replaced as sheriff after a scandal about Walter Simon's actions as deputy while Simons was away "for weeks" in Quebec. Walter reportedly handled badly two actions against debtors and ultimately, Simons accepted responsibility and settled for half of the usual fees. In July 1822, Simons did request a two to three week leave of absence to settle mercantile transactions in Montreal. This period of absence may be when the problem occurred. Letter from Simons to Hillier, July 22, 1822, *Upper Canada Sundries*, vol. 57, 29382–29384, microfilm C-4609, images 225–227.
325. Letter from Simons to Hillier, April 19, 1824, *Upper Canada Sundries*, vol. 66, 34963–34964, microfilm C-4612, images 1330–1331.
326. Armstrong, *Handbook of Upper Canadian Chronology* (Toronto: Dundurn Press, 1985), 98.
327. *Colonial Advocate*, June 1, 1826.
328. Various letters, *Upper Canada Sundries*, vol. 66, 34961–34969; Armstrong, *Handbook of Upper Canadian Chronology*, 170.

pointed to the more prestigious position of a magistrate/justice of the peace in Gore just three years later in 1827. Magistrates customarily added "Esq." ("Esquire") to their names and being appointed a magistrate was the "basic way of conferring civil status and civil power" and often the first step toward seeking elective office or national administrative appointment.[329] Magistrates had both ministerial (administrative) duties as well as judicial duties.[330]

Magistrates collectively set local tax rates to cover expected expenditures, and appointed and supervised the treasurer and tax assessors, collectors and all town officials. They administered oaths of allegiance to all local government officials. Magistrates also issued licenses and regulated public businesses such as taverns, ferries and markets. Magistrates "[a]t the local level were all-pervasive." Since English Poor Law was not enacted in Canada, the magistrates also attempted to alleviate poverty by such means as ordering fathers of illegitimate children to pay child support and binding poor children into apprentice positions until adulthood so they could learn a trade.[331]

The magistrates' primary duty was keeping the peace and they formed the lowest level of the judicial system (even though most had no legal training). They would hold Courts of Request (petty sessions) on the first and third Saturday of every month to hear minor misdemeanor cases such as those with £5 or less in dispute. They had no clerks to assist them and in effect made up law as they proceeded, trying to do what was fair. At the next highest judicial level, every January, April, July and October, the magistrates would meet with the sheriff at the district town's courthouse to conduct the Court of General Quarter Sessions of the Peace that heard assault and battery as well as petty larceny cases with the aid of local juries.[332] The highest court was the Court of the King's Bench that traveled to each district in Assizes to hear all capital and other important criminal and civil cases.

As a magistrate in 1827, Simons chaired a public meeting and a committee in the Gore District to once again propose building a gaol (jail) and courthouse in Dundas. Other petitions sought different locations

---

329. Johnson, *Becoming Prominent*, 61–68; Frederick H. Armstrong, *Upper Canada Justices of the Peace and Association 1788–1841* (Toronto: Ontario Genealogical Society, 2007), 13–16.
330. Weaver, *Crimes, Constables, and Courts*, 29.
331. Philip Girard, Jim Phillips, and R. Blake Brown, *A History of Law in Canada: Volume One, Beginnings to 1866* (Toronto: University of Toronto Press, 2018), 355.
332. Johnson, *Becoming Prominent*, 61–68.

such as Hamilton. Unfortunately, a motion in the House of Assembly to refer Simons' petition to a select committee for further consideration failed to pass by two votes.[333] Ultimately the gaol and courthouse were built in Hamilton starting with the laying of the cornerstone in August 1827.[334] These buildings were completed in 1832. In October 1827, Simons also was called to be chairman of a committee to examine how to open and improve the roads (and raise money for that task) from East and West Flamboro to the newly established town of Guelph. His magistrate commission may have ended by this time[335]—in fact, ending the same year it began, as explained in the following chapter.[336]

---

333. *Journal of the House of Assembly of Upper Canada,* December 5, 1826–February 17, 1827, 39. Simons is identified as "Esq.," which was common practice for magistrates. He was not explicitly identified as a magistrate but was chair of a committee containing other magistrates.
334. *Gore Gazette,* August 14, 1827.
335. *Gore Gazette,* October 20, 1827. In the road commission report, neither Colonel Simons nor Doctor Hamilton had "Esq." after their names, which was common practice for magistrates. Simons' selection as chair over several "Esquires" on the committee might suggest the community wanted to show its support for Simons after the trial. This matter is discussed in the next chapter.
336. Armstrong, *Upper Canada Justices of the Peace,* 56.

CHAPTER ELEVEN

The Tar-and-Feather Outrage

Simons was appointed but then removed as a magistrate in 1827 because legal proceedings were filed against him for allegedly participating in a violent mob tar-and-feather attack against George Rolph, an alleged adulterer. However, because Rolph's brother John had been elected to the House of Assembly on a reform platform in 1824, this attack is often interpreted as an illegal attack by tories against the newly developing reform movement.[337] Indeed, John Rolph refers in a letter to the tenacity of his enemies' pursuit of "me and my brother."[338] As noted in prior chapters, Simons previously had exposed reformers Joseph Willcocks and Richard Beasley so his opposition to reformers was well established.

Simons allegedly was joined in this latest attack by his young friend Dr. James Hamilton, a magistrate since 1820, his son-in-law Alexander Robertson, and others. Simons and Hamilton were found liable for damages by the jury in an 1827 civil trial and Robertson was found not guilty in a verdict directed by the judge in the same trial. A later criminal complaint named other participants but that case never went to trial as discussed below.

This chapter examines the attack and subsequent efforts by Rolph to obtain justice. The attack and related legal proceedings drew province-wide and even international attention and the courtroom for this

---

337. Riddell argues the outrage "was very largely political" rather than based on personal dislike of Rolph; see William R. Riddell, "The Court of King's Bench in Upper Canada, 1824–1827," *The Canada Law Journal*, 49 (1913), 126–134 at 128. In contrast, Dent notes the "outrage had arisen of private complications, and no political question arose in the course of the trial"; see John Charles Dent, *The Story of the Upper Canadian Rebellion* (Toronto: C. Blackett Robinson, 1865), 168. See generally, Ross D. Petty, "The 1826 Ancaster Tar and Feathers Outrage: Three Defendants' Perspectives," *Ontario History*, 114, no. 2 (2022), 196–220.
338. Metropolitan Toronto Library, W. W. Baldwin Papers Collection, B105, letter from John Rolph to W. W. Baldwin, May 5, 1829.

civil trial in August 1827 against three alleged attackers was packed "almost to suffocation."[339] The case was notable because gentlemen tories—leaders in their community and normally strong proponents for the rule of law—had, it was alleged, violently and lawlessly attacked the brother of a reform advocate to punish him for commiting adultery. This action suggested the tories believed themselves to be above the law. This outrage remained in the public eye for over two years as George Rolph with his attorney and brother John sought justice against the attackers. Other outrages occurred later, perhaps inspired at least in part by what came to be known as the "Ancaster Outrage." Eventually, government reform was accomplished after the Rebellion of 1837–38.[340]

Reformers were seeking changes including more input for voters on local issues and the election of local officials rather than their appointment by the lieutenant governor and executive council, both appointed by the crown.[341] During 1825–27, the House of Assembly debated the citizen status of American settlers who came to Upper Canada beginning in 1794 in order to obtain cheap lands—the so-called "late loyalists."[342] Reformers such as John Rolph supported the rights of late loyalists to both own land (something largely not disputed) and to vote and run for elected office in Upper Canada. Tories believed late loyalists would support reform and sought to limit their rights. Tories also supported the constitutionally established church supported by church reserve land leases. Reformers wanted those revenues to support other Protestant clergy, not just those of the Church of England.[343]

Background

The use of hot pine tar to attach feathers to a person's skin as punishment and humiliation dates back at least to medieval times, but it did

---

339. *Gore Gazette,* Aug. 25, 1827: 102; "Tarring and Feathering," *New York Spectator,* September 7, 1827. Nearly identical stories appear in *The United States Gazette* (Philadelphia), September 7, 1827: 2, and *The Lancaster Intelligencer,* September 14, 1827: 2–3. See also Leo A. Johnson, "The Gore District Outrages, 1826–1829: A Case Study of Violence, Justice, and Political Propaganda," *Ontario History* 83, no. 2 (1991), 109–26 at 110.
340. Dent, *Story of the Upper Canadian Rebellion.*
341. Gerald M. Craig, *Upper Canada: The Formative Years, 1784–1841* (Oxford: Oxford University Press, 1963).
342. Alan Taylor, "The Late Loyalists: Northern Reflections of the Early American Republic, *Journal of the Early Republic,* 27: 1–34
343. Robert W. Passfield, *Anglican Toryism in Upper Canada: The Critical Years, 1812–1840* (Oakville, ON: Rock's Mills Press, 2019), 189–196.

not become well known in North America until used (or threatened) by colonists on tax collectors before the American Revolution. For example, in Simons' ancestral home of Salem, Massachusetts, three collectors were attacked with tar and feathers in the summer and fall of 1768 alone. The practice soon spread to other colonies and was used or threatened against loyalists during the American Revolution and after. For example, in 1812 in Burlington, Vermont, the American commander threatened to tar and feather those who were disrespectful to the government.[344]

As loyalists Simons and his co-conspirators had no difficulty using the same practice against reformers, particularly because the practice was increasingly being used to punish behavior that the community considered immoral.[345] His New England ancestry makes it likely that it was Simons who came up with the tar-and-feathering idea for the attack.

George Rolph, the tar-and-feathering victim, was called to the bar of Upper Canada in 1816 and moved to Dundas, then in the newly formed Gore District, in the same year. In April 1816, Rolph was appointed clerk of the peace, clerk of the district court, and registrar of the surrogate court for the newly formed Gore district. All three positions would be a source of revenue for Rolph but the position of clerk of peace called for Rolph to assist the local magistrates with the administration of local government and petty justice.[346] Rolph came from a conservative tory family closely associated with Colonel Thomas Talbot, a tory who had been personal secretary to Lieutenant Governor John Graves Simcoe and a large landowner and settlement promotor.[347] Rolph was appointed lieutenant to the First Norfolk Militia in 1812 and captain in the First Gore Militia in 1823.[348] Rolph had all the appearances of a successful tory professional who would support the status quo of appointing crown loyalists to the vast array of government positions.

Rolph soon became the second-largest landowner in town but he was

---

344. *Kingston Gazette,* August 18, 1812 cited in Jane Errington, *The Lion, the Eagle, and Upper Canada: A Developing Colonial Ideology,* 2nd ed. (Montreal: McGill-Queens's University Press, 2012), 77.
345. Benjamin H. Irvin, "Tar, Feathers, and the Enemies of American Liberties," *The New England Quarterly* 76, no. 2 (2003): 197–238.
346. Paul Romney, *Mr. Attorney: The Attorney General for Ontario in Court, Cabinet, and Legislature 1791–1899* (Toronto: University of Toronto Press, 1986), 109.
347. Passfield, *Anglican Toryism,* 125.
348. J. K. Johnson, *Becoming Prominent: Regional Leadership in Upper Canada, 1791–1841* (Kingston, ON: McGill-Queen's University Press, 1989), 223.

aloof and refused to associate with or support the other town elites.[349] He chose not to attend their gala balls or assemblies and not to preside over or give toasts at their public dinners, according to a draft address to the jury.[350] Rolph did not fit in and if he were persuaded to leave, his position of clerk of the peace could be filled by someone who was more compatible with the magistrates and other local elite.[351]

The local elites' dislike for Rolph was compounded by their dislike for his brother John. John Rolph started as a loyalist tory serving as paymaster of the London militia during the war. After the war John Rolph traveled to England for three years in order to complete his education and converted to the reform cause.[352] He was elected to the legislative assembly as a reformer in 1824. His brother George probably was viewed as a likely reform sympathizer although there is little evidence he was politically active at that time.[353] Ironically, this attack may have caused George to take up the reform cause and certainly cemented his brother's views that government needed reform.

The Attack

According to allegations and testimony in the civil lawsuit, around midnight on the night of June 3-4, 1826, several disguised men invaded George Rolph's home after dining and drinking at Dr. James Hamilton's house. The group had discussed the rumored extramarital relationship between George Rolph and his married live-in servant Mrs. Evans. They reportedly sought to punish him for such immoral behavior. Mrs. Evans and her young child had left her abusive husband when she came to

---

349. T. Roy Woodhouse, *The History of the Town of Dundas: Part 1* (Dundas, ON: Dundas Historical Society, 1965), 20–25.
350. Josephine Phelan, "The Tar and Feather Case, Gore Assizes August 1827," *Ontario History* 68 (1976): 17–23 at 17.
351. As noted above, Riddell argues the outrage "was very largely political" rather than a result of personal dislike of Rolph (Riddell, "The Court of King's Bench": 128).
352. Passfield, *Anglican Toryism*, 126. Dr. John Rolph originally trained as a medical doctor, but was called to the bar in 1821 and was the fourth Bencher in Upper Canada. He practiced both medicine and law until 1832 when he transferred his legal practice to his brother George and became a member of the Medical Board. He remained active in reformist politics and was in exile in the United States from 1838 to 1843. Upon his return to Canada, he became a prominent teacher of medicine. See W. M. Canniff, *The Medical Profession in Upper Canada 1783-1850* (Toronto: William Briggs, 1894), 590-603, and Charles Godfrey, *John Rolph: Rebel with Causes* (Madoc, ON: Codam Publishing, 1993).
353. Carol Wilton, "'Lawless Law': Conservative Political Violence in Upper Canada, 1818-1841," *Law and History Review* 13, no. 1 (1995): 111–136 at 117–118, 128.

work for Rolph as a live-in servant. By the time of the trial Mrs. Evans and her child had returned to England so she did not testify.[354]

The timing of the attack was triggered by the arrival of Mr. Evans who stayed at the inn while seeking to persuade his wife to return to England with him. If he was successful, the local aristocracy would lose its opportunity to attack Rolph for his alleged immoral behavior. Furthermore, with Mr. Evans in town, the group could condemn him as well for "selling" his wife. Thus, before the attack on Rolph, a gang of men, all disguised except one, visited Mr. Evans at the inn and threatened to punish him for selling his wife. The gang carried Mr. Evans into the street and gave him "wholesome advice" about being a good husband. Afterwards, Evans did not appear hurt and seemed "quite satisfied" with his treatment according to a witness.[355]

Later that same night, a gang, whose membership at least partly and perhaps completely overlapped with the group that attacked Evans, invaded the Rolph home. In contrast to the allegedly satisfactory treatment of Mr. Evans, George Rolph was not satisfied at all with his treatment by his attackers. The Rolph attackers dressed in sheets, disguised their voices, and had blackened their faces or wore masks.[356] They dragged Rolph out of his bed and into the street while threatening dismemberment and castration. They stripped him naked while beating him and then applied tar and feathers to his body. (They had lost their feathers on the way to Rolph's house and had to obtain a fresh supply from one of Rolph's own pillows.[357]) They left the traumatized Rolph lying in the street naked.[358] They probably were frustrated by the fact that Mrs. Evans was not found in bed with him.

While Rolph was traumatized, mob members returned to their everyday routines. As discussed in the previous chapter, within a month of the

---

354. Phelan, "The Tar and Feather Case": 17. One source suggests she left the Rolph household the morning after the attack. "Tarring and Feathering," *New York Spectator,* September 7, 1827.
355. *Gore Gazette*, August 25, 1827: 102; Robin Christine Grazley, "Nothing 'Improper' Happened: Sex, Marriage, and Colonial Identity in Upper Canada" (Ph.D. thesis, Department of History, Queen's University, 2010), 228–229.
356. Riddell, "The Court of King's Bench": 126–134.
357. Romney, *Mr. Attorney*, 112. Simons later noted he was only ashamed of destroying one of Rolph's pillows (*Gore Gazette*, August 25, 1827: 102).
358. Curiously, John Rolph had sought to introduce a bill in the Assembly before the attack to punish people living openly in adultery (*The Canadian Freeman*, December 1, 1825). Perhaps he was already aware of the rumors about his brother and Mrs. Evans and sought to provide a legal means of punishing such conduct to avoid violence.

attack, on July 1, 1826, Colonel Simons hosted a banquet of about one hundred people in honor of Lieutenant Governor Peregrine Maitland's visit to Burlington Heights to commemorate the opening of the Burlington Bay Canal. Many of those attending had probably heard that Simons participated in and perhaps led the attack against Rolph a month earlier but that did not stop him from hosting this most important event.

Rolph's Quest for Justice

George Rolph, advised by his brother John Rolph (the reformer) and others, developed a plan for legal retribution.[359] This strategy can be divided into four stages. The first part was a November 1826 affidavit George Rolph sent to Lieutenant Governor Maitland urging him to investigate magistrate Dr. James Hamilton as one of the attackers.

Dr. James Hamilton had graduated from the Royal College of Surgeons in Edinburgh in 1816 at the age of 20. Two years later he settled in Ancaster as the only doctor in the area and spent most days traveling to visit patients. In 1820, he moved to West Flamboro and in 1823 he was appointed surgeon to the First Gore Militia in April before marrying Ann Draper Hatt, daughter of a prominent community leader, in December of that year.[360]

Rolph argued if he had to continue to work with Hamilton, it would be most painful and degrading to his office as clerk of the peace. Maitland responded that Rolph should prosecute Hamilton and other suspects himself because without a guilty verdict from a jury, Maitland could take no further action.[361]

Step two of Rolph's quest for justice occurred about ten months after the attack when he filed a civil complaint in the District of Gore Assizes against the three gang members he could identify: Simons, Hamilton and Alexander Robertson. Perhaps these three were identified because Simons had a disabled right arm while Hamilton and Robertson likely spoke with a Scottish brogue and were known to be close associates of Simons.

Robertson was Simons' son-in-law, having married his daughter Matilda in 1824. Robertson was an Ancaster merchant who ran an advertisement from February to June 1828 in the *Gore Gazette* offering to

---

359. William Warren Baldwin and his son Robert also acted as plaintiff's counsel in this case. John Rolph moved to Dundas in 1827 for four years—perhaps to be closer to his brother.
360. Canniff, *Medical Profession*, 410–412.
361. Romney, *Mr. Attorney*, 110.

trade "excellent whiskey" for wheat delivered to his mill (or perhaps a mill he had designated but that was operated by a miller). He also may have operated a general store in Ancaster as he would later in London with two of his brothers. Such stores at this time in Upper Canada were the intermediaries between wheat farmers and their needs for goods like tea, sugar, tobacco, and salt as well as hardware, textiles, clothing and footwear. Merchants would normally sell these goods to farmers on credit until the crop was harvested and also would accept wheat or flour in barter for other goods.[362] Robertson had migrated from Scotland in 1820 after killing a reform protester, when a mob assembled outside his family home threatening their safety and seeking guns. He likely had no love for reformers.[363]

Rolph chose to file his civil complaint in the quarterly assizes civil court before a visiting judge and a local jury in order to limit the influence of the Gore magistrates. George Rolph as clerk of the peace maintained a list of eligible jurors and may have been able to influence the sheriff regarding membership on jury panels including his own. Rolph sought £1,000 in damages for trespass on the premises and assault on his person. In his opening statement to the jury in the civil trial, John Rolph highlighted the social-class connotation of this case. He noted that the accused were all wealthy gentlemen of privilege and he congratulated members of the jury for being yeomen rather than gentlemen. He noted that no one of their rank had participated in this outrage.[364]

The Trial Proceeds

The jury trial began on August 25, 1827, before Mr. Justice James B. Macaulay who had been appointed as acting judge for the summer of 1827.[365] Like Simons, Macaulay had fought in the War of 1812 including

---

362. Douglas McCalla, "Retailing in the Countryside: Upper Canadian General Stores in the Mid-Nineteenth Century," *Business and Economic History* 26, no. 2 (1997): 393–403; Douglas McCalla, "The Internal Economy of Upper Canada: New Evidence on Agricultural Marketing Before 1850" in *Historical Essays on Upper Canada*, ed. J. K. Johnson and Bruce G. Wilson (1999), 237–260.
363. *Glasgow Herald*, April 7, 1820: 1; *Glasgow Courier*, April 6, 1820: 2; Peter Berresford Ellis and Seumas Mac a' Ghobhainn, *The Scottish Insurrection of 1820* (Edinburgh: John Donald Publishers, 1970), 155–157; Derek Parker, *A History of Elderslie* (Elderslie: Elderslie Community Council, 1983), 18–19.
364. *Gore Gazette* August 25, 1827: 102.
365. Macaulay's benchbooks are available at the Archives of Ontario, RG 22-390-1. He wrote a two-page report on his decision for the Lieutenant Governor, available online at Upper Can-

the Battle of Lundy's Lane. After the war Macaulay studied law with both Henry John Bolton (who represented the defense in the Rolph trial) and Bolton's father, who had been Attorney General. In May 1825, Macaulay was appointed to the Executive Council, so he was clearly a member of the tory elite.[366] The victim, Simons' two co-defendants and the judge are pictured below.

11.1. From left to right: George Rolph (1794–1875); Dr. James Hamilton (1797–1877); Alexander Robertson (1798–1855); James B. Macaulay (1793–1859)

At this civil trial, John Rolph argued the attack against his brother was premeditated. It was organized over dinner at Hamilton's home. The doctor had previously solicited at least one friend, John Paterson, to join them that night for the tar and feathering but Paterson refused (and later testified). The attack occurred at night by people who were "masked and disguised" showing a plan to avoid being identified. They traveled a significant distance to carry out the attack (a spontaneous mob would have been more likely to dissipate over distance and time). Lastly, they had to purchase and prepare the tar and feathers.[367]

In addition to this evidence that implicated Hamilton, Rolph presented evidence specifically against Titus Geer Simons. Witnesses testified that Colonel Simons had told James M'Nally (a neighbor) that the attackers entered through the door rather than a window and that Rolph begged for mercy—suggesting Simons was part of the mob. Simons also

---

ada Sundries, C-6864, 47269–47270; https://heritage.canadiana.ca/view/oocihm.lac_reel_c6864/1?r=0&s=1.

366. "Macaulay, Sir James Buchanan" in the *Dictionary of Canadian Biography* at http://www.biographi.ca/en/bio/macaulay_james_buchanan_8E.html. For discussion of the Tory elite, sometimes labeled the Family Compact, see Graeme Patterson, "An Enduring Canadian Myth: Government and Family Compact," in *Historical Essays on Upper Canada: New Perspectives*, ed. J. K. Johnson and Bruce G. Wilson (Ottawa: Carleton University Press, 1989), 485–511.

367. *Gore Gazette*, August 25, 1827: 102.

said the only thing he was ashamed of was that the mob had lost their feathers and had to cut up one of Rolph's pillows for feathers. As a member of the landed elite, he apparently felt property damage to Rolph's pillow was more significant than injury and humiliation of Rolph's person. Another witness saw Simons outside in the village around 2 a.m. but could not tell if his face was blackened or disguised.[368]

The defense team was led by Solicitor General Henry John Bolton (Mr. Justice Macaulay's mentor), in his capacity as a private attorney. The two other defense lawyers, Allan Napier MacNab and Alexander Chewett, appear to have been participants in the attack and refused to testify in order to avoid self-incrimination. George Gurnett, editor of the *Gore Gazette*, and Andrew Steven, deputy clerk for the crown (who was subpoenaed to testify and also argued the subpoena was improper), also refused to testify for this reason. When the judge questioned the self-incrimination defense of these four potential witnesses, Bolton acting in his private capacity rather than as the Solicitor General argued that the defense was proper in these circumstances. The judge deferred to the latter's purportedly greater legal knowledge in such matters and refused to compel the witnesses to testify by holding them in contempt and ordering them to be jailed until they cooperated. Instead, the judge suggested that the plaintiffs could sue the witnesses for damages if his ruling was overturned on appeal. This ruling seems to have upset the plaintiffs' strategy by not providing witnesses who could identify other perpetrators.

The defense did not try to establish the innocence of the accused but rather sought to exonerate them as guardians of community morals "who stood forward to vindicate the rights of an outraged community, [and] deserved praise, rather than punishment." They "had merely acted in accordance with the community's wishes, in keeping with the ideals of a patriotic, Christian manliness."[369] Macaulay refused to allow evidence that the attackers sought to separate Rolph from Mrs. Evans or merely punish Rolph for adultery since neither argument would legally justify the attack and there was no evidence Mr. Evans organized or participated in the attack.[370] Nevertheless, references were made to this defense

---

368. Ibid.
369. Ibid.; Grazley "Nothing 'Improper' Happened," 226.
370. LAC RG 5 A1, vol. 86, 47269–47270, Report of Justice Macaulay, November 10, 1827; Grazley, "Nothing 'Improper' Happened," 228.

when arguing to the jury. Defense counsel argued that Rolph's dismissal of Mrs. Evans after the attack indicated that Rolph understood the community was opposed to his immoral behavior.

The jury seemed to understand and largely agree with this public morality defense, returning a quick verdict requiring that Simons and Hamilton each pay £20 in damages—far less than the £1,000 requested. Macaulay directed that the jury acquit Alexander Robertson which it did so that he paid no damages. The only specific testimony involving Robertson came from the sheriff, who heard Robertson say he was not a party to the attack but was in Flamboro at the time, and from Robertson's brother William, who said he did not believe his brother would have participated in the attack.[371]

Gurnett's *Gore Gazette* published a full-page article on the trial and printed a few hundred separate single sheets of the report to be sold for a shilling each to raise money to help pay the damages. The *Gore Gazette* noted that "Col. Simons and Dr. Hamilton had age and standing in society on their side. As for the young engaged in it, he looked upon merely as the tools in the hands of the older and more experienced plotters in the business."[372]

The Appeal of the Civil Trial

The third part of Rolph's strategy was to file an appeal seeking a new trial both on the amount of damages and Alexander Robertson's innocence. This latter issue was virtually ignored in the actual appeal.[373] Rolph's team did argue on appeal that Robertson would have been convicted had the reluctant witnesses been compelled to testify: "it was generally believed that he was there."[374] However no other evidence on this point was presented and the *Canadian Freeman* later stated that there was no doubt on either side that Robertson was innocent.[375] Robertson would be described as a "pious, sober, church-going looking gentleman."[376]

The appeal occurred at the Court of King's Bench at the end of April

---

371. Benchbooks of J. B. Macaulay, LAC, RG 22, series 390, envelopes 1–2, 13–53; *Gore Gazette*, August 25, 1827: 102.
372. Ibid.
373. Phelan, "The Tar and Feather Case": 17–23.
374. *Canadian Freeman*, May 22, 1828.
375. Ibid., July 6, 1828.
376. Ibid., May 22, 1828.

1828 before Justices John W. Willis and Levius P. Sherwood.[377] Despite a letter from one of Rolph's attorneys requesting that he stay, the Chief Justice of the Court of King's Bench William Campbell had travelled to England for health reasons and because he believed there was no case on the docket where the two remaining justices would disagree.[378] Soon, he would be proven incorrect.

In this appeal, Solicitor General Bolton (again in his private capacity as defense counsel) argued that Steven was improperly subpoenaed and that Steven plus three others correctly claimed the right against self-incrimination in this civil trial. Bolton emphasized that two of these men were attorneys themselves and all were respected gentlemen in the community. Had their refusal to testify injured the plaintiff, he could have sued them for damages. In fact, the plaintiff presented sufficient evidence to win the case against two of the defendants and to receive £40 in damages, which the defense characterized as substantial—enough to qualify to be a juryman or run for the Assembly. Furthermore, the judge's alleged mistake of law on not forcing these people to testify was not justification for the burden of a new trial in a case where the plaintiffs were awarded substantial damages. Otherwise any plaintiff could simply pay an alleged witness to refuse to testify and request a new trial whenever the initial trial award was deemed insufficient.

These arguments ignored the fact that the judge deferred to the Solicitor General on this question of law and that the Solicitor General and Justice Macaulay told the courtroom if this ruling was wrong on the law, it could be overturned in a new trial.[379] They also argued that the trial court correctly found Robertson innocent and he should not be compelled to endure the stress of a new trial.

The co-counsels of John Rolph argued the outrage was sufficiently notable that only a new trial would result in justice. They cited several cases where permissible testimony had been compelled despite the right against self-incrimination such as cases of associates in crime who tes-

---

377. The appeal was covered in the *Canadian Freeman* from May 8 to June 5, 1828. For more on the Justices, see Alan Wilson, "Willis, John Walpole," in *Dictionary of Canadian Biography*, vol. 10 (University of Toronto/Université Laval, 2003–), accessed October 20, 2021, http://www.biographi.ca/en/bio/willis_john_walpole_10E.html; and Ian Pemberton, "Sherwood, Levius Peters," in *Dictionary of Canadian Biography*, vol. 7 (University of Toronto/Université Laval, 2003–), accessed October 20, 2021, http://www.biographi.ca/en/bio/sherwood_levius_peters_7E.html.
378. Phelan, "The Tar and Feather Case": 20–21.
379. AO, RG 22-390-1, Box 1, Env. 2, Benchbooks of Justice James B. Macaulay, August 1827, 52.

tify not about their own activities but about the conduct of others. Furthermore, they argued, a blanket waiver of all testimony was inappropriate. Witnesses could be asked questions about evidence or who else participated that would not incriminate themselves. The judge should rule on a question-by-question basis on whether the witness would incriminate himself by answering. Such additional testimony might lead to Robertson being found guilty or a greater damage award against the others. While the Rolph team persuaded Justice Willis to vote in favor of a new trial and holding the recalcitrant witnesses in contempt, Justice Sherwood voted against a new trial. With the third justice out of town, the tie meant the motion for a new trial failed due to lack of majority support. This appeared to end the litigation except John Rolph had developed an alternative plan.

Criminal Prosecution

Earlier in April 1828, the Rolph legal team set up stage four of Rolph's quest for justice—criminal prosecution. This may have been their end goal the whole time while pursuing the civil trial primarily to get testimony about other participants. Toward this end, Rolph's team compelled at least one witness to testify before a grand jury leading to a proposed criminal indictment in *King vs. Simons et al.* On April 12, 1828, George Rolph as clerk of peace advised the magistrates of the Court of Quarter Sessions there were no more cases for the petite jury to hear, so it was dismissed.

The grand jury then presented its "Representation" to the magistrates during the court of Quarter Sessions.[380] The grand jury requested that the magistrates transmit the representation to the Court of King's Bench and the Attorney General for the latter to criminally prosecute the ten named defendants before the Court of the King's Bench. In addition to the three defendants from the civil trial, the "Representation" named seven new defendants: two of their defense attorneys who refused to testify in the civil trial—Allan MacNab and Alexander Chewett; two other presumed participants who similarly refused to testify—Andrew Steven, deputy clerk of the crown, and George Gurnett, the editor of the *Gore Gazette*; and three others—John Law, clerk of the district court and two other gentlemen, Peter H. Hamilton and John D. McKay.[381]

380. LAC, RG 5 A 1/88/48678-48679, copy of Representation, April 14, 1828.
381. LAC, RG 5 A 1/90/49965-49966, Appendix Letter etc., September 19, 1828. This is one of several "appendices" sent by Rolph to Hillier. LAC, RG 5 A 1/49961-49962, September 19, 1828.

The magistrates sought to control this prosecution and repeatedly offered to treat the document as an indictment and immediately consider the prosecution themselves in Quarter Sessions rather than wait for the next King's Bench session in September. After all, the offense of assault and battery was within the authority of this court. The named defendants who were present in court also wanted an immediate trial in Quarter Sessions controlled by their friends, the local magistrates. Alan MacNab abusively argued that Rolph's attempt to bypass the local courts was an effort to discredit the charged individuals and create a public belief that this was an "official riot" conducted by government office holders.[382] He further predicted (correctly as it turned out) that the Rolphs would avoid actually conducting a trial because (MacNab predicted) they would lose. The arguments got so heated, Rolph refused to answer questions except in writing in order to avoid getting tripped up by repetitious questions.[383]

The magistrates ordered George Rolph to prepare indictments for the grand jury which he did during a two-day break. The grand jury protested, still insisting it had the right to send the representation to the higher court.[384] On Tuesday, April 15, 1828, after much argument, the court was prepared to begin trial when John Rolph produced a writ of mandamus signed by Justice Willis ordering the magistrates to stay all further proceedings against the defendants and send the indictments to the Court of King's Bench for trial before that court. The magistrates of the Court of Quarter Sessions fussed and fumed but ultimately decided to comply with the order from the higher court and required each defendant to post a £50 bond to guarantee their appearance at the future court session.[385] Although two men offered to post bonds for all of the defendants, Rolph insisted each person should have two sureties of £25 each with no overlap among the sureties. Two separate sureties for each defendant immediately volunteered from the court audience.[386]

---

382. LAC, RG 5 A 1/88/48754-48757, affidavit of E. Leslie, April 21, 1828; RG 5 A 1/90/49969-49976 at 49971, affidavit of John Binkley, September 19, 1828.
383. LAC, RG 5 A 1/88/48680-48681, G. Rolph answers, April 14, 1828; LAC, RG 5 A 1/88/48807-48812, affidavit of J. Lesslie, April 26, 1828 at 48808.
384. LAC, RG 5 A 1/90/49967-49968, appendix marked B, September 19, 1828.
385. The magistrates would later explain their actions to Lieutenant Governor Maitland. LAC, RG 5 A 1/89/48971-72, Representation of the Magistrates, May 10, 1828.
386. *Gore Gazette*, April 19, 1828: 30–31.

The *Gore Gazette* (whose editor was indicted) criticized the surprise production of a writ of mandamus as "disreputable," "trickery" and "dishonest" as well as "proof of such abandonment of all the principles which are essential to the character of a gentleman and an honorable man." John Rolph reportedly considered a libel lawsuit challenging this portrayal in the *Gore Gazette* story. The *Gazette* responded that its story was substantively accurate (although not verbatim) and it was Rolph's behavior, not the story, that may have cast John Rolph in an unfavorable light. The *Gazette* went on to argue that Rolph supported and praised the news media when it criticized the government but he hypocritically condemned the media for criticizing him.[387]

While it appears Rolph had outmaneuvered the defense with a questionable tactic, the defense also engaged in questionable tactics as illustrated by Bolton's arguments on self-incrimination. During the civil appeal, Justice Willis of the King's Bench strongly denounced the actions of the Solicitor General for both privately representing defendants that potentially could be subject to criminal prosecution and then not criminally prosecuting those who refused to testify. Furthermore, when defense counsel Alexander Chewett and Allan MacNab were accused of persuading several witnesses not to testify, the Solicitor General simply held the supporting affidavits for eight months before delivering them to the Attorney General, so there was no witness testimony to aid in the appeal.[388]

Although Rolph had won the right to a trial, he did not appear at the scheduled hearing in September 1828, thereby releasing the defendants from any further actions.[389] Two years and two months after the outrage occurred, litigation concerning it was finally over. Correspondence during this time period indicates that Rolph did not pursue the hearing because he thought the attorney general had a duty to criminally prosecute.[390] It also is likely Rolph gave up because he believed he would not be successful in the criminal prosecution. The civil trial demonstrated that the Rolph attackers were determined not to testify, making it difficult to tell who was in the mob.

Furthermore, Justice Willis was suspended ("amoval") from the Court

---

387. Ibid.: 38.
388. Romney, *Mr. Attorney*, 111–115; Johnson, "The Gore District Outrages": 113.
389. Johnson, "The Gore District Outrages": 109–26.
390. LAC, RG 5 A 1/90/49964-49966, George Rolph, September 19, 1828 letter to Hillier, Appendix Letter A, September 19, 1828; Romney, *Mr. Attorney*, 113.

of the King's Bench in June 1828[391] and replaced by a conservative judge, Christopher Hagerman.[392] Hagerman clearly believed in vigilante actions by the aristocracy since he whipped early reform advocate Robert Gourlay in 1818 for publishing an unfavorable article about his brother. Gourlay was later jailed for sedition and expelled from the province in 1819.[393] Hagerman also was married to a sister of trial court Justice Macaulay.

The Aftermath

Curiously, one month after the King's Court referral, a group of independent electors recommended that James Hamilton (and another) step forward to become candidates for colonial parliament from Wentworth.[394] Apparently, they did not think the pending criminal prosecution should disqualify or diminish popular support for him; however, Dr. Hamilton was not elected.[395]

Although the criminal prosecution by the attorney general never occurred, Rolph could take some solace in his July 1828 election victory against nine other candidates for one of the two seats in the House of Assembly for the Halton riding of Gore. As noted above, there is little evidence George Rolph was politically active before this, but at this point he clearly became allied to the reform movement. Reform advocates dominated the tenth Parliament of 1829–30, including defense team members John Rolph from Middlesex and Robert Baldwin from York. However, after conservative John Beverley Robinson was appointed Chief Justice in July 1829, George was not re-elected and his brother John Rolph decided not to run for re-election.[396]

391. The treatment of Justice Willis was a scandal itself. See Dent, *The Story of the Upper Canadian Rebellion*, 162–194, and Wilson, "Willis, John Walpole," in *Dictionary of Canadian Biography*.
392. Phelan, "The Tar and Feather Case": 22; Johnson, "The Gore District Outrages": 116 n.39; Robert L. Fraser, "Hagerman, Christopher Alexander," in *Dictionary of Canadian Biography*, vol. 7 (University of Toronto/Université Laval, 2003–), accessed October 18, 2021, http://www.biographi.ca/en/bio/hagerman_christopher_alexander_7E.html.
393. S. F. Wise, "Gourlay, Robert Fleming," in *Dictionary of Canadian Biography*, vol. 9 (University of Toronto/Université Laval, 2003–), accessed September 12, 2021, http://www.biographi.ca/en/bio/gourlay_robert_fleming_9E.html; Carol Wilton, *Popular Politics and Political Culture in Upper Canada: 1800–1850* (Montreal: McGill-Queen's University Press, 2000), 27–36.
394. *Gore Gazette*, May 17, 1828: 47.
395. Hamilton remained active in tory politics. For example, he spoke at a "Durham" meeting in the fall of 1839 (Wilton, *Popular Politics*, 200).
396. Frederick H. Armstrong, *Handbook of Upper Canadian Chronology* (Toronto: Dundurn Press, 1985), 84–85, 98, 105; Robert E. Saunders, "Robinson, Sir John Beverley," in *Dictionary of Canadian Biography*, vol. 9 (University of Toronto/Université Laval, 2003–), accessed October 25, 2021, http://www.biographi.ca/en/bio/robinson_john_beverley_9E.html.

While the Ancaster Outrage litigation was over, the struggle for political reform continued up through (and beyond) the Rebellion of 1837–38.[397] Five days after the tar and feathering, a reform newspaper office (*The Colonial Advocate*) in Toronto operated by reformer William Lyon Mackenzie was ransacked by tories. During this "Types Riot," the attackers terrorized MacKenzie's mother and apprentices who fled, but no one was physically attacked. The attackers destroyed private property—the printing press and other equipment—with no resistance and even signs of approval from some observers who had gathered.

The rioters eventually faced civil charges in October 1826 and were ordered to pay Mackenzie £625 in damages, a relatively harsh punishment. The sting of the punishment was diminished, however, when the fine was paid through a collection taken up among the family and friends of the young men. Ironically the money Mackenzie won allowed him to replace his printing press and continue publishing the *Advocate*, which had been in dire financial straits when the June riot occurred.[398] Carol Wilton describes this outrage as "the most celebrated episode of conservative political violence in Upper Canada."[399]

There were many other incidents of political violence during the late 1820s and 1830s including two in the Gore District at the end of 1827.[400] However, outrages in the Gore District and Ancaster area subsided after the death of Colonel Simons in August 1829. One such attack was a November attack against Jacob Hagle, an elderly magistrate in Dundas. This attack, occurring after the Rolph verdict but before the appeal, was reportedly motivated by morality rather than politics as the attackers contended Hagle was too old to take a wife, which he had done recently. Hagle accepted the reprimand and refused to prosecute. Some suggest this attack was made by the same group who attacked Rolph.[401] This suggests that the Rolph attack may have been motivated more by morality and less by politics. The attackers may have been

---

397. Dent, *The Story of the Upper Canadian Rebellion*. Alexander Robertson was a militia cavalry captain during the Rebellion of 1837–38; see *History of the County of Middlesex* (Toronto and London: W.A. and C.L. Goodspeed, 1889), 151.
398. Paul Romney, "From the Types Riot to the Rebellion: Elite Ideology, Anti-legal Sentiment, Political Violence, and the Rule of Law in Upper Canada," *Ontario History* 79 (1987): 113–44.
399. Wilton, "'Lawless Law'": 111. Paul Romney describes the Types Riot as a *cause célèbre* ("From the Types Riot": 113).
400. See, for example, Wilton, "'Lawless Law'": 118–119.
401. *Canadian Freeman*, December 6, 1827; Johnson, "The Gore District Outrages": 112.

emboldened by the small awards made by the jury in the Rolph trial.

After losing seats in the election of 1828, it appears as though some tories attempted to defuse the accusations of political violence against them by trying to appear themselves as reformers engaged in an outrage. In January 1829 some people in Hamilton hung an effigy of Lieutenant Governor John Colborne for not freeing imprisoned journalist Francis Collins. This outrage gained province-wide notoriety in part because the tories promoted it as an example of lawlessness by the reformers and the *Gore Gazette* further reported that a gang of fifty resolute fellows from the Gore District were organizing to free Collins from jail in York by force. The House of Assembly conducted hearings on this "Hamilton Outrage."[402] Tory witnesses again refused to answer questions about who was involved. The *Report of the Select Committee* concluded the report of a gang of fifty was the wishful thinking of one man and the outrage was "unworthy of public notice."[403]

As a member of the Assembly, George Rolph did get the satisfaction of voting in favor of a motion to arrest Allan MacNab (an accused attacker against Rolph in the criminal complaint) for refusing to answer some questions about the Hamilton Outrage. MacNab spent ten to fifteen days in jail but was treated as a hero when he returned to Hamilton.[404]

It is interesting that MacNab refused to testify about the views of his neighbors about this outrage but then contributed to the reward fund seeking information. Also of interest, Simons apparently started the reward fund with his pledge of £25, the largest individual contribution and more money than the amount of his civil fine in the Ancaster Outrage, which his attorneys had argued was "substantial." Apparently, he was trying to demonstrate that his wealth was unimpaired by his previous fine and that he remained loyal to the King and his representatives.

Ultimately, total amount of the reward for information on the Hamil-

---

402. Upper Canada, House of Assembly, *Journals*, 10 Geo. 1 (1829); *Gore Gazette*, February 7, March 3, and March 16, 1829; Johnson, "The Gore District Outrages": 118, 119.
403. W. W. Baldwin, chairman, "Final Report of the Select Committee to which was referred the matters of the outrage committed at Hamilton and the alleged threatened release of Francis Collins by force," *Journal of the House of Assembly of Upper Canada, From 8th January to 20th March 1829*, 10 Geo. 1 (1829) 43 Appendix.
404. Woodhouse, *The History of the Town of Dundas, Part 1*, 26; Johnson, "The Gore District Outrages":119; Peter Baskerville, "MacNab, Sir Allan Napier," in *Dictionary of Canadian Biography*, vol. 9 (University of Toronto/Université Laval, 2003–), accessed October 18, 2021, http://www.biographi.ca/en/bio/macnab_allan_napier_9E.html.

ton Outrage increased from £282 on February 7, 1829 to £527 on March 16. The number of sponsors grew to more than 110, including several who were criminally charged in the tar-and-feathering outrage. Hamilton pledged £10 as did Allan MacNab and Alexander Chewett. Alexander Robertson pledged £2, 10 shillings and George Gurnett pledged £5. If the effigy outrage was in fact staged by tories to make reformers look like they were violating the law and disrespecting the lieutenant governor, the reward program might have functioned as a public commitment not to provide information that would lead to the payment of the promised rewards.

Repercussions of the Ancaster Outrage

Although only two attackers were held civilly liable, the Ancaster Outrage eventually resulted in other repercussions for the parties involved. The continuing controversy caused the Lieutenant Governor to not renew the magistrate appointments of both Simons and Hamilton at the end of 1827.[405] George Hillier, civil secretary to the lieutenant governor, further noted that if they had "grounds for disputing the justice or legality" of the verdict perhaps the outcome would be different. As he had done with past setbacks, Simons first thanked Hillier for informing him of the Lieutenant Governor's decision. He also expressed his regret about having lost the confidence of the Lieutenant Governor.[406]

Simons then interpreted Hillier's attempt to appear reasonable regarding a legal appeal as a possible opening to appeal based on the facts of the case and his trial tactics. In early 1828, Simons obtained and forwarded two affidavits from respected community members who swore Simons was with them on the night of the attack and could not have participated in it. The first was from John M. A. Cameron who swore that he and Simons conducted business that day into the evening until they heard screams and dogs barking from the direction of Dundas. They

---

405. LAC: RG7 G16/18/5, Hillier to Simons and Hamilton, November 24, 1827; RG5 A1/86/47297-47299, Simons to Hillier, December 4, 1827. Romney, *Mr. Attorney*, 122, says Hamilton's dismissal did not take effect for several months and Simons was listed on the commission of the peace (the list of magistrates) in April 1828. Frederick H. Armstrong, *Upper Canada Justices of the Peace and Association 1788–1841* (Toronto: Ontario Genealogical Society 2007), 37, notes that Dr. James Hamilton served as a magistrate in Gore from 1820–1838 having received five commissions with no mention of any gaps in service. Finally, George Rolph's September 19, 1828 letter to Hillier, Appendix Letter A, describes James Hamilton as "late" justice of the peace just as Titus Geer Simons was "late" sheriff—a position he lost earlier. LAC, RG 5 A 1/90/49964-49966.
406. LAC, RG 5 A 1/86/47287-89, Simons to Hillier, December 4, 1827.

decided to investigate but at one point Cameron advised Simons to wait while he checked to see if it was safe. When Cameron returned Simons was gone.[407]

The second affidavit, that of George Patton, continued the same story. Patton was a clerk to Mr. Cameron at the time of the outrage but a merchant at the time of the affidavit. Patton saw Simons standing alone and joined him. A small group of men approached and asked what they were doing and they replied they were waiting for Cameron. One person in the group recognized Simons and humbly begged his pardon. The group left and Patton and Simons walked home thinking Cameron would overtake them. But he did not.[408]

Simons argued that these two affidavits proved his innocence and he was justified in not calling the affiants as witnesses in the trial. If he had called them, they would have to testify more generally and might have identified some of Simons' friends as possible participants. He did not wish his friends to potentially have to pay heavy damages for "a transaction which appeared to give such general satisfaction throughout the district." Furthermore, presenting defense witnesses would have given Rolph the right to the last word to the jury under procedural rules at the time. Simons argued that by not calling these witnesses, he had disrupted the plaintiffs' tactics to get new evidence in cross examination and secured the right to make the final argument to the jury. He argued this strategy was largely successful because only a light damage award was awarded.[409] As noted above, when arguing against an appeal, his attorneys characterized the total damage award from Simons and Hamilton as substantial.

In addition to the "de-magistrating" of Simons and Hamilton, George Rolph also suffered after the outrage. Not only did he immediately dismiss his servant Mrs. Evans, but he was suspended by the Gore magistrates as their clerk and they temporarily replaced him with John Burwell.[410] Rolph argued they lacked authority to dismiss him and 17 members of the grand jury who worked with Rolph objected to his treatment, noting he had performed his duties for 13 years and they had nev-

407. LAC, RG 5 A 1/87/47652-56, Simons to Hillier, January 10, 1828.
408. LAC, RG 5 A 1/87/48347-50, Simons to Hillier, March 12, 1828. Simons blamed the two-month delay between these two affidavits and letters on his own ill health.
409. Romney, *Mr. Attorney*, 110–111.
410. LAC, RG 5 A 1/88/48807–48812, affidavit of J. Lesslie, April 26, 1828 at 48808; LAC RG 5 A 1/88/48833–48835, G. Rolph to Hillier, April 28, 1828.

er observed him acting improperly or in any way that would disrespect the legal system.[411] The magistrates requested that Lieutenant Governor Maitland dismiss Rolph but the Lieutenant Governor refused to do so. In response, 21 magistrates dismissed him for misconduct in the discharge of his duties in open court on April 16, 1829. Five charges were listed to justify this dismissal including repeated disrespect and refusal to answer magistrate questions except through his attorney.[412] In a lengthy letter the magistrates explained their decision to the new (as of August 1828) Lieutenant Governor John Colborne, who then affirmed Rolph's dismissal.[413] A select committee of House of Assembly held hearings presenting several witnesses and a petition signed by 16 grand jurors in support of George Rolph's performance of his duties. The final 1830 committee report condemned the magistrates, in part for not allowing Rolph to defend himself.[414]

As noted above and adding insult to injury, George Rolph was defeated in the 1830 elections.[415] Fortunately for him, he acquired his brother's law practice in 1832. This occurred after Judge Sherwood refused to issue written rulings: John Rolph tore off his lawyer gowns in protest and never practiced law again. Instead he got his license to practice medicine in Dundas in 1829. In 1836, George married Georgina Clement in Wales. Despite his embarrassment from the outrage and his personal unpopularity, George Rolph and his new bride returned to Dundas where he lived until his death in 1875. He dedicated some of his land for a town park and was the clerk of the surrogate court for 54 years.[416]

Colonel Simons died much earlier than Rolph in August 1829 but the ramifications of the outrage continued after his death. Alan Napier MacNab wrote a letter to John K. Simons, the deceased's brother, indicating that Hamilton and Colonel Simons' estate were being levied their

---

411. LAC, RG 5 A 1/89/49360-49363, Statement of the Grand Jury in favor of Geo. Rolph, Esq., June 1828.
412. *Gore Gazette*, April 20, 1829: 2; Woodhouse, *The History of the Town of Dundas: Part 1*, 26.
413. LAC, RG 5 A 1/94/52174–52187, Lt. Gov. Colborne from the Magistrates of the Gore District, May 9, 1829 (the microfilm copy is difficult to read); Johnson, "The Gore District Outrages":116. Colborne became Lieutenant Governor in August 1828.
414. Report of the Select Committee of the House of Assembly, on the petition of George Rolph, Esq. against the proceedings of the magistrates of the Gore District (York: W.J. Coates, 1830), https://www.canadiana.ca/view/oocihm.89477/3?r=0&s=1, accessed October 20, 2021.
415. *Montreal Gazette*, November 1, 1830: 2. The 9th Parliament was dissolved in 1830 because of the death of King George IV and new elections were held that year.
416. Woodhouse, *The History of the Town of Dundas, Part 1*, 26.

share of £90 for the price of the tar and feathers. He proposed that each of them (who shared in the "honor" of the tar and feathering) pay £10 each.[417] Presumably there were nine co-conspirators who were expected to share the financial burden.[418] Son-in-law Alexander Robertson was a co-executor on Simon's estate but left town after that, joining his brothers in London at least by 1832. As an Ancaster merchant, his reputation with farmers might have been damaged by the trial even though he was found innocent.

One final possible ramification of this outrage might be a reconsideration of what the attackers had done, at least by Alexander Robertson (if in fact he participated). His aunt and uncle in Scotland suffered a break-in, robbery, and assault on June 14, 1829. Robertson's uncle, William Robertson, was stuck a total of five times and he and his sister were tied up while the thieves escaped.[419] In just over four months (compared to over two years in the outrage), two of the thieves were caught, confessed and hung on October 29, 1829, before a large crowd in Paisley, Scotland.[420] William Robertson forgave them for their attack. When Alexander Robertson, his wife, father-in-law, and close friend Dr. James Hamilton heard of the horrors of this attack, they might have drawn parallels to the attack they had inflicted on George Rolph (and perhaps Jacob Hagle). Perhaps they came to regret their attack. In any event, they certainly were grateful not to be criminally prosecuted and punished for their actions.

Perhaps this lesson in litigation and the importance of law in Upper Canada contributed towards Robertson's oldest son (and Simons' grandson), Thomas, becoming a lawyer, member of Parliament, and ultimately judge in the court of chancery.[421] One case heard by Mr. Justice Robertson harks back to his father and grandfather's trial for tarring and feathering an alleged adulterer. The case was brought by a Mrs. Lellis against a Mrs. Lambert for alienation of affections of the former's husband. Mr. Lellis visited Mrs. Lambert's house late at night and left early in the morn-

---

417. Mabel Burkholder, "Out of the Storied Past: Colonel Titus Geer Simons Took Prominent Part in Affair at Dundas in which Resident was Tarred and Feathered," *Hamilton Spectator*, August 1, 1953: 138.
418. Alexander Robertson and his wife moved to London, Ontario, around this time to join his brothers there. We don't know if he was one of the nine expected contributors.
419. Precognitions (recorded testimony), AD/14/29/238.
420. Alex F. Young, *The Encyclopaedia of Scottish Executions 1750–1963* 104 (1998).
421. See *A Dictionary of Hamilton Biography*, vol. 2, 1876–1924 (1981), 130–131, and *Hamilton Spectator*, September 7, 1905: 10.

ing, causing a scandal that resulted in neighbors rolling him in the mud. While this was not as bad as being tarred and feathered, Justice Robertson, like his grandfather, showed no sympathy for the alleged adulterer. When Mr. Lellis testified, claiming that he and his wife fought constantly over money and that she hit him with a stick, Justice Robertson commented, "So you are the hero of this story," eliciting laughter from those present. When Mr. Lellis finished testifying, the Justice remarked: "You have left a most splendid reputation behind you." When he charged the jury, he characterized Mr. Lellis as a "gay lothario." Not surprisingly, the jury found in favor of the estranged wife, awarding her $2,250 in damages—far more than the minimal £20 award against Justice Robertson's grandfather Titus Geer Simons in the civil tar-and-feathering case.[422]

Conclusion

We may never know the actual reason (or if there was just a single reason) for the attack on George Rolph. Academics tend to favor the political theory that it was an anti-reform attack. However, George Rolph did not appear to favor reform at that time; he simply did not engage with his fellow tories. Furthermore, in prior Simons attacks on Sheriff Willcocks and Colonel Beasley, Simons raised the issue of their support for the reform movement, although it was only relevant to the charges in the former case. Yet, in the George Rolph litigation, Rolph's alleged reform leanings are not mentioned.[423] If the attackers sought to condemn the reform movement, why not attack reform leader John Rolph directly?

What is most discussed is George Rolph's alleged adultery. At a time when tories were loyal to the Church of England, this is the explicit reason for the attack and perhaps should be given more weight as the fundamental reason for the attack. Under today's standards, attacking a community member for committing immoral acts might be difficult to accept, but such attacks were not uncommon in Upper Canada—a society where church-going was a cultural norm. It was clear that if Mr. Evans persuaded his wife to return to England, the justification (or pretext) of adultery would depart with them. Therefore, adultery does appear as reason for the timing of the attack.

Lastly, it seems clear that the attackers had expected George Rolph to

---

422. *The Globe and Mail*, November 6, 1895: 6.
423. Dent, in *The Story of the Upper Canadian Rebellion*, vol.1, 168, argues "The outrage had arisen out of private complications, and no political question arose in the course of the trial."

be a loyal tory and they invited him into tory patronage and tory society. He apparently rebuffed their efforts and was genuinely disliked for his aloof nature. This may have made his attackers eager to attack him on the pretext of immorality. Of course, any individual in the mob may have his own reasons for participating beyond disliking adultery or reformers. Perhaps some just sought to fit in with the local elite.

CHAPTER TWELVE

The Death of Titus Geer Simons

Despite his loss of prestigious government positions, Simons remained interested in politics. For the 1828 elections, Simons wrote a letter to his fellow electors in support of John Beverley Robinson, who was again re-elected to Parliament from York despite many other seats going to reformers. The July 1 letter, signed "A Yorkite," pleaded with the reader not to be blinded by prejudice or ignorance and extolled Robinson's pride and loyalty as a British subject as well as his past service and knowledge of the law and his ongoing protection of liberty. The opposition was characterized as ignorant barbarians who were arrogant enough to think, based on no experience, that they could govern better.[424] Robinson was elected to represent the town of York for the third time.[425]

Simons continued to petition the government. In December 1828, he was one of a handful of signatories on a petition requesting that John Chisholm be freed from prison to be able to support his aging mother. Apparently, Chisholm had been imprisoned until he was able to pay a fine but could not raise the money to pay the fine while in prison.[426] Simons also was one of a larger group of petitioners in early 1829 seeking funds to build a turnpike from Dundas to the Head-of-the-Lake.[427]

Simons died later that year on August 19, 1829 at the age of 64, a mere five years after the death of his father. The officers of his militia unit at-

---

424. AO, Number F 906 in container B294760.
425. Frederick H. Armstrong *Handbook of Upper Canadian Chronology* (Toronto: Dundurn Press 1985), 112.
426. Petition to John Colborne from Ralph Lemming, December 24, 1828, LAC Civil Secretary's Correspondence, Upper Canada Sundries, RG 5, A 1., vol. 91, 50306–50825, microfilm C-6866, images 1125–1126.
427. Petition to John Colborne from Absalon Shade, LAC, Civil Secretary's Correspondence, Upper Canada Sundries, RG 5, A 1., vol. 92, 50826–51344 at 51342–51343, microfilm C-6867, images 116, 117.

Figure 12.2. New gravestone for Simons

Figure 12.1. Simons in uniform

tended his burial in full uniform.[428] His will was entered into probate court on September 18, 1829.[429] Above is a photograph of his new grave marker at the West Flamboro cemetery, which is now maintained by Christ Church. He was, however, colonel of the Second Gore not the Second York militia as stated on the grave marker. His original grave marker is located in the same cemetery.[430]

Titus Geer Simons' Will

Titus Geer Simons' will (Appendix Four) was drafted on August 10, 1826 and probated on September 6, 1832. It sheds light on his family relationships. First, the will demonstrates that Titus Geer Simons was not happy with his second wife and leaves her the legal minimum of property in his will: land in Nissouri in the London district and household furnishings. He makes it clear that "all of which I declare and order to be given her as full compensation for all further charge or claims on my estate in the way of living or any other whatsoever." He later says:

> I cannot help mentioning in this place, although I have long since forgiven her cruel, unfeeling unmotherlike treatment to my poor motherless daughters, in advising and encouraging them to their destruction, thereby entailing on me sorrow, mortification and

---

428. John Robinson Simons, "The Fortunes of a United Empire Loyalist Family," *Ontario Historical Society Papers and Records* 23 (1926): 470–483.
429. Archives of Ontario, RG 22-155 Court of Probate estate files, microfilm MS 638, reel 65.
430. https://billiongraves.com/grave/Titus-Geer-Simons/11446985. However, he is not listed in the Ontario Genealogical Society transcription of West Flamborough Municipal Cemetery (Bullock's Corners) or the Christ Church Anglican Cemetery at Bullock's Corners.

unheard of trouble, in return for my having brought up and educated her Children and without making any charge against them for it, God forgive her?

He later explains:

I could wish that Charles Slaven, a brute in the Shape of Man, who aided and encouraged by my wife, seduced from the path of duty and from a fond father's protection, my poor and unthinking motherless infant Elizabeth Jane, should not anticipate any of the property given to my dear child, if my Executors can possibly prevent it

It seems clear that Elizabeth Jane was the daughter of Titus Geer Simons' first wife, the late Elizabeth Green. Since Simons refers to his motherless daughters in the plural, it is not clear whether Hannah also mistreated Charlotte in some way, perhaps in her marriage to Benjamin Markle. It also seems clear that contrary to his statement of forgiveness, Simons had not forgiven his second wife. He appoints Matilda and her husband Alexander Robertson to be guardians of his two minor (as of 1826) daughters Hannah and Bell Gore rather than allowing their mother to be their guardian.[431] Furthermore, his stepchildren from Hannah's first marriage are ignored other than noting that they were raised and educated by Simons. They received no property from Simons, but of course could inherit from their mother one day.

In contrast to his stepchildren with Hannah Coon Van Every, Titus Geer Simons was more generous to his half-siblings whom he refers to as brothers or sisters. He left personal property to both of his brothers and 100 acres of land to his sisters: Jerusha, Mary Elizabeth and Anna. His sister Sophia received a note of money due from her husband—an apparent forgiveness of an existing debt. However, it appears he might have conflated Mary Ann and Elizabeth into a single person and he omits his sisters, Amelia and Lucinda.

He treats his daughters in two different ways. His two oldest, Charlotte and Elizabeth Jane—daughters of Elizabeth Green—received 200 acres

---

431. It seems that at this time the father had authority to appoint a guardian for minor children even if the mother were still alive. See "The Law as to Custody of Children," *Upper Canada Law Journal* 9 (August 1863): 197–201.

and 300 acres in Nissouri respectively. His three youngest daughters, Matilda, Hannah and Bell Gore (daughters of Hannah Coon), received personal property (with the bulk of it going to Bell Gore, the youngest). He also expressed the wish that at least one and as many as all three of the younger daughters would keep the Flamboro Cottage homestead.

Daughter Hannah is recognized as particularly capable since she is the only child named executrix in the will "when she shall obtain the proper age." She also was appointed to receive a list of estate inventory as soon as possible to prevent possible theft, even if she was still a minor at the time of his death. Titus Geer Simons left Hannah his "Encyclopedia and Atlas" so perhaps he felt she was the smartest of his daughters. Even though Hannah's mother was not on good terms with Titus Geer Simons, he must have been confident that daughter Hannah would be loyal to his wishes and not manipulated by her mother. (Hannah married Ross Robertson, Alexander Robertson's brother, in 1832.)

From the perspective of future researchers, Simons' son Alexander is a mystery.[432] He received no personal property; no keepsakes from his father. He was excluded from inheriting the family homestead of Flamboro Cottage, which normally would have been his as the oldest son. He only received an equal share with each of his sisters of the remaining estate. Lastly, Alexander was not named as guardian to his minor sisters nor as co-executor of his father's estate.

The only other information we have about Alexander Simons is his mention as one of Titus Geer and Elizabeth Green Simons' children in the diary of Titus Geer Simons' nephew George Hill Detlor.[433] In addition, Alexander Simons also was recognized in John Kingsley Simons' will: "[I] bequeath unto my nephew Alexander Simons my heir at law the sum of five shillings in full of all demands against my estate."[434] John Kingsley, Titus Geer Simons' other brother, had no son named Alexander.[435]

432. There is an Alexander Simons listed as a laborer with his family in the 1851 Canada Census of Stormont. They are listed again in the 1860 U.S. Federal Census for Hammond, New York. These censuses indicate this Alexander Simons was born in Canada about 1818–1820, which seems too late for him to be a son of Titus Geer Simons, particularly a son born to his first wife. This Alexander could be a grandson of Titus Geer Simons through the latter's son Alexander, born in the early 1800s. Titus Geer Simons only recognized namesake grandsons in his will.
433. George Hill Detlor, *Journal of Diary of George Hill Detlor* (commencing September 25, 1851) on page 5 or 685 of part 2.
434. Archives of Ontario, MS 638, reel 65, June 9, 1832.
435. One party on myheritage.com suggests Alexander was a nephew of Simons who was treat-

In contrast to his treatment of his son Alexander, Titus Geer Simons was generous to his son-in-law Alexander Robertson, husband of daughter Matilda. This Alexander was named as guardian to Simons' minor daughters and also named as co-executor of the estate. Robertson, a captain in the militia cavalry, also was specifically named to receive Simons' military saddle and bridle.[436] Another of Simon's sons-in-law, Benjamin Markle, who married daughter Charlotte in 1817, is not mentioned in her father's will.

The final category of heirs recognized in the will was Titus Geer Simons' namesakes. They are listed second in the will, only after his wife, and ahead of his sisters, children and other heirs. His grandson Titus Markle was to receive fifty dollars' worth of sheep and cows and his nephews Titus Cummings and Titus Simons (Walter William Simons' son) each were bequeathed twenty-five dollars' worth of sheep and cows. Titus Markle also would receive his uncle's poaching gun and Titus Simons his uncle's fishing tackle. Other grandchildren and nephews were not recognized with a specific bequest, suggesting Titus wanted to recognize a special relationship with his namesakes.

Titus Geer Simons' Estate

The Titus Simons family businesses in West Flamboro were developed by both father and son. Any underlying properties of the businesses initially owned by Titus Sr. appear to have been inherited by Titus Jr. who also owned some additional properties. Titus Geer Simons (Titus Jr.) would directly distribute plots of land to Simons' wife, three sisters and eldest two daughters. His more developed property in Flamboro and Ancaster would be sold at auction. The Titus Jr. estate was substantial and valuable as shown by the October 18, 1834, auction announcement from the *Montreal Gazette* reproduced on the next page. The three properties in the auction are listed with a total minimum bid value of £2,300, which would be worth about 115 times that today—over a quarter of a million pounds sterling.

The most valuable property was Flamboro Cottage (Lot 4, Conces-

---

ed like a member of the family. The only nephew I have found is Alexander Wellesley McNab (1812–1891), son of Titus Geer's sister Mary Ann (1783–1810). I have found no evidence that this nephew was close to Titus Geer Simons, who explicitly recognized some other nephews as such in his will.

436. Given the will's specific naming of son-in-law Robertson and son Alexander, it seems clear these were distinct people.

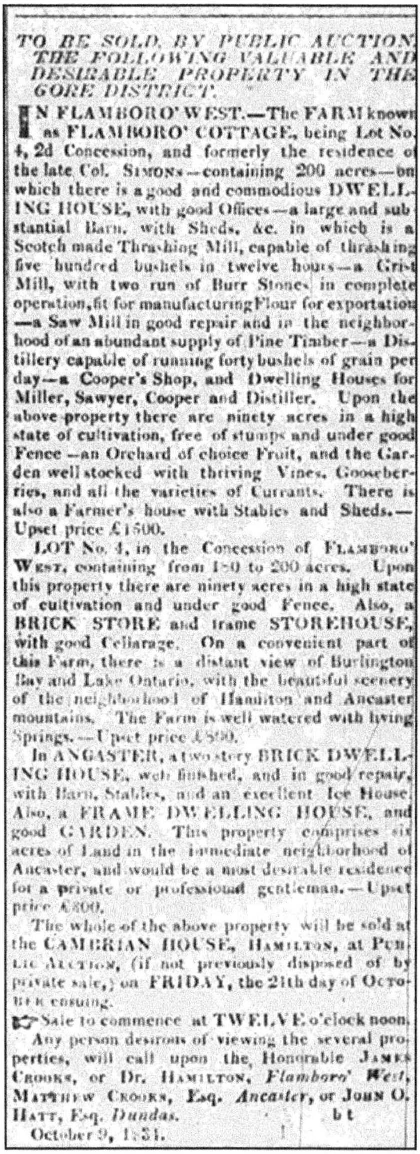

sion 2) that contained a large dwelling house with offices, a substantial barn with sheds containing a threshing mill (that could produce up to 100 bushels in 12 hours), a grist mill, a sawmill with plenty of pine timber, a distillery (processing 40 bushels of grain per day), and a cooper's shop. The property also held dwellings for the thrasher, miller, sawyer, and distiller. Of the 200 acres of this property, about 90 acres were extensively cultivated with fruit orchards and gardens. Finally, there was a farmer's house with stables and sheds. Apparently, in the short term, this property did not stay in the family as Simons wished but Arabella Gore Simons Miller acquired it about 1837 and built a house, which was called Stormont. Some say Titus Geer Simons started construction on it just before he died.

Nearby there is a second property on Lot 4 in West Flamboro consisting of 180–200 acres, about 90 acres of which were under cultivation, fed by a spring on the property. This lot also included a brick store and wooden frame storehouse with good cellarage. Finally, the third property at auction is a lot in Ancaster containing a two-story brick dwelling house with a barn, stables and ice house. This property included a second wood-frame dwelling with a good garden. The sale of such a substantial estate must have brought in a lot of money (the starting auction prices totaled £2600) for the residual heirs—Simons' six children.

Figure 12.3. Montreal Gazette Auction Announcement

CHAPTER THIRTEEN

Conclusion: From Loyalist to Tory in One Generation

> Neither my Father or Mother, Grandfather or Grandmother, Great Grandfather or Great Grandmother nor any other Relation that I know of or care a farthing for have been in England these 150 years. So that you see, I have not one drop of Blood in my Veins, but what is American.
> —John Adams, future U.S. president, in 1785[437]

According to his diary, the above quotation is how John Adams replied to the suggestion by a foreign ambassador that he was English or at least of English extraction. He bristled at the suggestion he was British rather than American. By contrast, though able to make a similar claim to American ancestry, Titus Geer Simons was a steadfast loyalist to Great Britain just as he had been raised by his loyalist father. Unlike the Adamses, both father and son Simons presumably were proud of the English blood in their veins and their status as British citizens. Titus Sr. had two grandparents born in England but both came to the colonies in their youth, so it seems unlikely that this modest difference explains the difference in attitude between him and John Adams.

We may never know why or exactly when Titus Simons Sr. became a loyalist when so many of his community, his father, and at least two of his brothers came to favor the rebellion and American independence. Around the time of the revolution, loyalists most often objected to some British policies just as patriots did. The difference was that loyalists felt

---

437. Nancy Isenberg and Andrew Burstein, *The Problem of Democracy: The Presidents Adams Confront the Cult of Personality* (New York: Viking, 2019), 87.

the proper way to address these policies would be to petition the colonial and British governments for change. Some proposed that colonial legislatures should have final approval or at least input over the crown's colonial policies. However, loyalists were frequently persecuted by their neighbors and often their property was confiscated or destroyed. So they sought shelter and protection in British-controlled cities and many like Titus Sr. enlisted in loyalist regiments to protect their property and families.[438]

Perhaps the most likely explanation of the loyalty of Titus Simons—both father and son—was the fact that both sought to make a living as merchants. They would prefer to be merchants inside the largest trading empire in the world with the benefit of favorable terms and protection of shipping by the British fleet. Indeed, this loyalty to Britain may have been one reason why Titus Simons Sr. and his family left Connecticut in the early 1770s to settle in Vermont and avoid the anti-British feeling of family and community. Of course, there also may have been better land and business opportunities in Vermont.[439]

In any event, moving to Vermont did not save him. Simons became known as a loyalist; the local committee on safety condemned and imprisoned him (twice) and sought to deprive him of his property. There is no evidence that he tried to hide his convictions. He also was angry enough about his persecution to follow his ancestors in joining the militia to fight, thus rejecting the option to migrate immediately to Canada with his wife and children. Such a decision must have been difficult because he would leave his wife and family living in Vermont where they were at risk.

While in the loyalist militia, Titus Sr. performed his duties but appeared to have little interest in seeking revenge against the rebels, in battlefield glory, or even in advancing his own rank. He was simply a mild-mannered regimental quartermaster who followed orders and probably withstood a beating without complaint from a superior officer. After his battlefield experiences, Titus Sr. was content to help the British Army by foraging for supplies and building fortifications. Later, he also was content to be an occasional deputy sheriff in Montreal, never seeking to serve as sheriff anywhere. In short, Titus Sr. was a committed loy-

438. Thomas B. Allen, *Tories: Fighting for the King in America's First Civil War* (New York: HarperCollins, 2010), xix–xxi.
439. Kenneth S. Lynn, *A Divided People* (Westport, CT: Greenwood Press, 1977), 91.

alist to Britain who joined the militia and did what he could to advance militia efforts against the revolution. He did not seek advancement or high social standing.

Titus Jr. was a committed loyalist, like his father, but became a committed tory. Not only did he support Canada staying part of the British Empire but also he believed in the British political philosophy of a hierarchical society ruled by an aristocracy. The ruling class ruled in the best interests of the masses (at least in theory) and the masses in turn were deferential and respectful to the ruling gentry.[440] Whereas membership in the British aristocracy status was largely inherited, Canadian class status was at least partially based on merit and successful merchants were typically considered members of the local gentry. Tories generally believed in the importance of the rule of law and the enforcement of contracts and property rights.[441] However, Titus Geer Simons, along with other members of the local gentry, seemed to believe that tories should create the law but it should not be applied to them.

In contrast to his father, Titus Jr. wanted to rise in the hierarchy as far as he could. Indeed, he had some success being appointed to various government positions. Perhaps Titus Sr. encouraged his son's ambitions or Titus Jr. might have developed his own ambitions after experiencing his family's sacrifices in support of the British crown. Titus Jr. may have felt entitled to some reward for his family's efforts and sacrifices.

Titus Jr's journey began at least as early as age 15, when started working with his father in the militia. Even before that he helped his parents with household chores in both Vermont and Canada. Like many sons before the industrial revolution, Titus worked with his father, learning from his father and seeking his father's approval. Titus Simons Jr. would work with his father and family until his early thirties, when he became the official government printer. After a few years as printer, Titus Jr. returned to working with his father as the two developed various businesses on the Flamboro land grant properties that would provide opportunities for Titus Jr's two half-brothers and support the growing family. It appears that Titus Jr. was more ambitious than his father and therefore may deserve most of the credit for the success of the businesses. However, Titus

---

440. Carol Wilton, *Popular Politics and Political Culture in Upper Canada: 1800–1850* (Montreal: McGill-Queen's University Press, 2000), 125–126.
441. Robert W. Passfield, *Anglican Toryism in Upper Canada: The Critical Years, 1812–1840* (Oakville, ON: Rock's Mills Press, 2019).

Sr. must have played a key role in managing the business during the War of 1812 when Titus Jr. and his brothers were in the militia.

The War of 1812 was the perfect opportunity for Titus Simons Jr. to demonstrate his loyalty and ambition to advance as a militia officer. Before the war, he shopped around various militia units and negotiated an initial rank of captain by the time the war started. He soon was promoted to major—second-in-command of the Second York. Simons proposed the idea of an Incorporated Militia which would receive extra training and fight alongside regular army units in exchange for land grants after the war. He was rewarded by being the first to enlist in the new corps. He was a successful staff officer at headquarters but also successful as a leader of troops in the field. He organized and managed boats for two successful amphibious invasions of American positions. He barely survived injuries received while leading his troops on horseback at the Battle of Lundy's Lane.

Unfortunately, Titus Simons Jr. was not only ambitious but also haughty and disdainful of those he deemed his inferiors. This pride would not allow him to avoid a fight when challenged by a lieutenant. Simons lacked the judgment to avoid fighting in front of enlisted men. He was forced to leave the Incorporated Militia regiment that he had created and commanded and return to the Second York.

He did not hesitate to challenge those who favored government reform, including a sheriff before the war and his own militia commander after the war. The latter was ultimately stripped of his commission. Government reform in Upper Canada focused on American ideas like equality among (free) men and the right of these voters to elect government officials who represented their views—in other words, popular sovereignty—as opposed to representatives who were appointed by the crown upon the advice of other government officials in Upper Canada. These officials were supposed to be men of independent means who would rule wisely in the public good.[442]

Ultimately, Simons' ambition led him after the war to be appointed militia colonel (the highest possible rank), the sheriff of the Gore district and a magistrate in the same district. He apparently ran (or at least considered running) for the House of Assembly but was not elected. But his lack of judgment and belief that rules should not be applied to him led

---

442. Ibid.

to his losing the latter two positions. It appears he lost his sheriff position by refusing to delegate authority to his brother, whom he appointed only as a temporary deputy and whose actions he then countermanded. He lost his position as magistrate after organizing or at least participating in the tar and feathering of an adulterer and brother of a reformer that led to nearly two years of litigation and notoriety. He admitted only that he was ashamed of destroying the victim's pillow to obtain feathers but was not ashamed of the brutal attack itself. As a member of the local aristocracy, he valued the legal protection of property above the personal well-being and safety of an opponent.

Despite their differences, the old adage that the acorn does not fall far from the tree still applies here. Both father and son believed in a hierarchical society. Just as Titus Sr. may have taken a beating from a higher-ranked officer, Titus Jr.'s first reaction to being in trouble was to humbly thank the aristocrat who caught him for informing him of the problem, express gratitude for the aristocrat having faith in him, and also express his sorrow that he had disappointed the higher-ranking official. Titus Jr. seems more likely to offer a defense of his actions while Titus Sr. only complained about being unable to do his duty after being humiliated.

In a broader perspective both were loyalists, both sought to take care of their immediate families, and both contributed funds to build churches. Both also worked hard to provide opportunities for other members of their family and were willing to take cues from their ancestors to migrate for better opportunities. They both settled in West Flamboro before the War of 1812. However, there also is much contrast between father and son. Titus Simons Sr. does not appear particularly ambitious but perhaps he was busy simply trying to provide for his growing family.

Figure 13.1. Stormont.
The house was built c. 1837 by William Miller, the husband of Arabell Gore Simons, daughter of Titus Geer Simons.

In contrast, the ambitious Titus Geer Simons sought improvement by seeking ever higher militia and government appointments. However, overall, his record is mixed. He had some noteworthy accomplishments both in the War of 1812 and afterwards in his community. However, he also committed some lamentable actions in both contexts. Thus, the father faded anonymously into the pages of history while the son rose to some level of distinction. Perhaps the simplest way to sum up the differences between father and son is to note that the latter sat for a portrait in uniform showing his high rank while so far as we know his father did not sit for a portrait at all.

Violence proved to limit Titus Geer Simons' advancement. His willingness to fight may be related to his father's acceptance of a beating from a superior officer without objection. Imagine if he had avoided the officer's mess fight. He would not have been transferred back to the Second York and been disabled at Lundy's Lane. Instead, he would have finished his tour of duty in the Incorporated Militia as the person who conceived of it and became its first member. He might have become known as the highest-ranking Canadian on the general's staff, an officer who successfully managed numerous boats to launch successful attacks against Americans at Buffalo and Black Rock. It seems likely he could then have achieved more political success based on his military success. Although he might still have mishandled being sheriff, if he had avoided the violent attack on George Rolph he almost certainly would have continued as a magistrate until his death.

APPENDIX ONE

Children of John Simons and Sarah Geer

Name	Birth/Death Dates	Spouse
John, Jr.	19 March 1724–22 April 1797	m. 1748 Miriam Jones; 10 children
Sarah	22 August 1726	Probably died young
Paul	11 September 1729–24 May 1778	m. 1750 Mary Isham; 11 children
Ebenezer	19 February 1731/2–1 March 1755	
Asahel	7 April 1734–3 June 1811	m. 19 June 1759 Mehitable Isham; 2 children
Charity	27 July 1736–17 February 1737/8	
Charity	4 September 1738–13 June 1805	m. 19 November 1761 John Abbe III; 9 children
Bathsheba	24 January 1740/1–4 October 1742	
Titus	7 June 1743–1824	m. 20 January 1763, Sarah Simons, d. 1824; 2 children including **Titus Geer** b. 30 January 1765; m. (2) 1 February 1774 Jerusha Kingsley; 9 children
Bathsheba	9 June 1748–30 April 1754	
Edward	3 September 1750–14 December 1750	

APPENDIX TWO

Children of Titus Simons Sr. and Jerusha Kingsley[1]

Name	Birth/Death Dates	Spouse(s)
Jerusha	17 March 1775–12 September 1847; Land grant petition, 8 July 1801[2]	John Detlor m. 8 Jul. 1801; 10 children
Elizabeth	Montreal, 20 August 1781–22 August 1846, Belleville, ON; Land grant petition, 23 June 1803[3]	Dr. Seth Meacham m. 12 Mar. 1807; 1 child
Sophia	Montreal, 1782–2 October 1864; Land grant petition, 16 Auust 1804[4]	John Carpenter; (2) Dr. William Brown; 1 child
Mary Ann	1783–10 August 1830; Land grant petition 7 September 1802[5]	John or Simon McNab m. 7 September 1802; 5 children
Walter William	Montreal, 1784[6]–23 July 1834; Land grant petition, 14 May 1816[7]	Elizabeth McKay m. 14 May 1816; 4 children
Annie	1785–12 February 1829	John Thompson, m. 3 June 1824, Bath, Ontario; no children
John Kingsley	Kingston, 20 February 1786[8]–27 May 1832; Land grant petition, 21 March 1809[9]	Margaret Fraser; no children

1. Adapted from Ross D. Petty, "Titus Simons of Hartland, Vermont, and Flamborough Ontario," *Vermont Genealogy* 25, no. 2 (Fall 2020): 99–110 (Fall 2020) at 109–110. People listed in this table were half-siblings to Titus Geer Simons.
2. Upper Canada Land *Petitions,* v. 151, D5, pet. 31, C-1743.
3. Upper Canada Land Petitions, v. 453, S6, pet. 42, C-2809.
4. Upper Canada Land Petitions, v. 453, S7, pet 14, C-2809.
5. Upper Canada Land Petitions, v. 332, M6, pet. 28, C-2194.
6. John Robinson Simons, "The Fortunes of a United Empire Loyalist Family," *Ontario Historical Society Papers and Records* 23 (1926): 473.
7. Upper Canada Land Petitions, v.456A, S10, pet. 219, C-2811.
8. Simons, "The Fortunes of a United Empire Loyalist Family": 473. Age calculated from gravestone in the West Flamborough Municipal Cemetery that lists his death date as 28 May 1832.
9. Upper Canada Land Petitions, v. 454, S9, pet. 68, C-2810; his probate file is available at RG 22-255, microfilm 638, reel 65.

Name	Birth/Death Dates	Spouse(s)
Amelia	Kingston, 1793–14 May 1837, St. George, Ontario; Land grant petition, 2 April 1816[10]	John Purvis Lawrasons m. 2 April 1816; 6 children
Lucinda	1795–? ; Land grant petition, 27 November 1815[11]	John Angle Cummings m. 27 Nov. 1815; 2 children; (2) Lawrence Daniels m. 4 Dec. 1827; 1 child

10. Upper Canada Land Petitions, v. 286, L10, pet. 53, C-2126.
11. Upper Canada Land Petitions, v. 98, C10, pet. 119, C-1651.

APPENDIX THREE

Children of Titus Geer Simons

Person	Birth/Death Dates	Spouse(s)
Charlotte	1798 or 1799 (gravestone and censuses)–1882. Close in age to Aunt Lucinda.	12 July 1817 with parental consent, Benjamin James Markle; 8 children
Alexander	Ancestry.com estimates from 1802 to1811–? The only documentation of Alexander Simons seems to be in the TGS and JKS wills and in George Hill Detlor's diary.	
Elizabeth Jane	1804 according to familysearch.com. or based on her marriage as an "infant" (< 21) according to TGS' 1826 will[12]	Before August 1826; Charles Slavan[13]
Matilda Ann	26 August 1808.[14] Baptized October 29, 1815 when Hannah was listed as her mother.[15] Died 1 August 1855 according to her tombstone.	10 March 1824 Alexander Robertson; 10 children

12. Eliza Jane must have been married as an "infant" (14–21 years old) before the will was drafted in August 1826. If 1826 were her marriage year, she must have been born after 1805. Of course, if she was married earlier then 1826 then her seven-year range of birth years from 1805–1812 would shift earlier as well, making 1804 a strong possibility.
13. An Elizabeth Slavin (described as a "washerwoman") lived alone in Toronto in 1870 according to Robertson and Cook's *Toronto City Directory*, 199 (1870). A widow, Mrs. Elizabeth Slavin, was living in St. John, New Brunswick, in 1871 according to a City Directory on Ancestry.com, but she seems to have been married to James Slavin. The will requests that his executors strive to prevent Charles Slaven from obtaining any property he devises to Elizabeth Jane.
14. Francis Beverley Robertson Family Bible. The gravestone in Maitland Cemetery in Goderich, Ontario, indicates that Matilda Robertson died on 1 August 1855 at age 47 which is consistent with a birthdate of 26 August 1808. This birth date also is indicated in Emma Siggins White, *The Kinnears and their Kin* (1916), 136.
15. Ontario Historical Society Papers and Records, vol. 3, 7–73 (1901), records of St. Marks and St. Andrews of Niagara by Rev. Robert Addison at 34.

Person	Birth/Death Dates	Spouse(s)
Hannah* Rosanna	1813 or 14 (censuses) (she presumably would be the infant carried to Lundy's Lane). She died after the 1861 census when she is listed living alone in Goderich.	21 September 1832 Ross Robertson, younger brother to Alexander above; 5 children
Arabella* Gore	The Dundas Historical Museum and her gravestone in the West Flamborough Municipal Cemetery (Bullock's Corners) lists her birthday as 19 February 1816. Her death was given as 1 January 1902.	23 September 1835 William Henry Miller (1811–1860); 9 children

* NOTE: Hannah and Bell are noted as under age (less than 14 years old) in Titus Geer Simons' will, which was drafted 10 August 1826. At this time, women could get married with parental approval at age 14, but fathers had the sole right to name guardians even if the child's mother was still alive.

APPENDIX FOUR

Will of Titus Geer Simons, drafted 1826, probated in 1829[16]

In the name of God, Amen, I Titus Geer Simons of Flamboro West in the Gore District and province of Upper Canada, being sound of mind and memory for which blessing I thank My God, do make and publish this my last will and testament and request that it may be received by all Concerned as Such:

After the payment of my funeral charges, which I request may not be extravagant, and all other just debts, I give and bequeath to Mrs. Hannah Simons, lot number 23 in the third concession of the Township of Nissouri in the London District containing two hundred acres of land more or less and to her heirs and assigns forever, and also the bedsted, bed and bedding and curtains on which we usually lay, and one third of the table linen, and six cups and saucers, teapot, milk pot, and six plates and six knives and forks and three silver teaspoons, one dining room Breakfast Table and three chairs, one frying pan one common pot, one teakettle and one milch cow, all of which I declare and order to be given her as full compensation for all further charge or claims on my estate in the way of living or any other whatsoever ____. I cannot help mentioning in this place, although I have long since forgiven her cruel, unfeeling unmotherlike treatment to my poor motherless daughters, in advising and encouraging them to their destruction, thereby entailing on me sorrow, mortification and unheard of trouble, in return for my having brought up and educated her Children and without making any charge against them for it, God forgive her?

Second, I give and bequeath to my Grand Son Titus Markle fifty dollars to be laid out in sheep and cows, as may seem just to my executors, and to be paid out at interest or share to some reputable farmer until he shall become of age, when he is to receive the whole but in the event of his death while still a minor this legacy is to be divided among his brothers and sisters of the same mother.

Third, I give and bequeath to my nephew Titus Cummings twenty five dollars to be laid out in sheep and cows and to be put out on shares for him until he should become of age, when he is to receive the whole, and in the event of his death while a minor the legacy to go to his sister Hannah.

Fourth I give and bequeath to my nephew Titus Simons (my brother Walter's son) twenty five dollars to be laid out in sheep and cows and to be put out in shares for him, until he shall become of age, when he is to receive the whole, but in the event of his death while a minor, the legacy to be given to his sister Eliza.

Fifth, I give and bequeath to my namesake Titus G. Simons Neville, twenty five dollars to be

16. Archives of Ontario, RG 22-155, Probate Court Estate Files 1793–1859, MS 638, reel 65.

laid out in sheep and cows and to be put out for him on shares until he shall become of age when he is to receive the whole, and in the event of his death to be given to his youngest sister.

Sixth __ I give and bequeath to my brother John K. Simons, my double barrelled gun, reticule, flask and shot bag.

Seventh__ I give and bequeath to my brother Walter William my favourite mare, Nell, saddle and bridle, and in the event of her death, another horse.

Eighth ___ I give and bequeath to my daughter Charlotte Markle lot number twenty four in the third concession of the Township of Nissuri in the London District being two hundred acres, to her heirs an assigns forever, I also give her two cows and four sheep.

Ninth ___ I give and bequeath to my daughter Elizabeth Jane lot number one in the sixth concession and also the south half of number four in the same concession of the Township of London making three hundred acres to her, her heirs and assigns forever.

Tenth ___ I give and bequeath to my daughter Matilda my piano forte with all the music, all my pictures, map and History of England and a horse with saddle and bridle.

Eleventh ___ I give and bequeath to my daughter Hannah my Encyclopedia and Atlas, bedsted, bed and bedding, my two mirrors, and one half of my estate, a horse saddle and bridle.

Twelfth___ I give and bequeath to my daughter Bell Gore, the residue of my library, spy glass, pier glass, bedsted, bed and bedding, side board and the remaining half of my estate. The table, chairs and kitchen furniture to be equally divided between her and my daughter Hannah and I give to my daughter Bell Gore my favourite case of pistols, my watch bearing my initials with gold chain and seal, the seal with my initial, I hope she will keep while she lives, and I also give her my own picture, and request that my military maps be equally divided among my last three daughter named. My best sofa to my daughter Bell Gore, and also the chest of drawers -- with pleasure sleigh and waggon and horses. My poacher's gun I give to my grandson Titus Markle, and my holsters to my brother John K. My fishing tackle to my nephew Titus Simons, (Walter's son).

Thirteenth ___ I give and bequeath to my son-in-law Alex Robertson my Rifle and gun cleaning traps with case and my military bridle and martingale.

Fourteeth ___ I give and bequeath to my sisters Jerusha, Mary Elizabeth and Anna one hundred acres of land each of them, to each of their heirs and assigns forever out of my military tract—being in the Township of Eramosa and to my sister Sophia I gave her husband's note of hand dated Sept 14, 1822 for 60 pounds 10 shillings 7 pence which is more than I have been able to give another of my affectionate and dear sisters.

Fifteenth __ I put and place the residue of all my property real and personal after the payment of all my just debts, into the hands of my Executors, herein after named, and by them to be equally divided, as near as may be, to be kept by one, two or three or more of my six children namely Charlotte, Alexander, Matilda, Hannah, Bell Gore and Elizabeth Jane, and the others to have an equivalent in money or other property as may be agreed on by the parties. It is my earnest wish that the homestead lot No. 4 in the 2nd Concession of Flamboro West (Flamboro Cottage) should be kept in the family, for on it I have spent the vigor of my youth in rugged industry to make a small pittance for my dear children and relatives, and it has pleased God to bless my labors and increase my share and for which I feel truly thankful. I could wish that Charles Slaven, a brute in the Shape of Man, who aided and encouraged by my wife, seduced from the path of duty and from a fond father's protection, my poor and unthinking motherless infant Elizabeth jane, should not anticipate any of the property given to my dear child, if my Executors can possibly prevent it—and as I have before mentioned I wish lot number four in the second concession of Flamboro West known by the name of Flamboro Cottage with all its mills should be kept by one of my three children, namely Matilda, Hannah and Bell Gore or by the whole of them with share and share alike in the profits thereof if agreed, not to be sold out of the family if it possibly can be avoided and should it be so managed that the said Flamboro Cottage and its appointees be kept by one of my said children or more, the others (residue of b) are to have the equivalent of other property. Or in money as may be agreed on by the parties concerned and my Executors herein after named.

I particularly request of my said Executors, and enjoin it upon them, that the[y] do <u>immediately</u> after my death take appropriation of my Estate real and personal and a faithful inventory of all <u>within</u> as well as without doors and give a Copy of same to my daughter Hannah, for I have been so often robbed by those whose duty it was to protect me and my property, for I believe some advantages will be taken of my death as heretofore been done of my absence to carry off property and given to those whom I have only received the basest ingratitude, the world knows what I have done for them, and I advise my children to shun their dwellings, if they value their own peace and happiness.

I do hereby nominate, constitute and appoint John K. Simons, W. W. Simons and Alexander Robertson Esq. my true and lawful Executors and my daughter Hannah when she shall have attained the proper age my executrix.

In witness whereof I have hereunto set my hand and seal this tenth day of August in the Year of Our Lord one thousand eight hundred and twenty six. And I do also appoint Alexander Robertson Esq. and Matilda his wife guardians of my infant children Hannah and Bell.

Signed sealed, published and Declared by the Said Titus Geer Simons to be his last will and Testament in the Presence of us

H. Neveill
Richard Hatt
John H. VanEvery

INDEX

For clarity, Titus Simons Sr. is referred to in this index as *Titus Simons*, and Titus Simons Jr. is referred to as *Titus Geer Simons*.

Abbe, Charity (Simons), 27
Abbe, John III, 27
Abbe, John, 14–17
Abbe, John, Jr., 20
Abbe, Thomas, Sr., 15, 16, 20, 21, 22
Adams, John, on being American, 154
Agricultural societies, 80
Allan, William, 77
Allcock, Henry, 70
Allen, Joseph, 61–62
American Revolution, 38–48; impact on ordinary people, 1
American settlers in Upper Canada, 85–86
Ancaster Outrage, see Simons, Titus Geer
Andover, Vermont, 8, 35, 36, 37, 50

Baldwin, Robert, 139
Bateau (boat), 45, 46, 57, 94, 95
Black Rock, Battle of, 96, 97
Beasley, Richard, 87, 102, 104, 111, 120, 122
Besserer, Lieutenant, 81
Bolton, Henry John, 133, 135, 138
Bosworth, Alice, 12
Brock, Isaac, 85, 89, 90
Buffalo, N.Y., 96, 97
Burgoyne, Gen. John, 40, 44, 45, 46
Burlington Board of Agriculture, 80
Burwell, John, 143

Cameron, John M. A., 142–143
Campbell, William, 120, 135
Canadian Volunteers, 95
Canso raid, 28
Cataraqui, see Kingston
Charlestown, Mass., 8, 10
Chewett, Alexander, 136, 138, 142
Chisholm, John, 148
Clark, James, 62
Colborne, John, 141
Committee of Safety, 41
Constitution Act (1791), 64
Coon, John, 83
Crooks, James, 116
Crysler's Farm, Battle of, 94–95

Danvers, Mass., 12
Davis, Anne (Kingman), 23
Davis, Robert, 23
Declaration of Independence, 39
Detlor, George Hill, 83–84, 151
Detroit, invasion of, 89
Dundas, Ontario, 117

Edwards, Jonathan, 24
Enfield, Conn., 11, 13, 18–22, 29, 32–36; transfer from Massachusetts to Connecticut, 30
English Civil War, 6
Evans, Mr., 129, 133
Evans, Mrs., 128, 133, 134

Fairfield, Elizabeth (Knight), 14
Fairfield, John, 14
Fairfield, Sarah (Abbe), 20
Fairfield, Sarah (Skepper), 6, 14, 15, 16
Fairfield, Walter, 14–15, 17
Fort Erie, 95, 102
Fort George, 92, 93, 95
Fort Niagara, 95
Fort York, 97–99
Fosdick, Demaris, 10
Foster, Eli, 32
Foster, Judith (Keyes), 32
Franklin, Benjamin, 39
Free Church of Ancaster (Old Free Church), 118–119
Freemasonry, 117–118
French and Indian War, 29

Geer, Deborah (Davis), 19, 23
Geer, Sarah (Abbe), 19
Geer, Shubael, 19–20, 35
Geer, Thomas, 19, 20, 21, 22, 23
Glorious Revolution, 17
Gore, Francis, 81
Gore Gazette, 138, 141
Gourlay, Robert, 139
Great Awakening, 24
Great Migration, 5, 6
Great Swamp Fight, 16–17
Green, John, 68
Green, Mary (Davis), 68
Greensville, 69
Grout, Elijah, 43–44
Gurnett, George, 133, 136, 142

Hadlock, James, 10–13, 17
Hagerman, Christopher, 139
Hagle, Jacob, 140, 145
Hamilton Outrage, 141–142
Hamilton, Ann Draper (Hatt), 130
Hamilton, James, 125, 130, 132, 134, 142, 145
Hamilton, Ontario, 117
Hamilton, Peter H., 136
Hartland, Vermont, 34
Hillier, George, 142
Howard, John, 63
Hull, William, 89
Hunt, Terrence, 63
Hutchinson, Bethia, 12
Hutchinson, Rebecca, 10, 11
Hutchinson, Richard, 10–13

Incorporated Militia, 91–93, 95, 97

Jackson, John Mills, 80, 81
Jarvis, William M., 122

King Philip's War, 16–17, 18
Kingman, Henry, 23
Kingman, Joanne (or Jane), 23
Kingston, Ontario, 56–58, 64, 65

Lambert, Mrs., 145–146
Land grants, 1, 18, 33, 34, 68, 70, 76, 80, 91, 113, 114, 157
Late loyalists, 85–86, 126
Law, John, 136
Lellis, Mr., 145–146
Lellis, Mrs., 145–146
Louisbourg, 28, 29; siege of, 29
Loyalists, 1, 2, 33, 41–47, 50, 66, 153–154; arrival in Canada, 47, 50; in militias, 54; townships, 57; refugee camps, 52–53
Lundy's Lane, Battle of, 104–107

M'Nally, James, 132
Macaulay, James B., 131, 132, 133, 135
Mackenzie, William Lyon, 140
MacNab, Allan Napier, 133, 136, 137, 138, 141, 142, 144
Magistrates, duties of, 123
Maitland, Peregrine, 130
Markle, Benjamin, 150, 152
Markle, Charlotte (Simons), 151, 152
Massachusetts Bay Colony, 5, 9, 17
McKay, John D., 136
McLean, Neil, 63–64
Merchants, role in economic development, 115; "incapacitating" from serving as sheriffs, 121
Militia myth, 89–90
Militia, in Upper Canada, 84–113; Incorporated, see Incorporated Militia
Miller, Arabella Gore Simons, 83, 153

Nevills, Titus Geer Simons, 83
New England, Dominion of, 17
New Hampshire grants, 33–34

Newark, Ontario (in Niagara), 64, 66–67; set fire by Americans, 95
Newspapers in Upper Canada, 73–78
Niagara, 66, 68, 75n., 88, 89, 94; see also Newark, Fort Niagara

Paine, Thomas, 39
Paterson, John, 132
Patton, George, 143
Pearson, Thomas, 103–104
Peters, John, 42, 43, 54, 55
Pilgrims, 5
Plymouth Colony, 5
Political reform, in Upper Canada, 140
Puritans, 5, 6

Queen's Loyal Rangers, 42, 45, 48, 53, 55
Queenston Heights, Battle of, 89–90

Riall, Phineas, 102–103
Robertson, Alexander, 125, 130, 131, 132, 134, 136, 142, 145, 152
Robertson, Ross, 151
Robertson, Thomas, 145–146
Robertson, William (brother of Alexander Robertson), 145
Robertson, William (uncle to Alexander Robertson), 145
Robinson, John Beverley, 139, 148
Rolph, George, 125–147
Rolph, Georgina (Clement), 144
Rolph, John, 125–147
Roy, Louis, 73

Salem Town, 8–11
Salem Village, 10–13; religious controversies in, 12–13, 15; witch trials, 15
Saratoga, battles at, 45–47
Sheriff, duties of, 119, 121
Sheriff, William, 62
Sherwood, Levius P., 135, 136
Short, Charles, 97–98, 101
Simcoe, John Graves, 64, 127
Simons vs. Allen, 61–62
Simons, Alexander, 83, 151
Simons, Asahel ("Ashna"), 30, 39
Simons, Charlotte, 69, 83
Simons, Dorcas (Foster), 31–32
Simons, Ebenezer, 27, 29
Simons, Elizabeth ("Lizzie") Green, 68, 82
Simons, Elizabeth (daughter of Titus), 53–54
Simons, Hannah Coon (Van Every), 82–84; children of from first marriage, 83
Simons, Hannah, 83, 151
Simons, James, 31
Simons, Jane Elizabeth, 83
Simons, Jerusha (daughter of Titus), 38, 69
Simons, Jerusha (Kingsley), 37, 68
Simons, John Jr., 24, 29, 30, 35, 39, 50, 51
Simons, John Kingsley (K.), 69, 87, 103, 116, 144
Simons, John, 27, 28
Simons, Matilda, 83

Index

Simons, Paul, 29
Simons, Sarah (daughter of Titus), 32
Simons, Sarah (Geer), 19, 20, 27
Simons, Sarah (Hadlock), 11–12, 20, 21
Simons, Sarah (Hadlocke), 17
Simons, Sarah, 31, 32; death, 32
Simons, Sophia (daughter of Titus), 55
Simons, Titus (grandson of John Jr.), 51
Simons, Titus Geer, 1, 32, 42, 52–53, 72; possible early military service, 55–56; education, 60; living in York, 67–68; selected as government printer, 68, 73, 74, 76; meets first wife, 68; nuclear family, 69; in Niagara, 70; in York, 70; jury duty, 70, 71; as newspaper publisher, 74–77; moves printing business to York, 75–76; dispute with Silvester Tiffany over poem, 77; dismissed from post as government printer, 77; land petitions by, 78; land purchases by, 79; in Wentworth County, 79; shop in Dundas, 79; role in agricultural board, 80; attends dinner party at home of John Mills Jackson, 80–81; swears affidavit against Willcocks, 81; contributes toward building gaol, 81; serves as tax assessor, 82; as a loyalist tory, 82; finds second wife, 82–84; children of by both marriages, 83–84; militia service, 86ff.; appointed lieutenant in Second West Riding Regiment of Lincoln, 86; military ambitions, 87; service in Second Gore militia, 87; service in Second York militia, 88ff.; suggestion of Incorporated Militia, 91; service at headquarters, 94; return to field, 94; role in capture of Fort Niagara, 95–96; role in Battle of Black Rock, 96; assessment by superiors, 96–97; role in guarding prisoners of war, 97; participation in scuffle at Fort York, 98–99; under arrest, 99; court of enquiry, 100–101; resigns from Incorporated Militia to return to Second York, 101–103; injured at Lundy's Lane, 104–106; medical treatment by Hannah Simons, 106; disability of, 106, 110; pension, 109–110; seeks command, 111–112; role in Beasley inquiry and court martial, 111–112; appointed colonel of Second Gore, 112; hosts banquet for Maitland, 112–113, 130; resumption of land acquisition, 113; erects house, 113; builds mills in West Flamboro, 114; as shop keeper, 114; creates "industrial empire" in West Flamboro, 115–116; as distiller, 116; taxes assessed on, 116–117; business interests in Montreal, 117; as a Freemason, 117–118; lays church cornerstone, 118–119; appointed sheriff, 119; reluctance to share authority, 119–120; complaint against as sheriff, 120; called before grand jury, 120; dismissal as sheriff, 122; encouraged to run for election in 1824, 122; appointed magistrate in 1827, 122; promotes gaol, 123; participation in tar-and-feather outrage (Ancaster Outrage), 125–147; civil trial, 131–134; verdict, 134; appeal, 134–136; criminal prosecution of, 136–139; starts reward fund related to Hamilton Outrage, 141–142;
not reappointed as magistrate, 142; levy on estate for cost of tar and feathers, 144–145; reasons for attack on Rolph, 146–147; petition to free John Chisholm, 148; death of, 148; grave marker of, 149; will of, 83, 149–152; unhappy with second wife, 149–150; appoints guardians of minor children in will, 150; bequests to half-siblings, 150; treatment of daughters in will, 150–151; names daughter Hannah executrix, 151; names Alexander Robertson guardian, 152; auction of properties, 152–53; loyalty to Britain, 154–155; tory views, 156; desire to rise in hierarchy, 156–158; belief in hierarchical society, 158; lack of judgement, 157–159
Simons, Titus, 1, 20, 21, 26–71; ancestors of, 3–25; nuclear family of, 27–28, 55; extended family of, 27–28; marriage of, 31; move to Vermont, 32–37; trial at Committee of Safety, 41; confiscation of property, 41, 50, 51; escape, 41; enlists in militia, 41–42; serves as quartermaster, 43–44, 53, 55; posted to St. Johns, Quebec, 48; capture of, 48; trial of, 48, 49–50; with family in Canada as refugees, 49–57; escorted to border by brother, 50–51; billeted in Machiche, 51–52; move to St. Johns, Quebec, 53; move to Vercheres, Quebec, 53, 55; beaten by James Rogers, 54; in Montreal area, 56; move to Kingston (Cataraqui), 56–57, 60; serves as deputy sheriff, 59–60; lawsuits, 61–63; sued by and sues Joseph Allen, 61–62; sued by James Clark, 63; sues William Sheriff, 62; sued by Terrence Hunt, 63; sues John Howard, 63; sues Neil McLean, 63–64; as innkeeper, 65; move to Niagara, 66–67; move to York, 69; jury duty, 70; possible militia service in 1804, 86; no longer listed in militia, 86–87; loyalty to Britain, 154–155; belief in hierarchical society, 158
Simons, Walter William (W.), 69, 87, 120, 121, 122
Simons, William Robert, 20
Simons, William, 11–12, 20, 21
Skepper, Sarah (Fisher), 14
Skepper, William, 14
Slaven, Charles, 150
Small, John, 70
Springfield, Mass., 16–17
St. David's, capture of, 103
St. Johns, Quebec, 47ff.
Stamp Act, 30
Steven, Andrew, 133, 135, 136
Stoney Creek, Battle of, 93
Stormont, 153, 159

Talbot, Thomas, 127
Tar and feathering, 126–127
Tar-and-feather outrage, see Simons, Titus Geer
Tiffany, Gideon, 70–76
Tiffany, Silvester, 70–77
Tories, 141, 146–147; attacks on reformers, 125, 126
Townshend Act, 9, 31
Types Riot, 140

Upper Canada Gazette, 73–74, 76, 77

Upper Canada, location of capital of, 64–65; growth in population and economy, 114–115

Vermont, convention, 40; formation of, 40; admitted as state, 64
Vincent, John, 92, 106

War of 1812, 1, 85ff.; end of, 108
Waters, William, 75
Wenham, Mass., 10, 14–16

West Flamboro, 79, 114
Westminster, Vermont, 38–39, 40
White, John, 70
Willard, John, 122
Willcocks, Joseph, 80, 81, 95
Willis, John W., 135, 136, 137, 138
Windsor County, Vermont, 36
Wright, Zadock, 37, 42, 43

York, Ontario (now Toronto), 67–68, 69

www.ingramcontent.com/pod-product-compliance
Lightning Source LLC
Chambersburg PA
CBHW061736070526
44585CB00024B/2690